The Advance of the State in Contemporary China

Since the Global Financial Crisis in 2008–2009, central-level, state-owned enterprises in China have extended their reach into the Chinese economy. Some have interpreted this development as a turning point in Chinese economic development; a decision for state capitalism and a stand against slow but steady marketization. In *The Advance of the State in Contemporary China*, Sarah Eaton suggests that the shift is a much slower-moving process and that this particular aspect of state sector reform can be seen to predate the financial crisis. She argues that the 'advance of the state' has in fact developed incrementally from an eclectic set of ideas regarding the political and economic significance of large and profitable state-controlled enterprise groups.

Drawing from case studies of China's telecommunication services and airline reforms, this fascinating new study offers illuminating insight into China's much-vaunted, but poorly understood, brand of state capitalism.

SARAH EATON is Professor of Modern Chinese Society and Economy at the Institute for Sociology and Department of East Asian Studies, University of Göttingen.

The Advance of the State in Contemporary China

State–Market Relations in the Reform Era

Sarah Eaton
University of Göttingen

CAMBRIDGE
UNIVERSITY PRESS

University Printing House, Cambridge CB2 8BS, United Kingdom

Cambridge University Press is part of the University of Cambridge.

It furthers the University's mission by disseminating knowledge in the pursuit of education, learning and research at the highest international levels of excellence.

www.cambridge.org
Information on this title: www.cambridge.org/9781107123410

© Sarah Eaton 2016

This publication is in copyright. Subject to statutory exception
and to the provisions of relevant collective licensing agreements,
no reproduction of any part may take place without the written
permission of Cambridge University Press.

First published 2016

A catalogue record for this publication is available from the British Library

Library of Congress Cataloguing in Publication data
Eaton, Sarah.
The advance of the state in contemporary China : state-market relations in the reform era / Sarah Eaton.
    pages cm
ISBN 978-1-107-12341-0 (Hardback)
1. Government business enterprises–China. 2. China–Economic policy–2000–
3. China–Politics and government–2002– I. Title.
HD4318.E28 2016
381.30951–dc23   2015028168

ISBN 978-1-107-12341-0 Hardback

Cambridge University Press has no responsibility for the persistence or accuracy of URLs for external or third-party internet websites referred to in this publication, and does not guarantee that any content on such websites is, or will remain, accurate or appropriate.

To my parents, Diane and Curtis Eaton

Contents

List of figures	*page* viii
List of tables	ix
Preface	xi
Acknowledgements	xvi
1 The advance of the state in China: the power of ideas	1
2 The ideas behind the advance of the state	28
3 The state's advance in the air: an analysis of airline reform	53
4 Advance of the state in telecommunications: the bricolage of managed competition	79
5 Is the state's advance coming to a halt?	109
Bibliography	125
Index	142

Figures

3.1	Airline passenger traffic, 1970–2008	*page* 58
3.2	Market share of the three largest (CR3) and eight largest (CR8) airlines, 1987–2003	66
3.3	Big Four airline groups' shares of passenger traffic, 2008	70
3.4	Corporate structure of Hainan Airlines Group (2005)	73
4.1	Increase in fixed-line subscriptions, 1980–2005	86
4.2	Competition in telecommunications basic services, 1994–2009	100

Tables

1.1	Mainland enterprises on the Fortune Global 500 list (2003, 2014)	*page* 7
3.1	Key industrial policies in airlines, 1980s and 1990s	58
4.1	Key industrial policies in telecommunications, 1980s and 1990s	83
4.2	Golden projects, 1993–2000	89

Preface

It is not every day that one hears a senior American policymaker admit that ideology has tainted his or her policy choices. In American political discourse, the word 'ideology' is typically reserved to describe the false beliefs held by the opposing team. One's own views do not sit on such unsteady foundations but rather stand firmly on the ground of Truth.

It was surreal, then, to see Alan Greenspan, Chair of the Federal Reserve from 1987 to 2006 – the man once known as 'The Oracle' to financiers – own up to an 'ideology' that he admitted had contributed to the Global Financial Crisis of 2008. In a congressional hearing during the darkest days of the crisis, Greenspan admitted he was in a 'shocked state of disbelief' because of the 'collapse' of an 'intellectual edifice' of risk management models (US Congress 2008: 13). Greenspan's *mea culpa*, however, did not satisfy the committee's chair, Democrat Henry Waxman, who pushed Greenspan to make a broader denunciation of his beliefs. He began by quoting Greenspan as having said 'I do have an ideology. My judgment is that free, competitive markets are by far the unrivaled way to organize economies. We have tried regulation, none meaningfully worked.' Waxman then asked whether Greenspan felt that his ideology had driven him 'to make decisions that you wish you had not made?' Greenspan replied that 'Yes, I found a flaw, I don't know how significant or permanent it is, but I have been very distressed by that fact' (ibid. 46).

This and other scenes in the dark days of the Global Financial Crisis pulled back the curtain on Anglo-American capitalism. Long held up by champions of the Washington Consensus as the endpoint of history, the crisis revealed that the intellectual edifice of financial capitalism in the twenty-first century is, like the shoddy 'tofu buildings' (*doufu lou* 豆腐楼) that litter China's urban landscapes, shaky to the core. It was an ungentle reminder of John Maynard Keynes' famous insight about the immense power of ideas 'for good or evil', gleaned in the blackness of the Great Depression (Keynes [1936] 1997: 384).

However, as Greenspan rightly pointed out during his congressional testimony, we all 'need an ideology' – what he defined as a 'conceptual framework ... [to] deal with reality'. The collapse of one dominant ideology simply triggers a search for the next. Since 2008, this quest has drawn many of the disenchanted to China's shores, where praise for the 'China Model' and the 'Beijing Consensus' has been warmly received by a leadership eager to be seen as offering something to fill the void. A few weeks before the Greenspan hearing, then-Premier Wen Jiabao declared in an interview with CNN's Fareed Zakaria that the secret to China's economic success was a rejection of the neoliberal injunction to enforce a rigid separation between state and market. 'Socialism can also practice market economy', Wen declared, when 'both the visible hand and the invisible hand are given full play in regulating the market forces' (CNN 2008).

Such claims have been met in the West with both thunderous applause from the left and anxious hand-wringing from the right. To long-time opponents of neoliberalism, like Martin Jacques, a prominent journalist and former editor of the British Communist Party's *Marxism Today* journal, China's extraordinary rise has served to expose the poverty of neoliberal development strategies (Jacques 2009). Jacques characterizes the coming 'age of China' as one in which the Chinese principles of policy pragmatism and gradualism will supplant the practice of development as the delivery of one-size-fits-all reform packages from Washington to all corners of the world. On the right, worried guardians of the American-led world order have also conceded that China's rise poses a deep challenge to the existing rules of the game. Political scientist Stefan Halper, a White House official under three Republican Presidents, argues in *The Beijing Consensus: How China's Authoritarian Model Will Dominate the Twenty-First Century* (2010), that there is a clear and present 'model threat' from China. He argues that China has now taken the lead in marketing its 'vision' of politics and economics to the rest of the world. But all is not lost, Halper tells us; if America were to commit itself to winning back the hearts and minds of the global public, the world could again be made safe for American supremacy.

The above illustrates an important point about distortions that have arisen in the post-crisis debates over ideology. As others have argued, 'the China case' – once the preserve of a small number of little-known economic historians – has now become a political football between left and right, and everyone in between, in rich capitalist countries (Ferchen 2013; Naughton 2010). How China-as-talking-point is characterized, however, is subject to the distorting lens of the particular commentator. It is an elusive, shape-shifting creature barely recognizable from one commentary to the next. Wherever it appears, though, it is a fearsome, clear-minded and patient animal.

Yet China does not see itself in nearly such certain terms. Indeed, what the China debaters have all too often overlooked is the extent to which China's self-understanding is a continually evolving and deeply contested subject (Ferchen 2013). Of course, certain features of the Chinese economy set it apart from the world's other major economies – the economic might of large state-owned enterprises (SOEs) in key industries, for example. But if we look more closely, we find this and other supposedly distinct features appear far less solidly outlined. We might expect, for example, that the extraordinarily rapid ascent of the Forbes Global 500 list by China's central-level SOEs – up from just ten in 2003 to fifty-one in 2014 – would be a source of national pride. And, indeed, for many Chinese, it is. But others within China view it grimly, as evidence not of the fruition of 'reform and opening' but instead as a betrayal of the reform pathway laid down by Deng Xiaoping. Indeed, at the time of writing, debate over the appropriate role and form of SOEs in the Chinese economy is arguably *the* economic issue in Beijing and a perennial topic of debate among policymakers, economists and the reading public.

This book puts under a microscope the question of how China's muscular state-owned national champions came into being. In much of the popular literature on China's brand of 'state capitalism', the role of large, centrally controlled SOEs in China's political economy is characterized as an almost inevitable consequence of China's gradual move towards a market economy within the structure of continuing Chinese Communist Party (CCP) authoritarian rule. As Ian Bremmer, an American political consultant, wrote in his popular *The End of the Free Market* (2010):

Certain that command economies are doomed to fail but fearful that truly free markets will spin beyond their control, authoritarians have invented something new: state capitalism. In this system, governments use various kinds of state-owned companies to manage the exploitation of resources that they consider the state's crown jewels and to create and maintain large numbers of jobs. They use select privately owned companies to dominate certain economic sectors. They also use so-called sovereign wealth funds to invest their extra cash in ways that maximize the state's profits ... in all three cases, the ultimate motive is not economic (maximizing growth) but *political* (maximizing the state's power and the leadership's chances of survival). This is a form of state capitalism but one in which the state acts as the dominant economic player and uses markets primarily for political gain. (Bremmer 2010: 4–5)

However, the reality in China is much more complex. Bremmer is right to point out that political motives and not purely economic considerations have given shape to China's national champions strategy. But the reality he describes is not, in fact, the result of the methodical execution of a blueprint from on high but rather of a thoroughly contingent and incremental process.

Things certainly might have been otherwise. Indeed, the growing wealth and clout of China's large SOEs – referred to as the 'advance of the state' (*guojin* 国进) in common parlance – actually represent a puzzling break with the past. Until quite recently, the conventional wisdom among China watchers held that Chinese economic reform aimed at a gradual, minimally disruptive transition to a free market economy by slowly ushering the state-owned economy – long an albatross around policymakers' necks – into retirement while simultaneously nurturing development of the non-state sector. One prime proponent of this view, Nicholas Lardy, characterizes Chinese economic reform as the triumph of 'markets over Mao' (Lardy 2014). And, for many years, the state sector's lethargic performance leading finally to a massive retrenchment in the late 1990s supported the view that SOEs were increasingly being relegated to the margins of the Chinese economy. However, this conventional view is much less easily accommodated to the precipitous rise of the state sector since the beginning of the new century. Thus, we are faced with the question: what accounts for China's turn towards state capitalism?

The answer provided in this book brings us back to ideas and ideologies. A commonly held (though by no means universal) belief among China's intellectual and policymaking elite is that large centrally controlled, state-owned enterprise groups are an indispensable pillar of China's refurbished system of socialist market economy. The existence of this belief is something of a puzzle. It is out of step not only with the tenets of neoliberalism, the pre-eminent global economic ideology since the period of China's economic reform began in 1978, but also with Maoist economic doctrine which idealized small-scale industrial enterprises and bequeathed a highly fragmented industrial structure to reform-era China. The rise of large SOEs is not, then, a simple story of path dependency. Tracing back the development of this ideological commitment to nurturing large state-owned national champions, we find that it was the result of a process of ideational 'bricolage' (Carstensen 2011) whereby policy entrepreneurs grappling with pressing issues at different junctures framed the 'large enterprise strategy' as the solution to various problems, both political and economic. The effect, over time, was one of sedimentation in which the addition of new rationales gradually added firmness and stability and a veneer of permanence to the institutions.

But the institutionalization and implementation of this idea have not always been smooth. In fact, the decision to create SOE oligopolies in key industries has been hotly debated at every turn. This analysis traces not only the development of this triumphant idea, it also highlights the many critiques within Chinese policymaking circles that have emerged along the way. This book demonstrates, first, that the advance of the state is not, and has never been, as has sometimes been asserted, a matter of the 'Beijing Consensus'. At every point there has been a persistent counter-narrative pushing against the development of state capitalist institutions. Drawing attention to this persistent counter-narrative is also important because China's state capitalist dissenters have articulated a starkly different vision of what the Chinese economy ought to be. If state capitalism in China collapses under its own weight, as some think it might, this vision-in-waiting might well provide the ideational foundation for new rules of the game.

In concentrating on the evolution of ideas and institutions regarding the role of large SOEs in the reform era, the analysis is necessarily drawn into the consideration of wider questions about state–market relations. The question of large SOEs is deeply entwined with – and ultimately inseparable from – a broad movement to recast the state economy in an era of almost unfathomable change characterized by torrid GDP growth, structural change, rural to urban migration on a massive scale and market liberalization. At the same time that policymakers wrestled with the extremely difficult question of what to do with SOEs, they were also confronted with a range of other equally thorny questions such as 'What ought to be the sectoral boundaries of the state economy?', 'What is a strategic sector?' and 'What constitutes appropriate market intervention in China's economy?' At the centre of this book is an analysis of policymakers' provisional answers to these thorny questions – answers that were very much the products of both contingency and contestation. The case studies of telecommunications services and airline reform, in particular, underscore the indeterminate and highly contested nature of the state sector's great transformation.

Acknowledgements

I wish to thank the outstanding and generous group of scholars who helped give definition to this project at its very earliest stages and saw it through to a completed dissertation and now to a book. Joe Wong and Lou Pauly were, and are, great advisors and mentors to me. As most of my writing was done far away from Toronto, first in Beijing and then in Vancouver, they had to give me a lot of rope and I can only hope they don't look back on that as a mistake! The drafts I sent them always came back quickly and with excellent and thoroughly practical commentary. And since I left the graduate school nest they have also helped me through the challenges, big and small, of setting out on an academic career. At several forks in the road, Joe brought the proverbial big picture into focus for me. I would feel like a success if, one day, I could manage to be half the mentor to my students that Joe has been to me.

Other committee members and examiners contributed to the project enormously. My third committee member, Richard Stubbs, has been a mentor since my Master's studies when he funded the trip to my first-ever conference presentation, in Singapore, and later took a leap on the decision to co-author a publication with me. Those two years at McMaster, where I also worked closely with Tony Porter and Will Coleman, were integral to defining the research interests around which my work revolves and, no less significantly, helping me to shed my shy, self-doubting undergraduate persona. I drew from Victor Shih's deep knowledge about Chinese political economy at several points in the dissertation process and was fortunate to have his invaluable feedback on the final draft. Todd Hall's comments on my dissertation provided me with the kernel of this book. At a later talk in Oxford, when I was approaching the end of writing the manuscript, Todd again had some excellent advice for me about how to sharpen the argument, which I hope to have done justice to here.

Various individuals and organizations provided invaluable support during the research for this project. The Chinese Academy of Social Sciences' Institute of World Economics and Politics in Beijing gave me a home base during an early period of library research and interviewing in 2008–9. I am especially grateful for help from the fine group of scholars there, above all Zhang Ming, Gao Haihong and Yu Yongding. During a crucial round of interviews in spring 2012, I was fortunate to have research assistance from Guo Xing with whom I enjoyed wide-ranging conversations about China's political economy. I also benefited enormously from two productive stints at the University Services Centre for China Studies library at the Chinese University of Hong Kong. I am especially grateful to Gao Qi for research support as well as interesting conversation during those visits.

Without research funding from a number of sources, this project would not have been possible. I am grateful to the Social Sciences and Humanities Research Council of Canada for support in the form of doctoral and postdoctoral fellowships, the Canada–China Scholars' Exchange Program, the Chiang Ching Kuo Foundation, the China Times Cultural Foundation, the Dr David Chu Scholarship Fund for Asia Pacific Studies and the Department of Political Science at the University of Toronto.

Since I began work on this project in 2008, many scholars and practitioners have generously shared with me their valuable insights and suggestions. They are Margaret Boittin, Loren Brandt, Kjeld Erik Brødsgaard, Cheng Xiaonong, Greg Chin, Jennifer Choo, Jae-Ho Chung, Matt Ferchen, Doris Fischer, Anthony Garnaut, Juliette Genevaz, Julian Gruin, Nis Grunberg, Sandra Heep, Sebastian Heilmann, Jeffrey Henderson, Roselyn Hsueh, Paul Irwin-Crookes, Kan Kaili, Thomas Kampen, Scott Kennedy, Wendy Leutert, Kun-Chin Lin, Winnie King, Alanna Krolikowski, Jonas Nahm, Barry Naughton, Miguel Otero-Iglesias, Margaret Pearson, Lea Shih, Kay Shimizu, Vivienne Shue, Marc Szepan, Eric Thun, Carl Walter, Wang Hongying, David Welch, Christine Wong, Wu Guogang, Yukyung Yeo and Zhang Weiying. I also received helpful comments at the Association of Asian Studies (2012) and International Studies Association (2011) conferences as well as at talks given at the University of Oxford (2014), Bristol University (2014), Heidelberg University (2013), the Copenhagen Business School (2012), the Chinese Academy of Social Sciences' Institute of World Economics and Politics (2009) and Tsinghua University (2008). Finally, I am extremely grateful to dozens of anonymous interviewees who generously shared their time and insights with me.

I am also very grateful for the support this book project has received from Cambridge University Press. Lucy Rhymer is a very patient and supportive editor who made very helpful suggestions on the manuscript. Two anonymous reviewers of the manuscript also provided excellent feedback for which I am grateful.

I thank the *China Journal* and the *Copenhagen Journal of Asian Studies* for permission to re-use material found in Chapters 2 and 3 which previously appeared in articles published in these journals.

Friends and colleagues provided welcome diversions throughout this process. At the University of Toronto, I was lucky to be surrounded by a group of entertaining and smart graduate students who made research and writing a much less lonely process than it otherwise might have been. My thanks especially to Bill Flanik, Wendy Hicks, Caroline Shenaz Hossein, Seth Jaffe, Mike Mastroeni, Andy Paras, Marie-Eve Reny, Charmaine Stanley, Steve Trott and Jenn Wallner. Alanna Krolikowski deserves particular mention here. In addition to being brilliant and witty she is also generous and kind and it was my extreme good fortune to overlap with her for much of my research stay in China. Other friends made my time in China enjoyable and memorable, particularly Chen Shu, He Weimin, Andrée Chenard, Cigdem Gül and Trinh Thuy Hang.

Well before I had ever thought about the advance of the state in China, a professor of Chinese history at Mount Allison University, Marilyn McCullough, nudged my life in a new direction. Her enthusiasm for her subject was completely infectious and after taking all of the courses I could with her, in 1999, I joined one of her annual summer exchange trips to Hangzhou. I was so enlivened by the experience that I knew from that point on that China would somehow play an important part in my life. Marilyn died too young and is missed and fondly remembered by her students.

The Eatons have also deeply shaped this book as well as its author. Growing up in an academic family, nightly dinner-table debate gave me an early taste for the give and take of academia and made me believe, audaciously, that I too could have such a life. A writer and professional editor, my mom, Diane, subjected my grade school essays to a level of scrutiny that was orders of magnitude more intense than what I ever received from my teachers. It is no exaggeration to say that everything I have learned about writing I learned from her. My dad, Curtis, tried hard to make an economist of me but I hope that my becoming a political economist is some consolation to him! Brett and Isabelle Eaton were kind enough to take a crazy husky into their busy lives while I was living in China. Although we now live on opposite sides of the world, the Eatons are never far from my thoughts.

Above all, I wish to thank Genia Kostka, without whom this book truly would never have seen the light of day. When this was but a half-conceived dissertation project she, fresh from her own Ph.D., helped me to articulate the argument and pushed me to get down to the business of writing without too much humming and hawing. My first draft then came together surprisingly quickly, thanks in no small measure to a brilliant incentive structure she devised to hold me to my time targets involving carrots for completing chapters on time (mojitos at Bed Bar in Gulou) and sticks for missing deadlines (cash donations to unsavoury organizations like the NRA – kindly, never enforced). A couple of years later, when it came to the work of drafting the book manuscript, our lives had become much busier with two academic jobs and the arrival of baby Quinn. In spite of weighty demands on her own time, Genia generously let my book project take priority and took the time to carefully read and comment upon every new draft. And she mostly bit her tongue when two consecutive lovely summers in Berlin were spent indoors and hunched over laptops. In that period, the large Kostka clan (Christine, Micha, Steffi, Nadja, Jule, Trine, Tanja, Niko and Peter) provided us with a home, a great volume of cheerful childcare as well as general merriment for which a big 'Danke an Euch alle!' is due.

While many have contributed to this project, its errors and omissions are my responsibility.

1 The advance of the state in China: the power of ideas

Two combinations of four characters have much to reveal about change in the Chinese economy. In 2004, Hong Kong economist Larry Lang raised the alarm about corrupt management buyouts (MBOs) of state-owned enterprises (SOEs) and applied the phrase 'retreat of the state, advance of the private sector' (*guotui minjin* 国退民进) to the ills of SOE privatization. Lang's public skewering of refrigerator tycoon Gu Chujun for acquiring state assets at below market value stirred controversy on the mainland, leading ultimately to Gu's arrest and an end to officially sanctioned MBOs. A few years later, the same characters arranged in slightly different order described a very different trend. In the wake of the 2008 Global Financial Crisis, a series of high-profile takeovers of private enterprises by China's central-level SOEs gave rise to a new, and quickly ubiquitous, phrase: 'advance of the state, retreat of the private sector' (*guojin mintui* 国进民退). In the span of less than a decade, in other words, hand-wringing about the Chinese economy has come full circle. Whereas concern once focused on curtailing private entrepreneurs' predations in the weakened state sector, policy debate now centres on how to shield private enterprises from the unwanted advances of massive and centrally backed SOEs (*yangqi* 央企). What has happened?

The analysis offered here finds that the advance of the state in China is a longer-term and slower process than the above vignette would suggest. Commentators have sometimes characterized central SOE assertiveness since 2008 as marking a turning point in Chinese economic development – as a decision for state capitalism and against slow but steady marketization (e.g. Wines 2010). A closer look at the evidence shows that the state's advance reaches much farther back in time. To be sure, the Chinese government's US $586 billion post-crisis fiscal stimulus plan, which heavily favoured the state sector, did play to the advantage of large SOEs and hastened the 'retreat' of private enterprises from several industries including steel, real estate and airlines. But this was a moment of culmination more than inception. Today's muscular *yangqi* are, in some measure, the product of twenty years of sustained effort to mould state-owned national champions in key industries. While previous work has focused on the contribution of institutions and interests to the advance of the state, this study demonstrates the formative role played by ideas, stressing the economic *and* political significance of state-controlled large enterprise groups.

The advance of the state: events, debate

The phrase 'advance of the state, retreat of the private sector' entered common parlance along with events linked to the Global Financial Crisis of 2008–9. While SOEs have long enjoyed privileged access to financial resources as compared to non-state enterprises, the government's 2008 fiscal stimulus plan was interpreted by some as having substantially boosted the competitive advantages of SOEs, above all SOEs under the authority of the central government, as well as hastening the retreat of private enterprises from certain industries. Unveiled in November 2008, the US $586 billion stimulus plan was subsequently tied to the implementation of the 'Ten Industries Revitalization Plan' (2009) which aimed to promote industrial consolidation via mergers and acquisition as well as technological upgrading in the steel, auto, shipbuilding, textiles, light industry, non-ferrous metals, equipment manufacturing, IT and logistics industries. Since industrial SOEs in these industries tend to be much larger than private enterprises, industrial consolidation often squeezed non-state enterprises into state-owned enterprise business groups (Economist Intelligence Unit 2009: 23). Perhaps the most audacious example of consolidation by administrative fiat took place in Shandong Province where the Rizhao Company, a thriving private steel enterprise, was heavily pressured by the provincial government into accepting a takeover by struggling state-owned Shandong Steel in September 2009. In the wake of the financial crisis, *guojin mintui* was also seen to be taking place in a number of other key industries. Chapter 3 examines the phenomenon of *guojin mintui* in the airline industry more closely.

As some domestic commentators have pointed out, China was hardly alone in marrying fiscal stimulus to industrial policy in the immediate post-crisis period. But the deep resonance, if also the fuzziness, of continuing debate about *guojin mintui* in China is distinctive. In late 2012, a little more than four years after the collapse of Lehman Brothers, at a time when public discussion had moved well past arguments for and against bank bailouts and nationalization of industry in other crisis-afflicted countries, *guojin mintui* was said to be the single most important matter of economic policy at the Eighteenth Party Congress, the occasion for Xi Jinping and Li Keqiang to take over national leadership from Hu Jintao and Wen Jiabao. Indeed, in his opening remarks to the Congress, outgoing General Secretary Hu Jintao strived to appease both camps. In one breath he called for 'enhancing the vitality of the state-owned sector of the economy and its capacity to leverage and influence the economy' before declaring that the government ought to 'unswervingly encourage, support, and guide the development of the non-public sector' (quoted in Rabinovitch 2012).

In the fray, it is not always clear just what, or whom, is being indicted. As Li Zheng points out, the phrase *guojin mintui* is very much open to interpretation:

> The 'state' (*guo*) and 'private' (*min*) in 'advance of the state, retreat of the private sector' are all unclear, making it easy to have misunderstandings. To be specific, *guo* can refer to the country, to the state economy or to SOEs. *Min* can indicate the public, the private economy or private enterprises. And 'advance' (*jin*) and 'retreat' (*tui*) could each refer to long term or short term, qualitative or quantitative, active or passive forms of advance or retreat. (Li 2010)

Indeed, defined as an aggregate ownership trend, a number of prominent economists have argued that *guojin mintui* does not in fact exist, since, economy-wide, the proportion of state ownership in industry continues to decline while the share of non-state forms of ownership marches ever upwards (Hu 2012; Ma 2010; Wei and Zhang 2010; Li 2010). Nicholas Lardy points out that, by 2011, SOEs produced just 26 per cent of industrial output with non-state firms accounting for nearly all the rest (Lardy 2014: 20).

Others contend that the aggregate trends do not do away with arguments for the existence of an advancing state. In a detailed analysis of *guojin mintui*, economists from the Unirule Institute, a think-tank known for advancing views at right angles to the official line, concede to *guojin mintui* sceptics that, while the share of SOEs contribution to gross industrial output continues to fall, 'in certain resource-based and basic industries, the role of state-owned capital has increased' (Sheng and Zhao 2012: 155). They also find that the degree of industrial concentration in several industries increased between 2002 and 2007, including elements of the non-ferrous metal, tobacco and oil industries (ibid. 132). The analysis concludes, too, that industries with the highest levels of concentration were those home to the largest proportion of SOEs.

Others understand *guojin mintui* as nothing less than an about-face in China's approach to economic development, one that, while difficult to pinpoint in the official statistics, nevertheless represents a profound break with the past. Wang Hongqie writes:

> Some scholars think that the current *guojin mintui* is not a few isolated events but has become a general trend; it is not the behaviour of a few individual enterprises, but is quite common among SOEs, especially central SOEs; it is not a few industries, but is widespread in many important industries; it is not limited to a few upstream, so-called related-to-people's-livelihood-and-state-security-natural-monopolies but touches on many other industries. (Wang 2010: 16)

As discussed below, to some participants in China's 'theory world' (*lilunjie* 理论界), *guojin mintui* has contributed to a reform stall.

What is beyond debate in this empirically murky and often emotionally charged discussion is that central SOEs are a force to be reckoned with. This is itself a remarkable turn of events and, to some observers, the growing economic clout, size and political influence of central SOEs constitutes the primary evidence for an advancing state and a retreating private sector, even if the aggregate numbers might suggest a different conclusion. Yasheng Huang (2008), for example, offers the controversial conclusion that the apotheosis of private sector development actually took place in the 1980s after which point the tide began to turn, slowly but surely, against rural private enterprises in particular, as government at all levels placed steadily greater emphasis on building up large, state-owned enterprises in urban areas. In recent years, the central government has stressed the importance of the hundred-odd central SOEs under the State Council 'going big and going strong' (*zuo da zuo qiang* 做大做强), by which is meant expanding the scale of SOE business groups via mergers and acquisitions while improving their competitiveness. One study finds that, in accordance with this policy, the largest state-owned business groups have rapidly scaled up in recent years. In 2000, 538 parent company SOEs controlled a total of 6,805 subsidiaries and had an average of 12.6 subsidiaries each; in 2007, a smaller number of parent company SOEs – 301 – held fewer total subsidiaries (5,002) but the average number of subsidiaries per SOE had risen to 16.6 (Lee and Kang 2010: 221). Within this group, the 131 business groups under the watch of either the State Council or central government are particularly dominant. Of China's 2,926 business groups, these central groups, which account for just 4.5 per cent of the total number of registered groups, held 48 per cent of total assets and contributed 42 per cent of total revenue in 2007 (ibid. 220). This, too, has generated controversy. In recent years, some have characterized the expanding scale of central SOEs as predatory: 'More than a few scholars as well a segment of public opinion see the efforts of central enterprises to get bigger and stronger as 'central ferocity' (Wang 2010: 16). Central SOEs are not only growing, they are also suddenly awash in cash.

Since China's debt-ridden SOEs were once albatrosses around the necks of Chinese leaders, the surging profitability of state-owned, large enterprise groups in the so-called 'monopoly sectors' (*longduan hangye* 垄断行业) is perhaps the most significant, and certainly the least anticipated, change in the Chinese economy since the turn of the century. In 1998 just 31 per cent of all SOEs were reported to be profitable, as compared to 57 per cent of SOEs in 2007 (Zhongguo Caizheng Nianjian 2008: 429). Yet these official figures largely reflect strong profitability among central SOEs. Many provinces with a large state sector continue to struggle even after the massive restructuring efforts of the late 1990s. Official figures record that between 2001 and 2009 central SOE net profits more than quadrupled. While there can be no doubt that state sector profitability has remarkably improved, there are good reasons to treat these numbers cautiously (Sheng and Zhao 2012: 51). First, despite notable improvements in data-gathering and measurement, official figures published by the National Bureau of Statistics are still seen as lacking reliability (Koch-Weser 2013). Second, economists caution that this surge in profitability (see Figure 1.1) should not be too easily interpreted as evidence of vastly improved economic performance. While today's SOEs tend to be better managed and shoulder lighter social obligations than they did prior to restructuring, state sector profits are padded by certain non-market benefits which are generally not extended to non-state enterprises. In particular, large SOEs often acquire resources at below market rates, enjoy lower financing costs than non-state enterprises and receive various forms of government subsidies (Sheng and Zhao 2012: 51–73).

The central SOEs advance is not taking place evenly across industry, however. They are the leading players in just a select few strategic industries, although their tendrils extend deep into many non-priority, 'competitive' industries. As defenders of the status quo have pointed out, this development is aligned with a government policy first outlined in the late 1990s. The Fifteenth Party Congress (1997) first established the guiding principle for pruning the once-universal state economy such that SOEs were to remain the 'commanding presence' in 'lifeline industries and key areas' but could begin to retreat from non-priority sectors in which non-state enterprises were expected to become the dominant force. Following years of clamorous internal debate about how exactly to define 'lifeline industries' and 'key areas' (cf. Eaton 2011: 86–93), the central government finally signalled, in late 2006, the industries from which SOEs would not retreat. Although the associated central government policy was actually more ambiguous and non-committal than many observers realized at the time, this was the first time a central bureaucracy had put a name to the 'lifeline industries' in which SOEs were to maintain absolute control, namely: defence, power grid, petroleum and petrochemicals, telecommunications, coal, civil aviation and shipping.[1]

---

[1] In December 2006, the State Council issued an important policy on SOE retreat and advance, which was widely interpreted as having clearly demarcated the industries from which SOEs should retreat and those in which they should advance. Indeed, in the official *Xinhua* media report of the press conference, the policy is made to sound crystal clear on the matter of which industries count as lifeline industries: 'the state sector should maintain absolute control in national security and lifeline industries including in the seven big industries: defence, the power grid, petroleum and petrochemicals, telecommunications, coal, civil aviation and shipping.' In fact, the actual text of the policy says only vaguely that the 'state's controlling force' should increase in 'important industries and key areas'. Interviewees suggested that the marked discrepancy between the *Xinhua* version of events and the actual text of the policy reflects a last-minute difference of opinion between SASAC and the State Council (10BJ0629; 10BJ0702). The press release version listing seven lifeline industries reportedly reflects the contents of a SASAC report

Central SOEs in these strategic industries – regarded as the stars of China's 'national team' (Sutherland 2001)[2] – are every bit a 'commanding presence' and, behind high administrative barriers to entry, they have contributed the most to the surge in SOE profits in recent years. In 2009, petrochemical enterprises industries that were relatively off limits to private capital accounted for 32 per cent of total SOE profits, and SOEs in telecommunications, another protected sector, contributed 20 per cent of the total (Sheng and Zhao 2012: 40).

And while the expanding market share of non-state enterprises in non-priority sectors explains why the overall proportion of state ownership continues to fall, the sprawling business groups under these national champion SOEs include lines of business well outside of their core domains. An internal report drafted by the bureaucracy charged with managing these behemoths, the State-Owned Assets Supervision and Administration Commission (SASAC), acknowledged that, in spite of a concerted effort to focus central SOE business on their designated core areas of business (*zhuye* 主业), national team subsidiaries remained 'too broadly' dispersed across Chinese industry and were found in fully eighty-six of China's ninety-five official industries (SASAC 2007: 166). The shadowy role of central SOEs in one such non-lifeline industry, China's booming urban real estate markets, has earned them public opprobrium as well as the epithet 'land kings' (*diwang* 地王). One study finds that a surge in real estate investment by central SOEs in connection with a flood of stimulus funds in the immediate post-crisis period fuelled a housing bubble in 2009, the effects of which are still being felt (Deng *et al.* 2011)

In the context of China's internationalizing economy, the so-called advance of the state has implications well beyond Beijing. The national team's increasingly bold 'going forth' (*zou chu qu* 走出去) into global markets has brought the phoenix-like rise of central SOEs to the world's attention. Anyone who has spent time in Beijing cannot fail to notice Sinopec's imposing headquarters opposite the Ministry of Foreign Affairs on Chaoyangmen Dajie, a potent reminder of the state-owned oil giant's record of multi-billion-dollar investments around the world. Besides the massive resource enterprises, China's

---

which had been submitted to the State Council and which was supposed to have accompanied the policy that was unexpectedly rejected by the higher level.

[2] There is some confusion about the precise origins of the term 'national team' in the literature on Chinese business groups. Dylan Sutherland (2001) was the first to use the phrase 'national team' in the English secondary literature to describe the so-called trial group enterprises under the central government's authority; however, it seems to have had some currency among Chinese policymakers and academics prior to that publication. For instance, a 1992 article by Sun Xiaoliang, a scholar and member of the State Commission for Restructuring of the Economy (SCRES), the organization with primary responsibility for the trial groups at the time, wrote of the importance of developing a 'national team' (*guojia dui* 国家队) to compete with global players (Sun 1992: 27).

Table 1.1: *Mainland enterprises on the Fortune Global 500 list (2003, 2014)**

	2014		2003	
	Number	% of total (Global 500)	Number	% of total (Global 500)
Total mainland enterprises	95	19	12	2.4
Total state-owned enterprises (SOEs)	71		10	
	Financial (Huijin)	Non-financial (SASAC)	Financial	Non-financial
Central-Level SOEs	5	46	4	6
Top five mainland enterprises (Fortune 500 rank)	1. Sinopec Group (3) 2. China National Petroleum (4) 3. State Grid (7) 4. Industrial and Commercial Bank of China (25) 5. China Construction Bank (38)		1. China Petrochemical Corp. (68) 2. State Power Corporation of China (77) 3. China National Petroleum Corporation (83) 4. Industrial and Commercial Bank of China (213) 5. China Telecommunications Corporation (228)	

Source: Fortune Global 500 annual ranking, available at: fortune.com/fortune 500.
*The year 2003 is chosen as a comparator since that was the first year that China's current state asset management system came into existence. With a few exceptions, China's central-level SOEs in non-financial sectors fall under the authority of SASAC. Responsibility for oversight of the largest central-level financial institutions lies with Central Huijin Investment Ltd.

service sector SOEs are also increasingly active in global mergers and acquisitions markets. And prior to the Global Financial Crisis, global capital markets were kept busy with a wave of big-ticket 'red chip' SOE initial public offerings (IPOs) that peaked with the world's biggest-ever listing: the Industrial and Commercial Bank of China's 2006 offering for US $19 billion. Yet these IPOs made the national team enterprises public companies in name only; foreign and non-state investors were sold minority stakes that did not entail a substantive transfer of corporate control away from the state (Walter and Howie 2010). The national teams' overseas listings have helped them quickly advance up the ranks of the Fortune Global 500, a closely watched list in Beijing which is often treated as a measure of central SOEs' success in 'going big and going strong'. In 2003, only twelve mainland enterprises were to be found on the Fortune 500 list, of which ten were SOEs. By 2014, the total number of Chinese companies had jumped to ninety-five, of which fifty-one are central-level SOEs.

The question now on people's minds is whether this 'advance' of central SOEs is a cause for celebration or despair. While the dramatic reversal of fortunes in China's state sector is understandably a source of pride for SASAC officials as well as senior SOE managers, the pages of a new corps of liberal-leaning mainland media outlets such as *The Economic Observer* and *Caixin*, as well as social media sites, are littered with complaints about profiteering and official corruption in the so-called 'monopoly sectors'. In a biting piece surveying the challenges and achievements of thirty years of economic reform, *éminence grise*, Wu Jinglian, described the state economy in perilous terms as evidence of a reform stall:

> In the beginning of reform, much of the initial resistance came from ideology but now it comes mainly from vested interests ... state-owned monopolies and government departments have been enjoying the fruits of reform for a long time and further reforms will harm their interests. Pushing reform of the state-owned monopolies and that of the political system means that the government will have to reform itself. Consequently, reform has entered a more difficult battle and progress has slowed significantly. (Wu 2009)

Scholars critical of the state's advance argue, too, that the huge increase in government investment and the ever-expanding base of SOEs is gradually dragging down the efficiency of the entire economy (Zhan 2013). Tian Guoqiang (2011) argues that *guojin mintui* is indicative of a mistaken approach to economic development in China, which he see as predicated on a 'three heavies, three light' (*san zhong san qing* 三重三轻) principle: 'heavy on government, light on market; heavy on national wealth, light on people's wealth; heavy on development, light on service'. Reflecting on such criticisms, former head of SASAC, Li Rongrong, articulated what many SOE reform insiders see as something of a bitter irony: 'I don't understand it: why it is that when SOEs did poorly you swore (*ma* 骂) at them and now that they are doing well, you also swear at them?' (quoted in Wang 2010: 16).

Other influential economists contend that what we are seeing is not the betrayal of reform but rather its fruition. Influential Tsinghua professor, Hu Angang, argues that the hybrid economy now emerging in China offers both a sensible and a durable basis for a market economy with Chinese characteristics, one which brings into play the relative strengths of private and state-owned enterprises:

> In the socialist market economic system, state-owned enterprises and private enterprises play different roles. In market competition, state-owned enterprises are more like an elite field army. They are resource-intensive, capital-intensive, technology-intensive enterprises and their core mission is to engage in fierce competition with the world's top 500 companies and Global 2000 enterprises. Their aim is not only to take their place in this group, but also to rise rapidly to become industry leaders. Private enterprises are more like regional forces. They are job-creating, labour-intensive and employment-intensive

enterprises, which can effectively help local development, while at the same time making use of private enterprises' advantages in flexibility and innovation to gain prominence in international competition. (Hu 2012)

Others with similar views suggest that when Wu Jinglian and other liberal-minded economists characterize the increasing heft of central SOEs as contrary to the spirit of reform, they in fact misunderstand the very spirit they invoke. Whereas liberal economists have assumed, or perhaps hoped, that China's gradual reform would lead SOEs to the margins of the economy and eventually into oblivion, others argue that this was never the outcome envisioned by state leaders in the reform era. Two Renmin University economists suggest that SOE reform has always been a task of curing and strengthening rather than harm reduction and euthanasia: 'The basic aim of SOE reform has been to use institutional innovation to help SOEs adapt to the requirements of market competition so that they could become the main body of the market (*shichang jingji zhuti* 市场经济主体) and develop strength in market competition, in this way fruitfully combining the socialist system of public ownership with the market' (Lin and Zhang 2013: 12).

The debate outlined above has at its heart the question of what an advancing state could portend for the future of China's economic development. For social scientists and others drawn to trying to form an image of reform-era China in the long view, there remains the all-important, backward-looking *why* questions to dissect. The following pages turn, for clues about the deep causes of the advancing state, to three master concepts of social science inquiry: interests, institutions and ideas. While there have been a number of interesting and insightful studies of this topic, broadly conceived, in the institutionalist and interest traditions, there has as yet been comparatively little analysis from an ideational perspective, a void this study begins to fill.

Seeking the origins of the state's advance

China studies scholars have sometimes been accused of engaging too seldom and too listlessly with theoretical developments in the social science disciplines (cf. Reny 2011; Kennedy 2011). While that may be true, the field is in no way isolated from theoretical innovation in the social sciences. The following brief review of the scholarship examining the factors behind the precipitous advance of the state shows that China scholars have drawn very strongly from two pillars of late twentieth-century social science thought, institutions and interests. The basic, powerful insight of institutionalism is that social life is shaped strongly by myriad 'rules of the game'. Since these rules supply many of the constraints in which actors operate, so the argument goes, theory with a purchase on the real world cannot avoid reckoning with institutions. In the late twentieth century, this stream of institutionalism was blended into the work of many leading rational choice scholars, for whom interests and preferences comprise the core variables. The vision of social behaviour given by rational choice is of purposive, goal-oriented choice-making under constraint; institutions come in as 'scripts that constrain behavior' (Shepsle 2006). While institutions serve to channel behaviour, interests are the hard ground of action in a rational choice world, 'the stable foundations on which actors' preferences over policy shift as their situation and the policy vary' (Milner quoted in Schonhardt-Bailey 2006: 23). In recent years, both institutional and interest-based modes of analysis have been brought to the analysis of the advancing state in China.

While a later section of the chapter summarizes the key attributes of the ideational approach to political economy, it is worth here briefly differentiating the ideational approach from its closest relative, institutionalism. Of course, the choice of brevity means trading off against accuracy to some extent since there is considerable ambiguity within the social sciences about both the meaning of 'institutions' and 'ideas' as well as the relationship between the two (cf. Searle 2005; Schmidt 2011). This study follows an important recent work in conceiving of ideas as 'the foundations of institutions' which 'give rise to people's actions and as those actions form routines, the results are social institutions' (Béland and Cox 2011: 9). Ideational analysis is seen as a necessary corrective to institutional approaches that tend to treat institutions as social givens rather than products of social construction with a story of their own. Key ideational variables encountered in this literature include 'theories, conceptual models, norms, world views, frames, principled beliefs, and the like' (Campbell 2002: 21).[3] In the arena of politics, various species of idea that meet with the right circumstances are 'able to become a durable or *institutionalized* part of life' (Berman 2013: 229), while others less fortunate wind up in the dustbin of history. To date, a number of scholars have provided a thorough inventory of institutions shaping the advance of the state in China but we have, as yet, much less work examining the ideational provenance of institutions and the process through which they came into existence.

---

[3] Certain institutionalists would consider some of these variables as institutional rather than ideational. Indeed, Schmidt (2011: 54) writes that 'In the sociological tradition, one cannot talk about a move into ideas as such, since ideas have always been at the basis of this approach – as norms, cognitive frames and meaning systems.' Recent work in comparative politics on informal institutions also includes in its ambit some social phenomena that others would think of as ideas. For example, Gretchen Helmke and Steven Levitsky's widely cited work gathers norms under its definition of informal institutions as 'socially shared rules, usually unwritten, that are created, communicated, and enforced outside of officially sanctioned channels' (Helmke and Levitsky 2004: 727).

The role of institutions

A number of studies have shone a light on the distinctive institutions, or rules of the game, that contributed to the formation of large, state-controlled business groups in the reform period. Critical of the neoclassical view that minimal government intervention in the economy and free competition between small firms furnish the best conditions for growth, Nolan (2001) argues, with evidence drawn from in-depth case studies of members of China's national team, that the various institutions established to support the development of large enterprise groups were largely beneficial to industrialization. Nolan also suggests that the increasing emphasis China's policymakers have placed on consolidating the state sector reflects a widely held view in government that these measures will help Chinese enterprises adapt to the realities of the 'global business revolution', the defining feature of which is a sharp increase in market concentration in many sectors over the last two decades. Lisa Keister's (2000) excellent study analyses the ways in which China's large-scale business groups developed in response to an industrial policy drive that began in the mid 1980s. Common to major works in this literature is an interest in evaluating the merits of these rules for both improving economic performance at the level of the firm and advancing towards developmental goals set by central policymakers. Dylan Sutherland's (2003) first-rate work both unearthed the policy origins of the large enterprise strategy and provided in-depth analysis of the development of business groups in the auto industry. In recent years, researchers in the business and management fields have taken the study of China's nebulous business groups in many interesting directions.

Business groups

Growing interest in China's business groups has coincided with an upsurge in business group research more generally. While the immense diversity of business group forms in different national settings presents some difficulties in coming to an agreed definition of the term (Colpan *et al.* 2010), Yiu *et al.*'s definition nicely extends across this diversity. They define a business group as 'a collection of legally independent firms that are linked by multiple ties, including ownership, economic means (such as inter-firm transactions) and/ or social relations (family, kinship, friendship) through which they coordinate to achieve mutual objectives' (Yiu *et al.* 2007: 1553). From the standpoint of classic economic theory, the 'ubiquity' of business groups outside the United States and the United Kingdom (Khanna and Yafeh 2007) presents a puzzle in the form of a 'second Coasian question', namely 'why is it that in every known capitalist economy, firms do not conduct business as isolated units, but rather form cooperative relations with other firms[?]' (Granovetter 1995: 94). The literature has produced a wide range of answers to this question, with some researchers characterizing business groups as 'parasites', formed primarily so that insiders may reap particularist benefits, while others see them as 'paragons' established in order to fill 'institutional voids' in emerging markets (Khanna and Yafeh 2007). Pyramidal business groups are seen by sceptics as especially prone to parasitism because they present hidden opportunities for 'tunnelling' – typically defined as the expropriation of minority shareholder wealth but which some see as extending to 'non-pecuniary benefits from controlling a vast business group – political influence, social status, power, over even a degree of impunity from the rule of law' (Morck 2010: 615). The paragon perspective suggests that there are compelling, non-corrupt incentives for firms to form groups in circumstances where finance, labour and product markets are underdeveloped, since choosing hierarchy over market can benefit firm development by bringing down transactions costs (Guest and Sutherland 2009: 618).

To date, research on China's business groups has tended to support the paragons hypothesis although recent contributions have presented a more nuanced picture.[4] Employing panel data on China's forty largest business groups between 1988 and 1990, Keister (1998) found that the presence of interlocking directorates and finance companies were significantly associated with better financial performance and productivity. In the context of roaring debate about privatization, Smyth (2000) concluded that advocates of privatization and downsizing at the World Bank had painted an excessively negative picture of the financial performance of China's large state-controlled enterprise groups and argued that there was good reason for government to promote state-owned enterprise groups. Guest and Sutherland's (2009) research on firms affiliated to the 'national team' business groups analysed their economic performance in terms of profitability, Tobin's Q and share returns. They came away with the 'surprising' result that affiliated firms outperformed other listed firms on all three performance variables.

Two recent articles offer more qualified conclusions. Lisa Keister's most recent work on this topic has found a declining benefit in group membership over time such that while 'business groups may be advantageous early in reform, increasing internalization of ties may create inefficiencies that have negative long-term consequences' (Keister 2009: 21). Sutherland et al. (2011)

---

[4] The National Bureau of Statistics defines an enterprise group in China as follows: 'a collection of legally independent entitites that are partly or wholly owned by a parent firm and registered as affiliate firms of that parent firm ... the core company of a business group in China should have a registered capital of over 50 million RMB plus at least five affiliated companies, and the business group should have a total registered capital (including the core and other affiliated companies) of over 100 million RMB' (quoted in Colpan et al., 2010: 10).

find that labour productivity has been steadily improving in all categories of Chinese business groups, above all in the national team groups. But their paper also points to the signs of parasitism. They analysed China's fifty largest business groups and concluded that eighteen of them are pyramidal in shape. Looking in detail at transactions within one such group, Shanghai Electric Group, they argue that such pyramids may have parasitical qualities and 'could form part of an entrenchment process of certain elites – mainly controllers of the non-listed group corporations – looking to enrich themselves personally as well as elevate themselves politically' (Sutherland *et al.* 2011: 176).

Contributors to this literature also draw attention to a ripple effect whereby business groups have proliferated beyond and below the national team. Dylan Sutherland (2003) took note of a boom in business groups at the sub-national level. In 1991, large 'provincial teams' had already emerged in Shandong, Guangdong, Shanghai and Jiangsu provinces with Liaoning, Jilin, Shanghai, Jiangsu and Fujian later following suit (Sutherland 2003: 153). Sutherland and colleagues highlight the large number of private business groups in existence – 1,290 nationwide in 2008 – although changes in data-gathering and reporting in 2006 make it difficult to identify trends (Sutherland *et al.* 2011: 168). While experts on the national team business groups concur that their formation was very much a product of the visible hand of the central state (discussed below), the more spontaneous emergence of business groups below the central level, and especially in the private sector, suggest prima facie the relevance of the 'institutional voids' perspective in explaining the development of Chinese business groups.[5]

In addition to identifying the key characteristics of Chinese business groups, this literature has also provided insight into the ideational foundations of the institutions behind their development. Contributors have emphasized how sharply Chinese policies have diverged from the policy recommendations of the world's leading development organizations. The conventional understanding of China's miraculous growth after 1978, what Nolan and Wang (1999) refer to as the World Bank's 'transition orthodoxy', emphasizes the contribution of small-scale, non-state enterprises – especially Township and Village Enterprises (TVEs) – to economic growth and characterize large SOEs as perennial laggards destined for privatization. Typical of this view, Harry Broadman, a lead economist for the World Bank, claimed in the year of China's WTO entry: 'It is increasingly recognized – both within and outside China – that the SOE sector is the Achilles heel of China's otherwise remarkable economic performance' (Broadman 2001: 849). Nolan and Wang (1999: 169) countered that Chinese policymakers did not then perceive SOEs as

---

[5] The author is grateful to an anonymous reviewer for sharing insight on this point.

'stagnant fossils waiting to die' and, through institutional innovations associated with the large enterprise strategy, had done much to transform target enterprise groups into increasingly vital and competitive entities. And Keister's field research in the 1990s uncovered a widespread belief in the benefits of scaling up among her interview subjects:

> [One] reason managers frequently cited for their willingness to join [enterprise] groups was *guimo*, literally 'scope'. *Guimo* is the collective power of the group derived from having many firms working together. Power can refer to economic, political or social aspects of the word, so *guimo* indicates not just economies of scale but also the increased influence over political issues that comes with size. When asked why they wanted to join a business group, many managers smiled and said (in English, in many cases the only English they knew) 'bigger is better!' Academics, particularly those who had read E. F. Schumacher's *Small is Beautiful*, were quick to mention that bigger may not be better. However, academics and managers both acknowledged that the economies of scale achievable though business group membership might help Chinese firms overcome the state of market development in their own country and allow them to compete globally. (Keister 2000: 74)

The following chapter presents evidence on the continuing relevance of Keister's findings for understanding the logic of Chinese industrial policy.

Yet, while the distinctive concepts behind the formation of large business groups has been carried over some period of time, this is not a simple story of institutional path dependence. We now know a considerable amount about how decisionmakers and market participants tend to regard the function and importance of large enterprise groups, but comparatively less about when, how and why these views came to be embedded in the institutions of Chinese policymaking. There is a puzzle here not simply because of the obvious disconnect between these views and the common knowledge circulating elsewhere in the world but also since, as the next chapter shows, this outlook was also quite out of step with China's official ideology as recently as the late Maoist period.

Political economy

The work of political economists has drawn us closer to the questions of what organizing principles and beliefs have informed these institutions. A number of scholars have looked at the norms underlying these interventionist policies. Margaret Pearson's (2005) widely cited piece argues that calibrating a state of 'managed competition' (*youxu jingzheng* 有序竞争) among large, mostly state-owned enterprises is a bedrock norm of the regulatory institutions overseeing the commanding heights of the domestic economy. In a subsequent contribution, she argues persuasively that the Chinese regulatory state is in fact 'tiered' (Pearson 2011). Whereas the state takes a relatively hands-off approach to a lower level of competitive industries in which non-state enterprises tend to be the main players, industrial policy is often employed in a middle layer of the economy containing pillar industries such as the automobile industry which brings together non-state, state-owned and hybrid forms of ownership. In the top-level strategic tier of the economy the state carefully manages oligopolistic competition between large SOEs through the medium of industry regulators, powerful economic ministries and enterprise managers themselves, who are entwined with officialdom through such institutions as SOE Party Committees.

Similarly, Ed Steinfeld's (2006) analysis offers clues as to why government officials have seen it necessary to exercise a high degree of market control in the strategic sectors. On the basis of long experience interviewing senior officials in the economic bureaucracy, Steinfeld concludes that officials tend to see the process of creative destruction among small local firms as largely beneficial and appropriate, but place much less faith in the market selection mechanism in industries populated by large enterprises: 'When such firms run into trouble, the conclusion is generally that something unrelated to the market has occurred, something that requires not the dissolution of the firm but rather a policy treatment' (Steinfeld 2006: 482). These analyses help to illuminate the significance of what Steinfeld characterizes as an idiosyncratic but widely held 'market vision' among Chinese senior officials in shaping the industrial policies analysed by Nolan and others. But here, too, Steinfeld's market vision comes into the analysis as explanans rather than explanandum.

Popular accounts

While scholars of Chinese political economy have focused on specifying the content of these idiosyncratic institutions, a number of more sweeping accounts of the ideas and purpose behind the modus operandi in China's political economy have appeared in recent years. A former senior editor of *Time* magazine, Joshua Cooper Ramo, first coined the term 'Beijing Consensus' to describe a set of novel ideas upheld by a commitment to pragmatic experimentation which he characterized as a compelling alternative model for developing countries. 'China's new development approach', he writes, 'is driven by a desire to have equitable, peaceful high-quality growth, critically speaking, it turns traditional ideas like privatisation and free trade on their heads' (Ramo 2004: 4). Mark Leonard's (2008) book, *What Does China Think?* has a similar purpose (and some similar limitations) although his knowledge of the terrain of economics and international relations debate in China is much firmer. Political consultant Ian Bremmer has branded China a state capitalist system, one that threatens to unseat liberal market economies as the normative ideal. Stefan Halper (2009, 2010) argued that China is actively 'exporting' the 'corrosive' idea of 'market authoritarianism', a trend which he see as a potent, indeed *the* greatest, threat to Western pre-eminence in the world order: 'The expanding appeal of China's governing model is shrinking the West – making our notions of society and government less relevant – and will do more to alter the quality of life for Americans and the West in the 21st century than any other development' (Halper 2009).

Both Ramo's sanguine view and Bremmer's and Halper's alarmism have found an enthusiastic readership worldwide, if considerably less praise among Chinese political economy specialists (cf. Ferchen 2013; Zhao 2010; Kennedy 2010; Naughton 2010). In a special issue of the *Journal of Contemporary China* examining debate over the 'China Model' of modernization, Scott Kennedy (2010) describes Ramo's Beijing Consensus as a 'misguided and inaccurate summary of China's actual reform experience'. Barry Naughton (2010) cautions against touting the pathway taken by reform-era China as a ready example for other countries to follow, since China on the eve of economic reform was characterized by a number of fortuitous, and uncommon, initial conditions which were subsequently crucial to rapid development. Matt Ferchen's (2013) excellent piece faults Ramo and Halper for failing to engage with ongoing debate within China between so-called 'New Left' and 'New Right' public intellectuals over how to define the country's system of economic governance. Ferchen argues that the complexity of the Chinese economy and conflicting trends therein – sides of contemporary China largely glossed over in the above accounts – defy any sort of easy categorization. Drawing from Pearson's work, Ferchen does, though, identify certain hard facts about Chinese political economy: 'This is not, however, an argument for absolute relativism. Among other things, China does not have a competitive political party system and it does seek to strategically regulate certain sectors of the economy in order to create national champions' (Ferchen 2013: 411).

In varying degrees of precision and accuracy, the works mentioned above have illuminated the institutions of central importance to the advance of the state in China. The work of business group researchers has shone light on the policies and practices that encouraged large enterprise groups, primarily but not exclusively state-owned, to form business groups and pursue means of expanding their market share in the 1980s and 1990s. The group of masssive central SOEs under the wing of SASAC and other central government ministries bear the legacy of these policies with their group structures and commanding position in priority sectors.[6] Political economists have added insight

---

[6] While SASAC assumed responsibility for many of the largest SOEs overseen by the central government, there are significant portions of the state-owned economy that remain beyond its range. Financial SOEs, principally the Big Four commercial banks along with a handful of state-owned securities companies, fall under a separate state asset oversight system. Beyond finance, the SASAC system also does not extend over the politically powerful rail SOEs and the state-owned tobacco industry.

into the question of why these institutions have come into being. Yet, in locating the institutions that give shape, substance and staying power to these policies, the basic question reappears one level down the chain of analysis. Somewhat ironically, casual observers of China writing for a non-specialist audience have been most ambitious in taking up the question of what particular ideas and purposes animate China's distinctive market vision. While China scholars have, for the most part, found these analyses wanting, there has as yet been little work on this important question to emerge from within the field.

Interests: the particularist view

A relatively recent trend in the study of Chinese political economy is the emergence of a literature employing the tools of interest group analysis to explain policy outcomes. At first blush, it would seem something of an awkward fit. What could an approach devised for the analysis of pluralist systems possibly have to reveal about the nature of policymaking in authoritarian China? Yet, as proponents of this approach contend, authoritarian China in 2015 is a world apart from the 1978 version. In an article cited widely among Chinese academics, Cheng Hao and colleagues from the Shenzhen University School of Management argue that a fundamental transformation in the nature of state–society relations has taken place in which 'the entire social interest structure has undergone differentiation and reorganization. The original structure of social interests has been broken and new interest groups and new strata of interests are forming' (Cheng *et al.* 2003: 63). The more powerful of these new groups are seen to have successfully tunnelled into policymaking circles at all levels of government – via *guanxi* ties, business associations and direct lobbying (Steinberg and Shih 2012; Deng and Kennedy 2010). In his pathbreaking book on corporate lobbying in China, Scott Kennedy (2005a: 3) argues that this amounts to a qualitative change in the nature of governance: 'The consequence has been a transformation of both the process and substance of public policy. China's national economic policies can no longer be viewed as the clear intentions of a strong state or as only the product of bargaining between government agencies.'

One species of interest group argument that has proven especially influential is Joel Hellman's Partial Reform Equilibrium (PRE) model. Hellman, a long-time specialist in the politics of economic reform transition at the World Bank, deeply shook established views about the dilemmas of transition with the 1998 publication of his *World Politics* article. To that point, Adam Przeworski (1991) and other proponents of the 'J-curve' theory were seen to have the most insight into the volatile politics in countries of the former Eastern bloc then trying to establish market economies (Przeworski 1991; Haggard and Kaufman 1992). Przeworski emphasized the potential for reforms to be derailed or even preempted by raucous political opposition from the prospective *losers* of economic reform. Since inflation, rising unemployment and goods scarcity are some of the more common short-term problems associated with the introduction of market reforms, the J-curve theory posits that the basic challenge facing reformist leaders is managing to, in effect, shield themselves from the demands of reform losers in order to maintain momentum through the deep valley of initial reform. Hellman effectively stood Przeworski on his head by arguing that the primary political challenge faced by reformers is not in fact pacifying reform losers, but instead minimizing the policy influence of the beneficiaries of early-stage economic reforms, the so-called 'short-term winners' who derive considerable rents from arbitraging between the price differentials in the planned and market segments of the economy.

In recent years, scholars thinking about the politics of China's transition have found the PRE model a useful heuristic. Perhaps the most widely read is Minxin Pei's (2006) account of China's 'trapped transition' which argues that there are deep problems written into China's gradualist approach to economic transition and continued one-party rule. Pei argues that the lure of short-term winnings, and not a general preference for prudence and experimentation in policymaking (as has often been claimed), explains why China eschewed a big bang approach to economic reform: 'Under the logic of political survival, the advantages of gradualism appear self-evident to authoritarian regimes. Unlike the big bang, gradualism allows the ruling elites to protect their rents in vital sectors and use retained rents to maintain political support among key constituencies' (Pei 2006: 31). Pei contends that this logic explains the state's 'selective withdrawal' from the economy such that 'low rent' sectors like agriculture were liberalized relatively quickly while 'high rent' sectors like telecommunications and oil and gas remain squarely within the state economy. Victor Shih (2006) employed the partial reform model in his study of financial reform in the late 1990s and his analysis of the determinants of financial policy under Premier Zhu Rongji challenges the widely accepted view of Zhu as a defiant technocrat reformer (e.g. Yang 2006; Naughton 2007; Heilmann 2005). Shih argues that various actions of the central government in the financial sector since the late 1990s – especially the recentralization of banking authority, the absorption of massive amounts of state-owned banks' bad debt, the maintenance of high barriers to entry for private banks and the failure to liberalize interest rates – were shaped strongly by the personal interests of 'politicized technocrats' in the policymaking elite. He contends that these policy choices served elites' interests by either padding their patronage resources or making them appear as indispensable problem-solvers. Finally, Zhang Qi and Liu Mingxing's (2010) study of local governance employs the PRE model in arguing that local political elites not effectively held to account by village elections will tend to devise means of selectively implementing reform policies in order to protect both their intake of economic rents and their future opportunities for rent-seeking behaviour.

While the above studies characterize government officials themselves as short-term winners stymieing reform, other close observers instead direct their attention to the shadowy networks of well-connected managers of SOEs in the so-called 'monopoly sectors' (*longduan hangye* 垄断行业). Indeed, discussion of central SOEs as an interest group (*liyi jituan* 利益集团) has become a regular feature of mainland news sources (e.g. *Xinhua* 2006a; Zhou 2009; Wu, 2009). Wu Jinglian's aforementioned 2009 *Caijing* article was another bold critique, the force of which may have contributed to his being sidelined in matters of economic policy and to accusations, printed in *The People's Daily*, that he was spying for the United States (Barboza 2009). Since the Third Plenum of the Eighteenth Party Congress in November 2013, a historic gathering which unveiled a bold slate of reforms (discussed in the concluding chapter), senior Party officials have often spoken of the need to curtail the influence of interest groups in the state sector as one of the fundamental challenges China now faces. The leadership's primary means of combating vested interests is a sweeping anti-corruption drive which has netted a large number of both 'flies' (low-level bureaucrats) and 'tigers' (senior leaders) since 2012.

A growing number of studies suggest that, in recent years, central SOE managers have exercised an increasing measure of power vis-à-vis government agencies and policymakers. Barry Naughton examined the complex interplay between SASAC and the central SOEs in its charge and found that when SASAC pushes hard against the interests of these enterprises, as it has in the effort to harvest their dividends for central government coffers, it 'makes progress only slowly and tentatively, as it grinds against the formidable power of large, wealthy, and politically connected organizations' (Naughton 2008: 8; Mattlin 2009). Drawing from Kjeld Erik Brødsgaard's (2012) recent work on the political implications of state-owned business groups, Carl Walter and Fraser Howie (2010) argue that the inclusion of the chair/CEOs of central SOEs on the Party's central *nomenklatura* list acts as a considerable constraint on the authority of regulatory bodies, since regulators often hold a lower official rank than the managers they are tasked with policing. Wang Junhao (2008: 57) said of the regulators' predicament: 'The cat wants to catch the mouse, but the mouse is bigger than the cat.' Besides their high official rank, which confers considerable power vis-à-vis industry rule-makers, central SOE CEOs also increasingly exercise a more direct form of power as members of the policymaking elite. In recent years, as growing numbers of central SOE managers have been appointed to senior positions in the government and Party, SASAC firms have come to be seen as 'incubators' for spots in the top leadership (*China Economic Review* 2013). Since the conclusion of the

Eighteenth Party Congress in November 2012, a number of leading government positions in the State Council and government ministries have been filled with former SASAC firm leaders.[7]

There is also evidence to suggest that central SOEs' power and influence have been developed into regulatory capture in industries where SOEs are the commanding presence. Erica Downs argues that the powerful National Oil Companies (NOCs) are becoming progressively 'more autonomous and less influenced by the party-state' (Downs 2008: 125). As an example of the power the NOCs wield vis-à-vis the fractious energy bureaucracy, she cites their influence in the National Development and Reform Commission's (NDRC) decision to partially liberalize the domestic prices of gasoline and diesel which have traditionally been kept artificially low to stave off consumer unrest. In 2005, as the spiralling price of international crude oil vastly outpaced modest domestic price increases, thereby putting considerable downward pressure on NOCs' profit margins, the companies began to use their considerable market power to pressure the central government to raise domestic prices. The NOCs' most effective tactic was selling a portion of their diesel and gasoline products into international markets, leading to widespread shortages at home. Outrage over the shortages combined with sustained lobbying by NOC bosses – three of whom were alternate members of the Central Committee at the time – reportedly resulted in the NDRC's capitulation in March 2006 when it raised domestic prices on petroleum products by 3–5 per cent and by a further 10–11 per cent in May of that year (ibid. 130).

Along with increased media scrutiny of state sector interest groups have come various proposals, sometimes from surprising corners, for reining in their influence and eliminating monopoly privileges. In early April 2012, then-Premier Wen Jiabao declared on a national radio programme that, due to their 'monopoly position', the four largest Chinese state-owned banks 'make profits far too easily' and concluded briskly that 'we have to break up their monopoly' (quoted in Chang 2012). Wen's surprising comments triggered a massive sell-off of the 'Big Four' banks' shares. 'New Right' economist Zhang Weiying claims that the most egregious forms of rent-seeking in China are found within the state economy and has called for the elimination of all administrative monopolies (e.g. Zhang 2006). Some leftist and statist thinkers have also considered this problem and proposed more moderate solutions. Hu Angang,

---

[7] They include: Guo Shengkun, State Councillor and Minister of Public Security who previously held top positions in both the state-owned China Nonferrous Metals Industry Corporation and the Aluminum Corporation of China; Wang Yong, a newly appointed State Councillor, who made his name in aerospace SOEs before joining SASAC, where he served as Director from 2010 to 2013; Miao Wei, new head of the powerful Ministry of Industry and Information Technology, who held leading positions in the Dongfeng Automobile Motor Corporation for many years.

for one, is in favour of increased government scrutiny of central SOEs business activities as well as a more determined effort to separate government from business (*zhengqi fenkai* 政企分开) in the state sector so that SOE managers may shed their dual identities as half 'political man', half 'economic man' and focus purely on the latter role (Cheng *et al.* 2003: 71).

Interests: the national view

Others seeking to explain the determinants of the hybrid nature of China's economy look not to the self-serving impulses of short-term winners but rather to central policymakers' dispassionate calculations of the *national* interest. In this vein, Roselyn Hsueh (2011, 2012) has offered the most sophisticated analyses to date. Seeking to explain the government's selective removal of FDI restrictions across industry, Hsueh argues that China has adopted a 'liberalization two-step' such that:

> it [China] employs a bifurcated strategy to meet its twin goals of complying with WTO commitments and retaining some control. In strategic sectors – those important to national security and the promotion of economic and technological development – the government centralizes control of industry and strictly manages the level and direction of FDI. In less strategic sectors, the Chinese government relinquishes control over industry, decentralizes decision making to local authorities, and encourages private investment and FDI. (Hsueh 2011: 3)

Hsueh's exhaustively researched work is excellent in many way but to readers in the field now accustomed to thinking of particularist interests as a driving force in China's political economy, the analysis seems to falter somewhat where it readily takes official pronouncements at face value. In an incisive review of Hsueh's book, Kun-Chin Lin stresses the difficulties of employing 'strategic value' as an explanatory variable 'without trapping oneself in the artifact of official categorization' (Lin 2013: 181–2). In the absence of corroborating evidence beyond the text of official pronouncements, one cannot easily dispense with the rival argument, offered by Minxin Pei and others, positing that the designation of strategic sectors in China is itself a highly politicized process in which the preferences of short-term winners play no small part.

Different species of interest-based analysis have become increasingly common in the China studies literature. This is an entirely natural and appropriate response to the particular changes to the Chinese state and society wrought by more than three decades of economic reform and opening to the global market. The insights offered in this body of work have significantly advanced the painstaking work of prying open the black box of the Chinese state in the reform era. Yet we should not lose sight of the fact that politics is about much besides interests. In the category of 'other' factors, ideas in particular loom large.

The difference that ideas make

Students of Chinese political economy have employed institutions and interest analysis to good effect, but the study of ideas, a recently resurgent area of inquiry in the social sciences, has, as yet, had comparatively little impact on the field. The following pages outline in brief the main tenets of ideational analysis, an approach which this author sees as crucial to understanding the advance of the state in China. While it is true that more than thirty years of reform have created a more 'porous' state (Kennedy 2005b), the People's Republic of China remains a steadfastly authoritarian polity in which a relatively small number of people wield enormous power over the national policy agenda. It is in no way naïve to suppose that the ideas such policymakers have about the world around them shape their decisionmaking. As Blyth (2002: 32) argued in his pathbreaking study, ideas 'are important because without having ideas as to how the world is put together, it would be cognitively impossible for agents to act in that world in any meaningful sense'. Likewise, institutional analyses have pinpointed the rules, regulations and norms that, in the manner of newly laid railway tracks, have propelled the state's advance. Yet they tell us little about the impulse to build the railway in the first place.

Ideas have been rescued from social science obscurity in recent years. To many early twentieth-century thinkers, the causal significance of ideas was very nearly self-evident. John Maynard Keynes famously concluded his *General Theory* with the grim assertion that 'soon or late, it is ideas, not vested interests, which are dangerous for good or evil' (Keynes [1936] 1997: 384). Max Weber ([1915] 1946: 280) staked a different position on the materialism/idealism debate but also saw considerable power in ideas: 'Not ideas, but material and ideal interests govern men's conduct. Yet very frequently the "world images" that have been created by "ideas" have, like switchmen, determined the tracks along which action has been pushed by the dynamic of interest.' Somewhat curiously, given the political context in which social science was conducted in the Cold War period, it was the Marxist view of interests as primary that formed the ontological basis of mainstream political economy. For many years, the literature was relatively silent on questions once seen as vitally important, namely how ideas, and not self-interest, shape policymaking (Campbell 2002: 21).

A growing number of scholars pressing for the resuscitation of ideational inquiry have drawn attention to the shortcomings of interest-based approaches. Many are troubled by circularity in some interest-based argumentation, especially the tendency to 'impute a comfortable "fit" between policy outcomes and structures of political interests' (Pierson 2005: 45) and failing to prove the hypothesized link between cause and effect (cf. Béland 2009; Blyth 2007;

Woods 1995). Daniel Béland (2009: 708) notes the errors to which this can lead: 'Although the concrete economic and institutional position of policy actors affects the way they mobilize and understand their interests, two actors who occupy the same basic economic and institutional position can have contrasted views about what their interests are.' Mark Blyth (2002) suggests that interests are particularly indeterminate in circumstances of crisis when 'Knightian' uncertainty prevails, i.e. when agents are not only unsure of the best means of pursuing their interests but are fundamentally uncertain about what those interests are. Under such circumstances, actors turn to ideas, which can be defined most economically as 'causal beliefs' (Béland and Cox 2011), for guidance about the content of their interests. For this reason, the emerging view in this literature is that interests and ideas are not, in fact, conceptual rivals but instead 'interdependent variables' or 'cluster concepts' (Blyth 2002; Steinmo 2003; Hay 2011).

The turn to ideas has also drawn momentum from institutionalists searching for a more satisfying theory of institutional change. Both rationalist and historical institutionalists have been accused of theorizing continuity more ably than change. Rational choice institutionalists tend to perceive institutional change as a path-dependent, evolutionary process, yet, in the eyes of one of the principal architects of this approach, Douglass North, theorists remain 'simply, ignorant' about the particular causal mechanisms driving this form of change (quoted in Campbell 2004: xvi–xvii). Along with path-dependent forms of change, historical institutionalists have also embraced concepts of radical breaks in order – 'punctuated equilibria' and 'critical junctures' – as sources of rapid institutional transformation, or 'moments when substantial institutional change takes place thereby creating a "branching point" from which historical development moves onto a new path' (Hall and Taylor, 1996: 242). While the salience of such historical contingencies is, to many eyes, plain to see, the study of exogenous shocks has been hampered by the absence of agreed criteria defining the precise features of such events (Capoccia and Kelemen 2007; Hogan 2006). As such, much of the empirical work employing these concepts is seen to have a certain ad hoc quality. Vivien Schmidt (2011, 2010, 2008) has argued that ideational analysis, or 'discursive institutionalism', is uniquely positioned to fill in the blanks since it 'endogenizes change, explaining much of how and why public actors bring about institutional change through public action' (Schmidt 2010: 21). Examples of such ideational modes of inquiry which have shed light on otherwise puzzling instances of institutional change include 'epistemic communities' (e.g. Adler and Haas 1992) – or networks of knowledge-based experts – and 'policy paradigms' (Hall 1993; Blyth 2002) such as Keynesianism. Policy paradigms are said to prescribe the content of policy options 'until they no longer provide answers to the problems these actors face' whereupon 'a search is launched for a new paradigm that, when found, ushers in a new set of policies and institutions' (Campbell 2004: xxvii).

Of particular relevance to this study is the work of ideational scholars who have looked in close detail at the policy process through which institutions become unstuck and eventually unseated by new institutions. Drawing on the work of John Kingdon (1984), some scholars have suggested that it is useful to distinguish between the operation of ideas at different levels, including 'policy solutions' and 'problem definitions' (Mehta 2011; Béland 2009). Regarding the former, Keynesianism and monetarism were, at different junctures, accepted by a critical mass of policymakers as appropriate and feasible solutions to economic crisis and, accordingly, came finally to topple prevailing orthodoxy. Jal Mehta argues persuasively for closer attention to the way in which such crises are defined: 'Homelessness, for example, can be seen as the product of a housing crisis, high unemployment, or a lack of individual gumption. The way a problem is framed has significant implications for the type of policy solutions that will seem desirable, and hence much of political argument is fought at the level of problem definition' (Mehta 2011: 27). The findings of Chapter 2, which examines the ideational and institutional foundations of the advancing state in China, lend empirical support to the claim that the particular framing of problems is integral to the selection of policy solutions.

This book brings the tools of ideational analysis to study the advance of the state in China. In common with the work of Blyth and others at the forefront of discursive institutionalism, the approach taken in this book does not deny the significance of interests and institutions, but holds that ideas comprise an important component of social science explanation. With regard to the particular subject matter of this book, ideational analysis has much to reveal about prominent puzzles in the literature, chief among them: *why* and *how* did rules of the game behind the advancing state come into existence? While the existing literature has examined the content of these institutions in close detail and analysed their consequences for firm performance as well as regulatory practice, this body of work reveals less about institutional provenance. Likewise, interest-based explanations give us only a partial account of the factors contributing to the advance of the state. In particular, these works tell us very little about the process by which these powerful interest groups came to develop into such a powerful force in the Chinese political economy. An argument developed here is that interests were not, in fact, the ground on which the institutions of the advancing state were built but rather the reverse: ideas and institutions supplied the conditions for the formation and effective expression of state sector interests.

Book overview and key findings

The core argument of the book is that the advance of the state in China has developed from a set of ideas regarding the political and economic significance of developing state-controlled large enterprise groups. The argument is based on extensive qualitative research involving semi-structured interviews and document analysis. The author undertook fieldwork in China at different points between January 2008 and June 2012. Interviews were conducted with a wide range of knowledgeable informants, including current and retired officials in central government ministries and regulatory bodies, government advisors, SOE managers, managers of private enterprises, journalists and scholars. In the text, interviews are referenced by the date and city in which they took place and take the form 'Year/City/Month/Day', e.g. '09BJ1205' denotes that the interview took place on 5 December 2009 in Beijing. The analysis also draws from a large volume and wide range of Chinese-language sources including Party periodicals, industry journals and national leaders' memoirs. Of particular value is the author's collection of dozens of internal documents drawn from issue-by-issue review of *Jingji Yanjiu Cankao Ziliao* (Reference Materials for Economic Research), *Neibu Wengao* (Internal Manuscripts) and *Gaige Neican* (Internal Documents on Reform) between 1985 and 2002.[8] These materials were especially helpful to examining the ideas behind the core institutions linked to the advancing state and provide much rich detail about the policy process.

Chapter 2 examines the ideational foundations of the institutions most closely associated with China's national champions strategy. The chapter shows that these institutions developed incrementally as solutions to a widening series of problems faced by China's leaders in the reform period. At different junctures since 1978 the development of large state-controlled enterprise groups was framed as a partial fix to pressing reform dilemmas. Economic concerns were, of course, central in this process, but so too were political leaders' apprehensions about the implications of economic opening for preserving political stability and continued one-party rule. Indeed, the push of China's national champions has clearly had a political dimension. In the

---

[8] The *Jingji Yanjiu Cankao Ziliao* series of documents covers 1985–97. The *Neibu Wengao* documents are from 1993 to 1999. *Gaige Neican* documents cover 1994 to 2002. Such internal documents are categorized into three levels of secrecy: 'top secret', 'secret' and 'confidential' (Yan and Zhao 1993: 75). The above publications fall into the category of internal reference materials, the function of which is to provide timely reports on current issues and theoretical developments to officials and which are typically accorded a low degree of confidentiality. In theory, these publications are to be distributed only to government officials. In practice, the internal reference materials consulted here are not viewed as especially sensitive and some mainland libraries and electronic databases have holdings of them.

context of a rapidly growing non-state sector and a teetering state sector, policymakers thought of state-owned large enterprises as key elements of the market-conforming model of state control they began to envision and work towards beginning from the 1980s.

Chapters 3 and 4 turn to the national champions themselves. The analysis is of the reform pathway of two 'lifeline industries' (*mingmai hangye* 命脉行业) now dominated by oligopolistic SOEs, airlines and telecommunications services. The two industries make for an interesting comparison because of their very different starting points. Whereas Deng Xiaoping himself designated airlines as destined for rapid reform and opening, policymakers took a much more cautious approach to telecommunications, and command economy institutions remained firmly in place well into the 1990s. Following the logic of Hellman's Partial Reform Equilibrium model, one would expect airlines' policymaking to be much less likely than telecommunications to fall prey to the politics of 'partial reform', since concrete steps towards market liberalization were taken relatively quickly and with sustained pace after 1978.[9] And yet, thirty years on, the airline and telecommunications service industries now have a relatively similar market structure in which central SOEs comfortably dominate the market. Prima facie, then, interests alone would seem a poor guide to explaining how similar outcomes could result from such different starting points.

Chapter 3 looks in detail at the process of airline reform in China. This chapter traces the circuitous route of China's airline industry into the ranks of China's strategic sectors. While the airline industry now belongs to a small group of industries characterized by oligopoly among state-owned enterprises, the initial reform pathway in airlines in the post-Mao era hinted at a different future. Indeed, a pronounced puzzle in the study of China's airline industry is why the trajectory of gradual state retreat was abruptly reversed in 1997 when regulators began a bold retrenchment leading finally to an administrative restructuring of the industry around the 'Big Three' state-owned carriers. This chapter argues that this policy reversal was shaped strongly by central policymakers' increasing emphasis on developing state-controlled national champions.

Chapter 4 analyses the gradual advance of the state in the telecommunications sector. It shows that every major turn in Chinese telecommunications policy has been preceded and shaped by vigorous debate about the role of

---

[9] In Hellman's (1998) rendering, early-stage partial reforms strongly predispose policymakers to adopt a more protectionist policy stance later on when short-term winners are well placed to capture the policymaking agenda in order to prevent the diminution of their rent streams. He suggests that more comprehensive approaches taken early on are more easily deepened at a later stage because the accumulated rents accruing to short-term winners are much less than they would be under a partial reform scenario.

telecommunications in China's rapidly changing economic and social structures. In these moments of uncertainty, different visions of the possible futures of Chinese telecommunications emerged, the merits of which were widely debated among academics, officials and, occasionally, the wider public. While the telecommunications industry exhibits a form of institutional change very different from the airline industry – a gradual form of 'bricolage' (cf. Carstensen 2011) rather than punctuated equilibrium – as in airlines, the anxious climate of the late 1990s gave rise to intense industry debate over telecoms' market structure. As new institutionalists would expect, debate was not far removed from questions of material benefit; in a manner similar to the process of the airline policy reversal of the late 1990s, short-term winners in the telecommunications industry argued powerfully for the ideas that they perceived as beneficial to their interests.

After reviewing the argument, the concluding chapter examines the future prospects of the advancing state. In recent years, debate between leftist and liberal thinkers has generated increasingly divergent, even incommensurable, visions of China's economic future. In the lead-up to the Third Plenum of the Eighteenth Party Congress the two groups vied for influence with the new leadership under Xi Jinping. The analysis finds that while reforms unveiled at the Plenum have altered the institutional environment of the state sector in significant ways – principally by raising the costs of corruption and increasing competition in the strategic sectors – this does not amount to a radical departure from the status quo, but is rather an effort to strengthen China's 'two-legged' economic system.

2 The ideas behind the advance of the state

This chapter investigates the drivers of a puzzling instance of policy change in China, one with great significance for the present-day advance of the state. Beginning in the late 1980s, central policymakers introduced a series of policies which had, as their common aim, the establishment and nurturing of large, state-controlled business groups in key industries. Enterprise groups selected for inclusion in the 'large enterprise strategy' (*qiye jituan zhanlüe* 企业集团战略) now under SASAC authority are now relentlessly called upon to 'go bigger and go stronger' (*zuo da zuo qiang* 做大做强) via scaling up and striving to attain global standards of competitiveness. This muscular SOE-directed national champions strategy is a surprising development, not only because it does not gel easily with a widely held image of Chinese economic reform as a process of gradual state retreat from the market, but it is also inconsistent with pre-reform practice, meaning that this cannot easily be explained as an instance of continuity from the command economy era. Indeed, China's sprawling state-owned business groups, some of which, like Sinopec and China Mobile, are now household names the world over, would have been anathema to the official ideology of the late Maoist period which upheld small-scale, non-specialized industrial enterprises as the economic ideal.

Using the tools of ideational analysis, the key finding of this chapter is that the push to develop state-controlled national champions in key sectors drew support and gathered institutional firmness incrementally as the solution to a number of problems – both economic and political – faced by China's policymakers at different points in time. Both these problems and the policy solutions are objects of inquiry in this chapter. As recent work has emphasized, policy problems are, like babies, not delivered by storks (Mehta 2011; Béland 2009). They do not arrive unbidden on policymakers' desks fully formed, but instead take their shape and develop under the care of individuals who strive to identify their nature and then persuade their colleagues and superiors of the urgent need to address them. In the process of problem definition, ideas inform both the formulation and the presentation of a given problem, as well as its reception by the policymaking audience. (A monetarist, for example, would be hard-pressed to persuade a group of hardened Keynesians that a modest increase in the Consumer Price Index is cause for alarm.) The various institutions that together comprise China's national champions strategy were understood by their advocates to be solutions to this sequence of problems. As such, this was a process of evolution more than one of rapid paradigmatic transformation. Moments of crisis, principally the 1989 Tiananmen Uprising, did have some effect on the course of change, but exogenous shocks served primarily to reinforce rather than destabilize nascent institutions in this policy area.

A number of 'cognitive mechanisms' which 'alter how actors perceive their identities, interests, and possibilities for change' contributed to this policy change (Campbell 2005: 43). In the early stages of policy development, advocates of change engaged in careful issue 'framing' in the process of defining various command economy inheritances as problems for reformers to solve. In particular, analysts in this period argued that allowing levels of industrial concentration to rise did not violate the tenets of Marxist-Leninist economics, and would in fact be highly beneficial to China's socialist development. 'Transnational diffusion' and 'translation' also contributed to the incremental development of China's national champions strategy (Campbell 2005; Béland 2009). Study groups played a key role in the diffusion of policy ideas from other countries, principally from other East Asian late-developer states, as well as the translation of these ideas to 'blend into and fit the local social and institutional context' (Campbell 2005: 54). In the effort to mould large enterprise groups, Japan's experience with *kereitsu* was a particularly important reference point, but these lessons were applied not to historically rooted, family-based business groups as they had been in Japan, but instead to SOEs facing the difficulties of market transition. A similar process of diffusion and translation describes how ideas were drawn from the Singaporean model of high efficiency and competitiveness combined with firm state control of the economy.

The chapter looks, first, at the process by which the problems that have fed this policy change were defined. Shortly after the launch of reform in the late 1970s, scholars in official policymaking circles defined both the Maoist-era inheritance of fragmented markets and the sorry state of the planning bureaucracy as urgent problems for policymakers to address. Successful problematization subsequently prompted much reflection on desirable market structures as well as forms of market intervention appropriate to a socialist market economy with Chinese characteristics. Whereas problem definition in this early reform period reflected officials' overarching concern with improving people's livelihoods and achieving rapid national development, the formulation of later problems relevant to this incremental policy change was shaped by the national leadership's concerns about how to maintain stability and control in an economy that was shifting underfoot. In the early 1990s, an influential group of 'neoconservative' scholars and officials characterized the poor performance of SOEs alongside the roaring success of the private sector as a grave threat to the CCP's monopoly on power. China's WTO entry excited similar concerns as policymakers and public intellectuals migrated to a more sceptical appraisal of globalization in the wake of the Asian Financial Crisis.

Policy solutions were shaped strongly by the concepts and perspectives embedded in these problem definitions. In the early reform period, industrial policies aimed at creating large, horizontally linked enterprise groups around industrial SOEs aimed to kill two birds with one stone: while providing a corrective to excessively fragmented markets, these large enterprise groups were also envisioned as lynchpins of Party control as the state shifted from the command-era model of 'mandatory planning' to a looser, more flexible form of 'guidance planning'. In the context of post-Tiananmen hand-wringing about mounting debt in the state sector, policymakers justified industrial policy to support a number of 'trial' enterprise groups in the name of revitalizing the state sector and, it was hoped, thereby steadying the foundations of CCP rule. As China's WTO entry approached, a global logic became much more apparent in efforts to support the national team. Helping the national team members learn to 'dance with wolves' in international markets remains the problem focus of policies in this area.

Problem definition in the 1980s: fragmented markets and planning bureaucracy

Among the inheritances of the late Maoist period was an industrial structure characterized by fragmented markets with extremely low levels of specialization. Under the Cultural Revolution's insistence on developing China's self-reliance, individual enterprises were encouraged to adopt industrial processes that brought the A to Z of production, from widgets to finished products, under one roof (Kirby 1985: 156; Marukawa 1995). These silo-like 'small and complete, large and complete' (*da er quan, xiao er quan* 大而全, 小而全) enterprises formed the foundations of autarkic local economies which, in ideal form, contained a full range of industries. Such enterprises were, unsurprisingly, not known for their efficiency or quality. In the early 1970s, a township government in Hunan decided to establish a local auto plant that would produce all the components as well as perform all the assembly in-house. The plant reportedly produced a total of two cars in one year, one of which never worked while the other made it 200 metres before falling apart (Kirby 1985: 156). Into the early reform period, thousands upon thousands of such enterprises were to be found in China. In 1983, the light machinery industrial system alone contained within it 60,000 enterprises, the overwhelming majority of which were small or medium-sized 'full capability factories' (*quan neng chang* 全能厂) (Yu 1983: 44).

In the early 1980s, a number of analysts argued that fragmented industry was a critical problem deserving of policymakers' attention. In the context of the centre's emphasis on reform as a means of improving the productive capacity of China's socialist economy, policy economists argued that this 'irrational' industrial structure stood in the way of the national goal of rapidly boosting industrial output. In 1980, Wu Jinglian and Chen Jiyuan, both members of the Chinese Academy of Social Science's (CASS) Economics Research Institute at the time, roundly criticized Jiangsu provincial leaders for aspiring to develop an 'independent industrial system' (*duli de gongye tixi* 独立的工业体系), and argued in favour of a new national production system based on regional specialization driven by comparative advantage. Others called orthodoxy into question by arguing that such fragmented markets were, contrary to the official ideology of the later Maoist period, not a requirement of socialist production. Socialism, they argued with frequent reference to V. I. Lenin's writing, was also wholly compatible with higher levels of industrial concentration (Li and Chen 1981). Still others focused on identifying the myriad problems generated by the irrational industrial structure including so-called 'duplicate production' (*chongfu shengchan* 重复生产): low-quality goods; low labour productivity; energy and resource waste; and under-utilization of enterprise equipment (Yu 1983: 44). International comparisons were also commonly employed in such analyses to bolster the claim that China's fragmented and undifferentiated industrial structure was, in fact, a significant problem. Underlining the dreadful performance of China's auto sector was a particularly common rhetorical device. One piece noted that, in 1978, China's 130 auto factories produced a paltry 150,000 vehicles, compared to Citroen's 800,000 and Toyota's 2.84 million in the same period (Li and Chen 1981: 69). A later internal document pointed out that China hardly needed all of its 100 auto factories and 2,000 spare parts production companies (Yin and Jia 1987: 4). One analysis commenting on this problem characterized the 'lack of concentration and dispersion based on specialized association' as 'the most serious defect of China's industrial organization' (Wang and Li 1989: 114).

Besides fragmented markets, the command economy period had also bequeathed a clunky and run-down planning apparatus quite unsuited to the task of guiding China's reform-era economy. It is worth stressing that, to the majority of participants in these policy debates, the problem was not state intervention in the economy per se but rather the particular form state intervention had taken in the late Maoist period. Indeed, while a range of views were expressed about what course reform of the economic bureaucracy ought to follow, debate was not defined by a clear-cut divide between advocates of market and plan. Robert Hsu's (1991) exhaustive survey of economic thought

32 The ideas behind the advance of the state

in China during the 1980s finds that even self-defined reformers held an image of the ideal marketplace fundamentally unlike that of their counterparts elsewhere in the world:

> Whereas Western economists regard a perfectly competitive market without government interference as the perfect market, the Chinese regard the state as an indispensable element of the perfect market. Without the state's guidance, market activities will become 'spontaneous' and therefore 'blind', and enterprise behaviour will become 'irrational', resulting in anomalies and wastes such as fraud and oversupply. (Hsu 1991: 50)

While there were, indeed, intense debates over the appropriate design of this new structure of market control, even many of the current crop of influential economists and decisionmakers hold to the principle that firm state guidance is needed to suppress the worst impulses of the market (Steinfeld 2006). A later section of the chapter describes how large state-controlled enterprise groups were conceptually linked to this discussion about the appropriate aims and exercise of state guidance of the reform-era market.

In comparison to the task of defining fragmented markets as a problem to be solved, the problematization of planning was a comparatively easier job. This was because the need for reform of the planning bureaucracy was plain to see for most insiders, as the planning system in the 1970s had fallen into an 'extraordinarily haphazard and unrealistic' state of affairs (Naughton 1990: 746). At the central level, the planning apparatus all but ceased to function during the Cultural Revolution, and Five-Year Plans were typically issued well into the planning period, while some simply never appeared at all (ibid.). In this chaotic period, local governments stepped into the breach and assumed control of resource allocation as well as enterprise management. Decentralization did not, however, open significant space for the emergence of local markets, since, in the radical political climate, even sideline operations in rural areas were branded 'tails of capitalism' and noisily suppressed (Hsu 1986: 385).

The obvious failings of the old system opened the way for a wide-ranging discussion of planning problems in the late 1970s and early 1980s. Reform-minded economists argued that a 'mandatory plan' (*zhiling xing jihua* 指令性计划), i.e. planning with compulsory and highly specific targets, was inappropriate for application to the entire economy, since the complex analysis needed to write high-quality plans was an extremely tall order given the frayed state of the planning system. Aside from the practical difficulties, some reform-minded economists also argued that mandatory targets were a bad idea for any sector of the economy because of their excessive rigidity. Many argued the merits of a looser, more flexible system with a much greater degree of enterprise autonomy (ibid.). Hsu reports that while some economists did call for the abolition of the plan altogether, this was a minority opinion at the time, and debate in the early 1980s centred instead on delineating the appropriate domain of the mandatory plan from areas of the economy suited to a looser form of 'guidance planning' (*zhidaoxing jihua* 指导性计划). The guiding slogan for this effort was 'macro control and micro flexibility' which reflected reformers' hopes of combining 'the best of the two worlds of planning and the market' (ibid. 385).

The official embrace of 'guidance planning' alongside the gradual elimination of 'mandatory planning' held out the promise of a system of state control in better fit with the rapidly changing economy. In the early stages of this policy shift, the central government embraced a three-tier division of the economy along the lines of a proposal first advanced by Chen Yun in 1956 (ibid. 383). The top tier of the economy comprising products 'fundamental to state plans and the people's livelihood' and 'key enterprises that affect the entire economy' would remain subject to mandatory planning and close state control. A middle tier serving a function 'relatively important to the development of economy and society' would be managed by a form of guidance planning that made use of indicative targets as well as market levers such as interest rates, prices, credit, etc. The bottom tier, in which non-essential goods were produced and sold, was to be left entirely to market forces (Naughton 1990: 756). As Naughton (1995) and others have shown, the top tier of the economy gradually 'grew out of' the mandatory plan in the 1980s and early 1990s. But hindsight shows that guidance planning was not so readily shed; indeed, instead of withering away, the commitment to a more flexible form of market guidance seems instead to have grown *with* the market in the upper tiers of the Chinese economy (Heilmann and Shih 2013; Pearson 2011).

Yet while guidance planning was adopted as a moderate solution to the problem of an outmoded system of state control, analysts now identified new questions and problems related to the practicalities of guiding fragmented markets. In this process, new sources of inspiration were supplied through transnational diffusion, and these policy lessons sought abroad were then translated into a form appropriate to China's circumstances. From the mid 1980s, a number of influential economists with close ties to officialdom undertook study trips to neighbouring East Asian states and argued in favour of incorporating aspects of the developmental state into China's growth model (Heilmann and Shih 2013; Xiao 2006; Kroeber 2011; Li 1989; Xü 1989; Kang 1989). In an excellent piece examining the activities of study groups in the early reform period, Xiao Donglian notes that Japan was the primary destination for study trips, as well as the source of the most academic and policy advisors travelling to China. Between 1979 and 1980, the journal *Jingji Yanjiu Cankao Ziliao* published more than thirty reports of study trips to Japan and seven pieces on Japanese economics experts' visits to China (Xiao 2006: 25).

Wang Huijiong of the State Council Development Research Centre (SCDRC) later emerged as a particularly influential admirer of the developmental state and was described by a knowledgable retired central government official as a powerful proponent of industrial policy in the early 1990s (12BJ0522). In a nearly 200-page long-range planning document, *China Towards the Year 2000*, Wang, together with a colleague from SCDRC, articulated the link between the move to guidance planning and the embrace of industrial policy:

> The means of China's macroeconomic management is now shifting from mainly direct control to mainly indirect control. This shift is a profound change. It signifies a change from the predominance of a mandatory product economy to that of a planned commodity economy; a change from control mainly by indexes to management mainly by policy; and a change from stressing growth rates to stressing economic returns ... The study of the industrial policy is dictated by the need to develop a socialist commodity economy and to further planning and reform. Indirect control mainly depends on policy, i.e. creating a macro-environment by means of a set of policies so that micro-economic activities will develop according to objective demands. The industrial policy which embodies these demands is the nucleus of this set of policies. (Wang and Li 1989: 108)

Advocates argued that industrial policy could 'coordinate various means of macroeconomic control', improve the allocation of resources and lead to improved labour productivity (ibid.). Yet they also identified a number of practical problems that had frustrated early experimentation with industrial policy. One missing piece was an industrial policymaking system as distinct from the planning bureaucracy (Wang *et al.* 1990: 29). Wang Huijiong argued that the failure of 1980s industrial policies was partly attributable to excessive dispersion of responsibility between departments during implementation as well as the misuse of policy tools (ibid. 29). The fragmentation of Chinese industry was itself described as a formidable challenge since the sheer numbers and small scale of enterprises were said to make the impact of both direct and indirect state guidance 'very limited' (ibid. 29).

In the first decade of the reform period, government officials and scholars identified two problematic legacies of the command economy – industrial fragmentation and a bureaucracy inadequate to the task of guiding the newly emerging marketplace. The proposal to nurture state-owned large enterprises in key segments of the economy would later draw support as a partial fix to both problems. What emerges from close examination of policy discussion in this period is that, as Sebastian Heilmann and Lea Shih (2013) have argued, the 'plan to market narrative' which has been a dominant theme in the literature on Chinese reform is rather misleading. While decisionmakers hoped that the incorporation of market mechanisms would both stimulate economic growth and enhance people's livelihoods, the aim of achieving 'macro control and micro flexibility', was not simply lip service paid to appease conservatives uneasy about the pace of reform under Deng's leadership. While the deficiencies of old-style planning were quite apparent to most, a majority of influential thinkers in this period did not envision a wholesale move to the market and the retreat of the state as the desired endpoint of reform. Instead, they thought about new methods of exercising state control in an economy that, while allowing sufficient space for a variety of ownership forms to develop, would preserve the 'leadership role' of the state economy (Hsu 1991: 25).

Problem definition in the 1990s: control dilemmas

Maintaining a firm grip on the economy was, of course, not just a matter of designing better bureaucracy and rationalizing market structures. Conservative elements of the Communist Party had long worried about the threats to authoritarian control suggested by the flourishing non-state sector in the 1980s and such fears were only heightened by the Tiananmen Uprising in spring 1989. With Zhao Ziyang at the helm, calls to constrain the growth of township and village enterprises (TVEs) had been largely held in check. However, to the stability-minded leadership group that assumed control after Zhao's fall, the burgeoning non-state sector and the floundering state economy posed significant political problems for continued one-party rule. Opening to the global economy via trade and investment liberalization also presented the leadership with control dilemmas. Behind state leaders' confident assertions that China would abide by the rules of the liberal global economic order in the 1990s, policymakers worried about the foreign takeover of domestic markets and turned to economic nationalist thought for guidance in the ways of maximizing the benefits of opening while minimizing the costs in terms of lost control.

Threats from the non-state sector after Tiananmen

In the immediate aftermath of the Tiananmen Uprising, the non-state sector came under fire for both economic and political reasons. The economic success of non-state businesses in the 1980s met with opprobrium from Deng's opponents, who had long been unhappy with reforms that encouraged investment to flow towards TVEs, bringing increased competition to bear on large and medium-sized SOEs (Fewsmith 2008: 40–1). The fall of Zhao Ziyang, who had been Deng's pick for General Secretary, shifted power towards Chen Yun's clique in the aftermath of Tiananmen and raised the stature of members of Chen's more leftist camp (*zuo pai* 左派), including Li Peng and Yao Yilin. The period was witness to much criticism of Zhao's liberalization measures, some of which suggested that economic reform had weakened the foundations of state power. Debate raged over the political implications of the increasing share of business conducted outside of the state economy. One widely read left-leaning piece claimed, as 'unquestionable fact', that reform had led to the formation of a bourgeoisie, while others maintained that private entrepreneurs had neither come together as a social class nor become any sort of political force (Yang 1998: 353). Premier Li Peng was associated with the former view and, along with other senior leftist figures, was said to have circulated internal documents claiming that large numbers of dissidents had gone into private business on the coast where they were awaiting the next democracy movement (Lam 1995: 96). Some have argued that such suspicions left a lasting, and negative, imprint on private sector development in China (Huang 2008; Haggard and Huang 2008).

Along with claims that the non-state sector posed significant problems for CCP's monopoly on political power, leftists also perceived danger in the weakening position of the state economy. The counterpart to diatribes against the political clout of the growing non-state sector were influential leftist critiques bemoaning the state sector's dwindling share of output, a sign to some of an impending class crisis (Misra 2003). In late 1991, the Hong Kong newspaper *Wen Wei Po* quoted an unnamed top-level State Council official as saying that the central government was extremely concerned that the state sector's share of industrial production had fallen to 59 per cent (Lam 1995: 54–5). The official was reported to have said that, since large and medium-sized SOEs anchored the public ownership system, 'this phenomenon is not only an economic but a major political problem' (ibid. 55). Ballooning debt in the state sector also fed the perception of crisis. Between 1985 and 1991, industrial SOEs debt-to-asset ratio grew from 40 per cent to 61 per cent (Cheng 2013: 323). Adding in state sector subsidies of 56 billion RMB, some commentators joked that stopping work in the state sector altogether would yield savings of 13 billion a year since SOEs were expected to contribute no more than 127 billion in profit and tax payments (Lam 1995: 71). While these numbers were alarming, by far the more worrisome development was 'triangular debt' in the state sector which totalled 300 billion RMB or 16 per cent of GDP in 1991 (Lin 2003: 55; Shih 2008: 145). As we will see later in the chapter, increased support for large state-owned enterprise groups in the post-Tiananmen period was largely a response to leftists' concerns about the economic *and* political implications of struggling SOEs.

Towards World Trade Organization entry: guarding against the global

In the context of China's opening to global markets via bilateral and multilateral trade agreements, in the latter half of the 1990s support for large enterprise groups was increasingly justified as a means of mitigating the attendant risks of

China's linking up with the global economy. China's General Agreement on Tariffs and Trade (GATT) re-entry negotiations began in the mid 1980s, but the phase of deep liberalization dates to 1995, when the leadership signalled its commitment to a course of tariff reductions and relaxation of foreign investment rules in order to support its bid to join the World Trade Organization (WTO). The final WTO Accession Agreement included unprecedented concessions in agriculture and finance, among other sectors. Yet, behind the leadership's outward displays of commitment to abiding by the liberal principles of the global economic order, there was much internal discussion about how the state should best adapt to the political and economic challenges of economic openness.

Initially characterized by Chinese intellectuals and officials as a salutary phenomenon, globalization came later to be seen by many as 'double-sided' and something to be carefully managed by the state (Garrett 2001; Deng and Moore 2004). Early discussions of globalization and related terms (internationalization, interdependence and integration) defined increasing global flows of goods and capital as at base a technological process, and one that had much to positively contribute to China's development (Deng and Moore 2004: 118). The occurrence of the Asian Financial Crisis of 1997–8, however, prompted many more sceptical appraisals. Fuelled by the widespread perception that Washington had badly mishandled the crisis, and perhaps out of cynical motives rather than simple policy error, Chinese policymakers increasingly took the view that while globalization had many beneficial aspects, it also bore the indelible stamp of *Pax Americana* and would have to be treated with caution and prudence. As Deng and Moore (2004: 121) write, decision-makers came to 'characterize globalization as an irresistible tide that no one can or should resist while emphasizing the need to manage the process proactively to maximize benefits and minimize harms'. The double-edged view of globalization is also very much in evidence in discussions in the late 1990s of how Chinese industry would be likely to fare after WTO entry. While Chinese economists identified likely 'winner' industries, such as textiles and consumer electronics, they cautioned that capital-intensive industries, in addition to finance, agriculture and telecommunications, would in all likelihood be unable to compete in the global market (Garrett 2001: 420).

The fragmented nature of many of these 'loser' industries was seen as a particular cause for concern. Without large national champions to anchor national interests in key industries, officials argued that low industrial concentration levels made the domestic market exceedingly vulnerable to foreign encroachment. A 1996 internal report by an official with the State Economic and Trade Commission (SETC) made the case with reference to the civil aviation industry:

As China's economy is gradually linked to the international economy, there will be more and more foreign companies and large corporations in the domestic market. This

38   The ideas behind the advance of the state

means that the domestic market will become even more a part of the international market, such that enterprise groups that stay within the domestic market will be in direct contest with foreign companies and large corporations. Objectively speaking, compared to the strength of large foreign companies and corporations from abroad, we are at a considerable distance. The total number of aircraft of our three airline groups ... is less than America's ninth largest airline, Southwest Airlines. The combined assets of our four aircraft manufacturing enterprise groups ... is less than 50 per cent of the total assets of America's McDonnell Douglas. (Liu 1996: 2)

Such analyses arguing that the domestic market was vulnerable to foreign encroachment lent support to a rising tide of economically nationalist interpretations of China's predicament (Gerth 2012). They were also an important factor in central policymakers' increasing support for industrial policy as a solution to the problem of 'how to make a frail domestic industry capable to bear the shock of trade liberalization' (Marukawa, 2001: 32). The following section describes how, from the mid 1990s forward, large enterprises came to be seen as key safeguards of the domestic market in a more open market environment.

Amidst all the uncertainty and momentous change engendered by economic reform, maintaining stability and control was (and is) perennially a top-of-the-agenda issue for Chinese policymakers. What the preceding analysis has shown is the salience of two control dilemmas in preparing the ground for the adoption of a muscular national champions strategy. In the aftermath of the Tiananmen Uprising, neoconservatives preached (to the converted, at the time) that it was a matter of political necessity for the state to keep a watchful eye on the non-state sector, while at the same time revitalizing SOEs and securing the guiding position of the state economy. As discussed later in the chapter, this lesson of Tiananmen was largely retained by the senior leadership even after the leftists lost influence following the leadership changes at the Fourteenth Party Congress. And while FDI poured into China following Deng's Southern Tour, behind closed doors, senior bureaucrats asked themselves what could be done to shore up China's frail, fragmented domestic markets prior to meeting global markets head on in the WTO club.

Policy solutions: the incremental national champions push

At different points in time, each of the above problems served as a powerful justification for developing policies to groom state-controlled champions in key sectors. The remainder of this chapter examines the way in which China's national champions policy push developed incrementally as a response to what policymaking elites had viewed in different time periods as pressing reform

Policy solutions 39

dilemmas. Early versions of the 'large enterprise group strategy' (variously referred to in documents and studies as *da qiye jituan zhanlüe* 大企业集团战略 and sometimes as *da gongsi zhanlüe* 大公司战略 or *da jituan zhanlüe* 大集团战略) were framed as partial solutions to the problematic inheritances of the Maoist period. Key developments of this policy line in the 1990s took shape as responses to problems formulated in the politically uncertain climate in the post-Tiananmen period and, later, in the anxious mood that prevailed before WTO entry. The analysis encompasses both the ideas behind government-linked scholars' proposed solutions as well as the content of the policies themselves.

Fixing fragmented markets: inspirations

Having arrived at the conclusion that China's fragmented markets were indeed a significant economic problem, a number of economists with close ties to officialdom called for the government to make increasing industrial concentration via market interventions a policy priority. In making their case, they drew eclectically from the annals of economic history in expressing the view that mounting industrial policy in support of large enterprise group development could, if done well, sharply accelerate China's economic development. From Marxian economics they learned that choosing the path of marketization would lead inexorably towards monopoly. From the East Asian developmental states they derived that this was not necessarily a bad thing; the example set by Japan, in particular, seemed to suggest that judicious state guidance of the process of 'centralization of capital' could effectively steer enterprises away from cronyism and indolence and towards meeting national development objectives.

According to one participant in the early 1980s economic policy debates, opinion on how to fix the problems faced by Chinese industry was divided between a 'structural' camp (*jiegou pai* 结构排) and a 'system' camp (*tizhi pai* 体制派) (12BJ0514). Proponents of a structural approach argued that the government ought to use policy measures to imitate other countries' large enterprises, while the system camp maintained that it was most important to focus on establishing the institutions of a market system and eschewed an industrial policy approach to addressing the burdensome legacies of the command economy. To structuralists, the establishment of large enterprise groups was an attractive means of mitigating the problem of fragmented markets. As mentioned, analysts of the problems caused by fragmented markets tended to focus particularly on the 'irrational' characteristics of the auto sector. Accordingly, they argued that large enterprise group experimentation ought to begin in this sector and they subsequently developed specific plans for its execution there. One internal report, written by officials with the State Commission for

40   The ideas behind the advance of the state

Restructuring of the Economy (SCRE), argued that China's thousands of small-scale automobile factories ought gradually to be brought under the control of the three largest automakers (Yin and Jia: 1987).

In arguing that large enterprise groups were *desirable* for China, proponents of this approach also worked to bury the old ideology that had given rise to the 'small and complete, large and complete' enterprises described previously. They did this by trying to make a virtue of monopoly within a Marxist-Leninist framework. Several early contributions outlining the case for industrial policy in support of large enterprise development drew from the Marxian concept of 'monopoly capitalism' in characterizing the 'centralization of capital' as the 'inevitable product' (*biran chanwu* 必然产物) of development (Sun 1987: 4). One document, written by an official from SCRE – the central bureaucracy with primary responsibility for large enterprise experimentation in the late 1980s – argued that the path charted by advanced capitalist countries could – indeed should – serve as inspiration for China's reform pathway:

When capitalism experienced large-scale production and the centralization of capital, namely after the merger of enterprises, the transition from free competition to monopoly was realized. This period produced short-term price agreements, cartels, syndicates, and concerns. Today, these organizations still continue to develop and evolve. The economic organization of socialism is also in accord with this rule. Economic system reform and horizontal combinations have resulted in a great liberation of China's productive forces. Industrial development is now being reorganized along the lines of specialization, collaboration and alliance-formation. Thus, the production of a new type of enterprise group fully complies with the laws of economic development. (ibid. 4)

Proponents of the large enterprise group strategy looked to advanced capitalist countries for inspiration, yet the 'laws of economic development' they induced from their Marxist reading of economic history are strikingly dissimilar from the 'laws' then on offer in much of the capitalist world. At the same time that policymakers in Thatcher's Britain and Reagan's America were intent on dragging government out of the marketplace in an effort to recover an era of free competition, these senior Chinese officials presented a very different causal story. They argued that capitalism's triumphs had come not from the flourishing of free competition but rather from its subsequent extinguishing by the advance of big business.

If economic history offered the conclusion that large enterprises were at once the inevitable and desirable products of economic development, the example set by large enterprises in Asia's developmental states provided policymakers with ready models and benchmarks with which to guide their own use of industrial policy. Beginning from the late 1980s, various wings of the central government sponsored studies of large enterprises in other countries, and Japan's experience was a particularly important reference point (Keister 2000: 66). A number of internal reports summarizing the findings of

Policy solutions 41

these studies present the view that Japan's post-war development had been led, to a large degree, by its six large enterprise groups (Li 1989; Xü 1989). One article argued, on the basis of the Japanese case, that increasing industrial concentration resulting from large enterprise development need not lead to 'stagnation' (*tingzhi* 停滞) or 'decadence' (*fuxiu* 腐朽). The writer surmised that 'the formation and development of enterprise groups in Japan involved the reassembly of monopoly capital in accordance with the objective requirements of large-scale socialized production' (Kang 1989: 9). And, by 'adjusting the relations of production, so as to better adapt to the objective needs of the development of social productive forces', these enterprise groups 'played a huge role in promoting economic development in post-war Japan' (ibid. 9). Instead of becoming leeches on the state, the author argued, Japan's *kereitsu* remained faithful servants to the cause of economic development: they helped the government maintain 'macro control' of the economy in the high-growth period; they intensified competition in both domestic and international markets; and they stimulated rapid increases in investment and exports (ibid. 9–11).

Fixing fragmented markets: policy solutions

Beginning from the early 1980s, policymakers drew from the ideas outlined above in devising policies to fix fragmented markets. The central government's first notable effort was the 'horizontal economy' (*hengxiang jingji* 横向经济) initiative that took shape in the early reform period (Zhou 1995: 2). Policymakers hoped to partially liberate industrial production from the constraints of the planning system by encouraging enterprises in different segments of industry and in different regions to form loose alliances with one another. In a 1985 *People's Daily* editorial, establishing horizontal economies was described as a critical element of correcting 'overcentralization and rigidity' in industry as well as laying the groundwork for an economic system more in tune with the global economy:

[Under the command economy] everybody was 'eating from the common pot' – enterprises relied on the state, employees relied on enterprises. This became the common feature of the vertical management structure. To overcome this fault, we must, in urban reform, firmly open the doors not only externally [to the world] but also internally [between enterprises], to facilitate all kinds of horizontal economic integration and affiliation among enterprises, eradicate the closely confined, rigid vertical management structure of the past, and gradually establish an economic structure characterized by open, multilateral economic networks. (Tong and Song 1986: 27]

Yet the economic results of these enterprise associations were not encouraging. Member firms saw the absence of centralized control within these structures as limiting their effectiveness (Lee and Kang 2010: 218). Local governments were also often opposed to such alliances since they feared losing control of the enterprises under their management (12BJ0517).

In its early phases, the large enterprise group strategy really served as an extension of these efforts to dismantle the choking Mao-era system. In the mid 1980s, Ma Hong from the SCDRC took the lead on a dialogue with industry leaders in the auto sector chafing under the constraints imposed by a bureaucracy that touched on every aspect of their business. On the basis of recommendations outlined in a SCDRC report, in 1987 the State Council formally designated Dongfeng Motor Company a 'discrete planning unit' (*jihua danlie* 计划单列) which meant a significant repositioning in the nascent guidance planning system. Instead of taking their marching orders from an industrial line ministry, Dongfeng was placed under the direct authority of the central State Planning Commission (SPC). It was hoped that the elimination of this one especially thick layer of bureaucracy would enhance the automaker's 'enterprise autonomy', the centrepiece of enterprise reforms in the 1980s. The same privilege was gradually extended to a small number of other manufacturing enterprises in the late 1980s.

Elements of a market-conforming model of state control: inspirations

As guidance planning gradually emerged as the basis of policymakers' vision of a market-conforming model of state control, proponents of the large enterprise strategy began to characterize large enterprise groups as key instruments of state control in the rapidly changing marketplace. As the planning apparatus shifted towards providing regulatory functions in the economy and directly guiding industry in only the most vital areas, insiders argued that the establishment of large enterprise groups would be important to the success of the new system. In particular, the gradual replacement of fragmented market structures populated by thousands of small players with industries dominated by a small number of large enterprise groups would, it was argued, make guiding key sectors an easier job (Kang 1989; Zhou 1995; Chen 1995). And looking to the example set by Korea and Japan, policymakers 'believed that it would be less costly and more efficient to implement industrial policies in an economy led by a few business groups' (Lee and Kang 2010: 218).

In the effort to craft markets and state structures conducive to a more market-friendly form of state control, analysts also looked closely at Singapore's experience with large enterprise groups. An internal document drafted by analysts from the China Merchants Group argued that Singapore held ready lessons for China in how to achieve meaningful 'government–enterprise separation' (*zhengqi fenkai* 政企分开) alongside continued firm state control of the economy:

Policy solutions 43

Singapore's state-owned enterprise economy occupies an important position in the national economy, and is known throughout the world to operate effectively. Its success is evident in the separation between management of state assets and enterprise operations, that is, government–enterprise separation. Singapore's state-owned economy is largely based on the government's establishment of four large holding companies as the core and with enterprise groups composed of government-linked companies. (Zhang and Liang 1995: 20–1)

In the years since, policymakers have drawn inspiration from both elements of the Singapore model – the commanding position of the state economy and their particular approach to government–enterprise separation. Indeed, support for an 'East Asiatic model' has been described as a hallmark of the Jiang Zemin era in which government support for state-controlled large enterprise groups crystallized. As leaders, both Jiang Zemin and Li Peng were said to share a belief 'in the co-existence of one-party dictatorship with "international" norms of doing business' and drew eclectically from the example set by ASEAN countries as well as Japan and South Korea in placing state-owned enterprise groups at the centre of their vision of Chinese capitalism (Lam 1999: 319).

Pillars of a revitalized state sector: inspirations

In the aftermath of the Tiananmen Uprising, support for large enterprise groups was closely linked to the leftists' emphasis on revitalizing the state sector as a matter not only of economic importance but also political urgency. Indeed, the development of the then incipient large enterprise group strategy was given a significant boost by Premier Li Peng's ascent in the leadership ranks and the prevailing leftist mood of the post-Tiananmen period. While the centrepiece of this post-Tiananmen period of retrenchment was a macroeconomic austerity programme that aimed to dampen the high inflation of the late 1980s, the Li Peng–Jiang Zemin administration also devoted significant resources to strengthening beleaguered SOEs. To some degree, the lessons of Tiananmen offered by influential 'neoconservative' (*xin baoshoupai* 新保守派) thinkers in the post-Tiananmen period of conservative rule (1989–92) were absorbed into official orthodoxy and survived Deng's famed Southern Tour and the subsequent decline of neoconservative influence.[1]

---

[1] So-called neoconservatives positioned their ideas in relation to that of Zhao Ziyang's 'neoauthoritarian' programme outlined in a series of 1987 speeches. Among other bold proposals, Zhao advocated strengthening inner-Party democracy and imposing a decisive separation between Party and government. (See the chapters in Wu and Lansdowne (2008) for analyses of the legacy of Zhao's proposals in various policy realms.) Neoconservatives incorporated some elements of neoauthoritarianism but argued that what was needed was not the diffusion of state power but instead its centralization in the hands of the CCP (Sullivan 1994). Leading proponents of

State sector policy initiatives drew inspiration from neoconservative views on how best to address the political dilemmas of economic reform identified by the leftists' following Tiananmen. The most influential exposition of the neoconservative creed came in a September 1991 internal document circulated following the unsuccessful coup against Gorbachev and said to have been commissioned by Chen Yuan and Deng Yingtao (Gu and Kelly 1994: 224). Viewed at the time as a 'direct consequence of a reaction to the democratic movement' (ibid. 229), the report articulated a seven-point programme to restore the stability and legitimacy of the Chinese state and avoid the Soviet Union's fate. The authors argued that, while staying the course of marketization was desirable, the Party would have to grasp not only the army but also the economy more firmly:

> Some scholars hold that a major reason our Party was able to grow large and strong was its grasp of the gun barrel, 'the Party controls the gun'. But this is only one aspect. Another still more important one is that the Party has to control the asset economy (*caichan jingji*). This is especially important under the present circumstances ... Party control of the asset economy is advantageous in stabilizing and advancing reform of the political system. If the Party owned the assets, political stability would have a carrier. Social progress can be guided by a powerful corporate interest and is not evidence of loss of control. (quoted in Gu and Kelly 1994: 226)

Influential Party elder Chen Yun was said to have read and received the neoconservatives' report enthusiastically. The Hong Kong press reported at the time that he circulated it among top leaders and may even have argued for its inclusion in the General Secretary's political report to the Fourteenth Party Congress in 1992 (Baum 1996: 330). Some of Jiang Zemin's speeches in this period were also suggestive of neoconservative influence, particularly a 'rigid and strident' July 1991 speech warning of bourgeois liberalization and calling for strengthened centralized planning and socialist ownership (ibid. 332).

Pillars of a revitalized state sector: policy solutions

Along with various measures to bail out SOEs, the central government's state sector revitalization plan included increased support for state-owned large enterprises in the name (if not entirely the spirit) of improved competitiveness.[2] At a high-level January 1991 meeting chaired by Li Peng, the assembled

---

neoconservatism included State Council spokesman Yuan Mu, propaganda official Xu Weichen, CASS scholar He Xin, and the 'princeling' son of Chen Yun, Chen Yuan (Baum 1996: 328).

[2] The leadership's SOE reform agenda, summarized in a presentation by Premier Li Peng to the Central Work Conference in September 1991 aimed primarily at the short-term goal of propping up the ailing state sector. The leadership pledged to extend the 'double guarantee' for SOEs (under which they were accorded priority access to bank loans and materials); subsidize their technological upgrading; adjust interest rates; and reduce the tax rate to 33 per cent. Tasked with

officials agreed that 'in order to increase the competitiveness of SOEs', SCRE, the State Planning Commission (SPC) and the Production Committee would jointly select 100 SOE enterprises to serve as pilot enterprise groups (Li 2007: 796–7). The meeting participants agreed that pilot enterprises should be granted broad foreign trade rights and have ready access to preferential loans (ibid.). The administration's plan for SOE revitalization later presented to the Central Work Conference, in September 1991, laid out the details of the 'large enterprise group pilot project', for which fifty-five pilot enterprise groups had already been picked, and pledged to expand the trial after sufficient experience had been gained (ibid. 858–60).

Behind the language of improved competiveness, however, lay more immediate concerns. In the context of a mounting financial crisis in the state sector, the establishment of large enterprise groups helped to relieve pressure on the state's financial resources, since politically unpalatable bankruptcies could be avoided by merging loss-making SOEs with stronger performers in enterprise groups (Cheng 2013: 332–3; Ma and Lu 2005). In 1997 the ranks of the incipient national team expanded to 120 with the addition of 63 enterprise groups. After the 1997 additions, a number of industries were represented by several pilot enterprises including electronics (ten), steel (eight), autos (six) and chemicals (seven). In picking multiple winners in key industries, policymakers had apparently been influenced by the views of the leaders of the influential Association for the Promotion of Business Groups who had travelled to Japan and South Korea to study how to promote oligopolistic competition between business groups (Sutherland 2003: 49).

In the 1990s, these 'pilot' enterprise groups were the beneficiaries of various forms of industrial policy. The most important of these were the diverse policy measures that served to minimize and channel the participation of foreign firms in priority industries (Nolan 2001: 18). Pilot enterprises benefited from the protections afforded by higher than average tariff structures as well as an array of non-tariff barriers including rules that limited foreign competitors' access to domestic supply chains; technology transfer requirements; and regulations obliging foreign firms to establish joint ventures with Chinese partner companies. Pilot enterprises also enjoyed a greater degree of 'enterprise autonomy', a policy priority of the time, than most SOEs in this period. In contrast to non-targeted SOEs, where business decisions were still strongly shaped by

---

solving triangular debt, new Vice-Premier Zhu Rongji's 'politically and economically savvy' solution was to lean on the banks to disburse loans of almost 80 billion RMB to the most heavily indebted enterprises who were, in turn, ordered to repay their debts to other SOEs, a method which succeeded in erasing 380 million RMB in debt (Shih 2008: 146). Shih (ibid.) points out that while Zhu's solution earned him accolades within the Party, the costs of this approach were ultimately borne by the financial sector since the banks were further exposed to the weakest performers in the state sector.

the priorities of various government bodies, pilot enterprises were granted broad autonomy over investment decisions, export and imports.[3] They were also permitted to retain their profits ahead of many other enterprises (ibid. 19). Finally, members of the national team were provided with major financial support from the state. Pilot enterprises were guaranteed capital funding through state plans which was disbursed primarily though soft loans provided by China Development Bank and the state-owned commercial banks, with whom most pilot enterprises had formal agreements designating one of them as its 'lead bank' (*zhu ban yinhang* 主办银行) (Yu 1998: 4). Among the commercial banks, China Construction Bank (CCB) was most strongly associated with the large enterprise policy line. Nolan (2001: 19) reports that CCB had 500 branches based in large enterprises which provided management with financial consultation and ready financing options.

It is almost a truism that Deng's Southern Tour in early 1992 effectively undercut the leftists and their neoconservative cousins and reignited the reform drive, in the process marking the post-Tiananmen period as a transitory phenomenon, nothing more than a brief pause in the process of reform and opening (e.g. Naughton 1995: 273). But the reality is perhaps a little more complex. As Willy Wo-Lap Lam has argued, the new leadership installed after the Fourteenth Party Congress held views on important matters of economic policy that were, in fact, quite consistent with the neoconservative outlook. Referring to Jiang Zemin and Zhu Rongji as 'neoconservative' leaders, Lam (1999) contends that the two top leaders, together with Li Peng, were united in the view that strengthening the state economy was of paramount importance and came to see shareholding reforms and other means of SOE restructuring (*gaizhi* 改制) as a means to that end. Insiders also reported in interviews that, contrary to his popular image as a brazen market reformer, Zhu Rongji was seen by many in the central government as an inveterate planner and was often at odds with senior officials, such as Qiao Shi and Tian Jiyun, who held more closely to Zhao Ziyang's vision of political and economic reform (12BJ0520).

One manifestation of the lingering influence of neoconservativism was policy debate about the appropriate domain of the 'state-owned economy' (*guoyou jingji* 国有经济) that began in earnest in the mid 1990s. At the same time that non-state enterprises established a firm footing in many industries, the central government began to consider how the state economy could continue to exercise a 'leading force' (*zhudao liliang* 主导力量) in the economy, a role mandated by the PRC's Constitution and emphasized by

---

[3] Survey data analysed by Cheng Xiaonong sheds light on the context of these privileges for 'pilot' enterprises. In 1993, while 89 per cent of SOE managers reported having decisionmaking autonomy in matters of production, just 15 per cent had autonomy over enterprise export and import decisions (Cheng 2013: 343).

Policy solutions 47

neoconservatives.[4] A 1994 internal report by researchers in the State Council noted that, at the time, there were two influential views on what 'leading force' actually meant: one camp argued that the state need only control certain key sectors of the economy in order to provide a 'leading force', while others took the view that the state would have to retain control of a large proportion of the entire economy in order to meaningfully fulfil this role (GWYYJSKTZ 1994: 27). At the time, the State Council report endorsed the latter view though senior policymakers subsequently leaned towards the former 'commanding heights' interpretation at the Fifteenth Party Congress (1997).[5] The state's plan for 'adjusting the layout of the state-owned economy' outlined at the Fifteenth Party Congress was that the state ought to retain a firm 'controlling force' (*kongzhili* 控制力) in 'lifeline industries' (*mingmai hangye* 命脉行业) and 'critical areas' (*guanjian lingyu* 关键领域). As will be shown later in the chapter, in the ensuing discussion about how the state ought to enhance its controlling force in priority industries, the development and expansion of state-owned large enterprises was described as an important method.

From the large enterprise group strategy to 'grabbing the large'

While references to the large enterprise strategy within Chinese officialdom petered out in the late 1990s – partly because Li Peng was replaced by Zhu Rongji as Premier and partly because the Asian Financial Crisis had badly tarnished the image of Asian business groups – one finds, nonetheless, a high degree of ideational continuity in later state sector initiatives. In particular, 'grabbing the large' – one half of the most controversial policy of 'grab the large, let go the small' (*zhua da fang xiao* 抓大放小) – carried forward the essential aims of the large enterprise strategy championed by Premier Li Peng in earlier years. In general terms, the idea was to focus the state's resources on supporting a group of 'elite SOEs' that would anchor a trimmer, fitter state economy (Lam 1999: 294). In the Fourth Plenary Session of the Eighth National People's Congress held in March 1996, the central government specified the terms of 'grabbing the large' in a document stating that the state would thereafter focus on transforming the thousand largest

---

[4] Chapter 1, Article 7 of the *Constitution of the People's Republic of China* reads: 'The state economy is the sector of socialist economy under ownership by the whole people; it is the leading force in the national economy. The state ensures the consolidation and development of the state economy.'

[5] *Mingmai hangye* is also a common translation of 'commanding heights'. The phrase 'commanding heights' was apparently first used by Lenin in 1922 in a speech explaining the Russian Communist Party's decision to switch to a form of state capitalism under the New Economic Policy. Lenin tried to reassure colleagues nervous about the Party's prospects under the circumstances of reduced dominance of the economy by saying that state control of land and crucial industrial sectors would serve to safeguard Party interests (Wu 2011a: 31, n. 9).

state-owned enterprises into the 'core of a modern enterprise system' (Xia 1999: 4). And as the text of the Fourth Plenary Session of the Fifteenth Central Committee's *Decision on Some Problems in SOE Reform and Development* makes clear, a primary goal of 'grabbing the large' was to cement the pivotal role of large SOEs in domestic and international markets. The Decision sets out the aim of transforming large enterprises into 'pillars of the national economy and the main strength in China's participation in international competition'.

In this period, state-owned large enterprises were also characterized as key lynchpins of state control in a pared-down state sector. The policy context was the Fifteenth Party Congress report's call to 'adjust the layout of the state sector' (*guoyou jingji buju tiaozheng fangzhen* 国有经济布局调整方针) such that majority state ownership would remain in 'lifeline' (*mingmai* 命脉) and 'pillar' (*zhizhu* 支柱) industries. In such priority sectors, the state pledged to increase its ability to control markets and improve SOE competitiveness. In all other so-called 'competitive' industries, the establishment of non-state enterprises was to be encouraged, while SOEs would eventually be encouraged to retreat. In the effort to parse this language for the purposes of implementation, policy debate subsequently focused on a number of key issues, including the precise definition of 'lifeline' and pillar industries; the means by which the state would exercise control in priority industries; the desired market structure in priority sectors; and appropriate forms of market regulation therein. In this context, encouraging the development and expansion of state-owned large enterprises came to be seen as one of the important means by which the state could enhance its control over priority industries. One internal report on the topic argued that as large state-owned business groups increased in size they would eventually be able to control domestic markets and lead the charge into international markets (Sheng 1997: 3).

Assembling a national team

Following Sutherland (2003) and Nolan (2001), in the late 1990s, elite pronouncements placed steadily greater emphasis on the pivotal role of large enterprises in China's internationalizing economy. As China's WTO entry negotiations entered the final stages and elements of economic nationalism featured increasingly prominently in intellectual and policymaking circles, supporters of the large enterprise groups began speaking of the 'pilot' enterprise groups as important defenders of China's national interests. In a 1997 speech, Vice-Premier Wu Bangguo made the case in stark terms: 'If we could have ten or twelve internationally competitive large enterprises we wouldn't just be a "big" economy, we could become a "strong" economy; we could take our rightful place in the international economy' (*Jin yi bu* 1997: 1).[6] Some documents from this period even called for large enterprises to engage in *Art of War*-style tactics in order to enhance their own position and undercut that of their competitors. In a 1995 speech addressing the challenges faced by the 'pilot' large enterprise groups in a liberalizing economy, Chen Qingtai, a senior central government official closely linked to the large enterprise group trials advised: 'We must not limit alliance formations to domestic enterprises; we should also make use of conflicting interests between international competitors and establish alliances with the competitors of our competitors; we must also consider attacking (*chuji* 出击) international markets and a number of new market areas, such as third world markets' (Chen 1995: 6).

In these uncertain times, large enterprises were described in some internal documents as providing a line of defence against foreign encroachment in the home market. The aforementioned State Council report on the economy noted that one of the rationales for supporting the development of large SOEs was China's increased vulnerability to foreign control of the economy due to the frailty of the non-state sector: 'In the context of a high degree of economic openness, in which market competition is intense and the private sector is weak, large state-owned enterprise groups should be established so as to safeguard the interests of the nation' (GWYYJSKTZ 1994: 27). Internal documents also reflect a preoccupation with large SOEs 'getting bigger and stronger' (*zuo da zuo qiang* 做大做强) in order to ward off the advances of foreign multinationals. The aforementioned SETC report on the sorry state of aviation, concluded that the solution to facing competition from the likes of McDonnell Douglas was to dance with the wolves: 'In the face of these powerful competitors, we must quickly adjust the organizational structure of enterprises; encourage competition; promote alliances and mergers; and make some strong enterprises that are in line with the country's industrial policy grow rapidly stronger' (Liu 1996: 2). In interviews with Chinese academics in the late 1990s, Keister (2000: 74) found wide support for the view that 'economies of scale achievable through business group membership might help Chinese firms overcome the state of market development in their own country and allow them to compete globally'.

It was also in this period that central policymakers began to emphasize the importance of the national team's expansion into overseas markets. Over the course of his time as Party Secretary-General, Jiang Zemin's speeches placed increasing emphasis on the twin concepts of 'bringing in' (*yin jin lai* 引进来) and 'going forth' (*zou chu qu* 走出去). An extended trip to Africa in 1996 apparently left Jiang deeply impressed with the continent's abundant

---

[6] Nolan (2001) and Sutherland (2003) first drew attention to similar statements by Wu Bangguo in this period.

natural resources and the many opportunities for China there (Chen 2009: 63). And from this point forward, his speeches made frequent reference to the importance of enterprises 'going forth' into global markets. In a January 2000 Politburo meeting, in an atmosphere of widespread uncertainty and anxiety about China's imminent WTO entry, Jiang explicated the links between *yin jin lai*, *zou chu qu* and China's fate in the globalizing economy:

In the last twenty years, we have focused on 'bringing in'. We have taken in foreign capital, technology, human capital and management experience and this was completely necessary. If we had not first 'brought in', it would be difficult to improve our products, technology and management ability; had we wanted to go forth, we would not have been able. The situation now is very different than twenty years ago. Our economic level has increased greatly so that we should, and possess the means to, go forth. It is only if we bravely go forth that we will be able to remedy our resource shortages and insufficient domestic market. Only if we go forth will we be able to introduce our technology, equipment and goods into foreign markets; this, in turn, will allow us to bring in new technologies and develop new products at home. Only this way will we be able to gradually shape our own multinational companies and better participate in international competition. Only in this way will be able to promote the economic development of developing countries; combat hegemonism and power politics; and protect world peace. (quoted in Chen 2009: 64)

Since the designation of 'going forth' as a 'major new action in the new phase of China's opening' at the Sixteenth Party Congress (2002), various levels and agencies of government have unveiled policies to promote overseas investment, including: soft loans for financing on key projects; simplified approval procedures; looser capital controls; and information and guidance on investment destinations in the Ministry of Commerce's *Guidelines for Investment in Overseas Countries' Industries* (Zhang 2005: 7–9).

This global logic is also a core mandate of the bureaucracy now tasked with guiding the national team – SASAC. Established in 2003, the central arm of SASAC was tasked with 'performing investor's responsibilities, supervising and managing the state-owned assets of the enterprises under the supervision of the central government (excluding financial enterprises), and enhancing the management of state-owned assets' for the 196 central SOEs placed under its care, many of which had previously belonged to the 'trial' large enterprise groups discussed above. SASAC was also given the ambitious goal of creating between thirty and fifty globally competitive enterprises by the year 2010. The bureaucracy also has an informal mandate to steadily reduce the number of central SOEs under its wing through merger or restructuring, a task which SASAC leaders have taken to with zeal: of the original 196 central SOEs, just 112 remain at the time of writing. A hallmark of SASAC practice under the leadership of its first powerful director, Li Rongrong, was consistent emphasis on central SOEs 'going big' in order to 'go strong' (*zuo da zuo qiang* 做大做强) against global companies in international competition

(12BJ0517). In the introduction to his co-edited volume, *Mergers and Acquisitions: The Only Way for Enterprise Development* (2004), Li argued that promoting consolidation in key sectors of the economy in the interests of creating first-class large enterprises would be nothing less than crucial to Chinese companies finding their place in a global economy characterized by oligopolistic competition between global firms.

SASAC's approach to coaching the national team blends old with new methods of state guidance. The bureaucracy's means of guiding mergers between central SOEs has at times resembled the 'forced marriages' (*lalangpei* 拉郎配) between large SOEs in the early 1990s in the interests of avoiding bankruptcy. While SASAC policy rhetoric emphasizes 'strong–strong mergers' (*qiang qiang lianhe* 强强联合), leading officials are under heavy pressure to reduce the members of the national team and prevent SOE losses and, as a result, some mergers between central SOEs under SASAC's watch have instead been motivated by a need to bail out weaker performers. For instance, a 2009 SASAC-engineered merger between weak China Eastern Airlines and its home-turf rival Shanghai Airlines is a case in point. New means of guiding, rather than commanding, the national team include the appointment of upper management (though in practice this responsibility is shared, and most often led, by the CCP Central Committee's Organization Department); annual review of SOE economic performance; and dispatch of supervisory panels to SOEs. Annual reviews, in particular, have proven to be a useful tool for guiding SOE investment decisions, but in practice SASAC is severely hamstrung by the fact that, while it has been tasked with fulfilling the role of shareholder on behalf of the state, it does not actually hold shares; shares are instead controlled by the shadowy group companies that sit at the apex of state-owned business groups. A number of local-level SASAC bureaucracies, including in Shanghai and Chongqing, have addressed this problem by establishing asset management companies and absorbing shares from the holding companies, but central SASAC's efforts to follow their lead have been plagued by dogged resistance from the powerful heads of these holding companies as well as the central government's own reservations about broadening central SASAC's powers in such a fashion (10BJ0702).

Conclusion

In shedding light on the ideational foundations of Chinese policymakers' embrace of a national champions strategy for large SOEs, the assembled documents offer insight into *why* Chinese policymakers chose this path. The assembled evidence reveals the importance of economic ideas in shaping this policy line. First, policymakers drew eclectically from the annals of economic history in forming the conclusion that mounting industrial policy in support of large enterprise group development could, if done well, correct costly policy mistakes made in the Maoist period and accelerate China's economic development. From Marxian economics they drew the lesson that choosing a capitalist road, even one with Chinese characteristics, would lead inexorably towards monopoly. From the East Asian developmental states they learned that this was not necessarily a bad thing; the example set by Japan, in particular, seemed to suggest that judicious state guidance of the process of 'centralization of capital' could effectively steer enterprises away from cronyism and indolence and towards meeting national development objectives.

But the promised benefits of developing state-owned large enterprise groups were not defined purely in economic terms. The national champions push also clearly had a political dimension. In the context of a rapidly growing non-state sector and a teetering state sector, policymakers thought of state-owned large enterprises as key elements of the market-conforming model of state control they began to envision and work towards from the 1980s. While there was undoubtedly an element of Marxist-Leninist correctness behind internal debate about how the state could continue to exercise its constitutionally mandated 'leading role' in a liberalizing economy, the fears informing this debate were nonetheless quite real. Indeed, the challenge facing them was immense: just how does a communist ruling party 'ride the tiger' of a marketizing economy? The blueprints in this category were truly few and far between and this fact helps to explain why, despite the vast differences between the two countries, Singapore emerged as an important model for Chinese policymakers' efforts to transform themselves into market-embracing communist authoritarians *while* staying on the tiger's back.

3 The state's advance in the air: an analysis of airline reform

This chapter examines a puzzling policy reversal in the course of airline reform. While the airline industry now belongs to a small group of 'lifeline' industries characterized by oligopoly among a small number of central SOEs, the initial reform pathway in airlines in the post-Mao era hinted at a very different future. Indeed, a core puzzle in the study of China's reform-era airline industry is why the trajectory of gradual state retreat was abruptly reversed in 1997 when regulators began a bold retrenchment leading finally to an administrative restructuring of the industry around the 'Big Three' state-owned carriers. The chapter finds that this policy reversal was shaped strongly by the policy backdrop discussed in the previous chapter, namely central policymakers' increasing emphasis on developing a national team of state-controlled national champions which gained momentum in the late 1990s.

As previous analyses of Chinese airline policy have argued, the occurrence of an industry crisis on the heels of a ticket price reform in the late 1990s was the proximate cause of market restructuring around the 'Big Three' state-owned airlines. Yet the move to oligopoly was shaped by more than just a normative preference for orderly markets. The creation of a state-owned oligopoly was part and parcel of a broad-based effort to bolster the market position of large SOEs in key industries under the banner of the 'large enterprise group strategy.' In recent years, the national champions mandate has only become more prominent in airline policy, even as the industry regulator has nominally retreated from the market.

The Maoist legacy and the early reform period

Civil aviation in China was ravaged by the succession of political campaigns that defined the Mao years. Between 1950 and 1976, the Civil Aviation Administration of China (CAAC) fell under the authority of, variously, the Central Military Commission, the State Council and the Ministry of Transportation before winding up as a division of the Air Force after 1969.[1] In the latter half of the 1960s, many cadres in the CAAC became targets for the Red Guard attacks and those linked to the 'Two Airlines Uprising' (*lianghang qiyi* 两航起义) were treated especially harshly.[2] Management of civil aviation was increasingly haphazard as the Cultural Revolution wore on. After becoming a military unit of the Air Force, the existing cost accounting system for air services was scrapped and replaced with a haphazard 'eating from one big pot' system (*da guo fan* 大锅饭) captured by a popular phrase of the time: 'fly a little or a lot, it's all the same; sell many or a few airline tickets, it's all the same; provide good service or bad, it's all the same; consume however much, it's all the same; lose money or make money, it's all the same' (Liu 2007: 483). Political campaigns also left their mark on the pattern of fixed-asset investment in the period as airports were constructed in the inland locations of Xichang, Lanzhou and Taiyuan as part of a massive and costly effort to erect a 'Third Front' in the event of foreign invasion. The safety of air travel was also severely compromised. Over the course of the Cultural Revolution, more than thirty serious safety incidents took place, resulting in the loss of a reported thirty aircraft and thirty-two lives (ibid. 482). At the time of Henry Kissinger's secret visit to China in 1971, the country had fallen so far behind international aviation standards that an airport staircase had to be built at short notice in order to deliver the US Secretary of State from his Boeing 707 onto the tarmac. Officials had rejected the embarrassing option of buying or borrowing one from a Western supplier and the staircase was instead hurriedly put together using photographs and published specs of the 707 (Fallows 2012: 46).

While China's civil aviation sector was clearly in a dismal state, it was political skirmishes between elites in the 1970s that set the stage for policymakers' decision to select a comparatively bold reform pathway in this sector.

---

[1] Yet throughout these administrative shuffles in the Maoist period, the principle of 'the primacy of military leadership' (*yi jundui lingdao wei zhu* 以军队领导为主) established the PLA as the final authority on important policies in the civil aviation sector (Chung 2003: 67).

[2] *Lianghang qiyi* is one of the most celebrated events in the Communist-era history of civil aviation. In November 1949, the general managers of two Kuomintang (KMT)-controlled airlines operating on the mainland, China National Aviation Corporation and the Central Air Transport Corporation, turned against Chiang Kai Shek's forces and handed their seventy-one planes and assets in Hong Kong over to the Chinese Communist Party. It was heralded as a major strategic victory for the Communists since the airlines had been supplying KMT outposts in the southwest provinces which were effectively cut off after the insurrection. Since Zhou Enlai (then vice-chair of the Central Military Commission) played the lead role in organizing the efforts of the Hong Kong Party underground to persuade the two businessmen to switch sides, in the years of the Cultural Revolution, denouncing participants as 'capitalist roaders whose death would not be worthy of regret' (*si bu gai hui de zouzipai* 死不该悔的走资派) amounted to a thinly veiled attack on Zhou himself. The official civil aviation history notes that, in all, seventy people with ties to *lianghang qiyi* were subjected to 'cruel attacks' and 'persecution' in this period (Liu 2007: 481).

The Maoist legacy and the early reform period 55

Following the death of Lin Biao in 1971 and the subsequent return of Zhou Enlai and later Deng Xiaoping to leading positions in the Party and government, the leadership declared civil aviation development a priority and depicted the development of long-distance international routes – 'flying forth' (*feichuqu* 飞出去) – as a crucial component of China's modernization and gradual opening to the outside world. In a speech made in August 1973, Premier Zhou declared: 'We must fly forth in order to open up. More and more countries are establishing diplomatic relations and exchange is increasingly frequent in the modernizing world. China cannot lock itself up; we must make flying forth a political responsibility' (quoted in Liu 2007: 484). To advance the cause of flying forth in the civil aviation bureaucracy, in 1973 Zhou personally intervened to rehabilitate a former acolyte and an experienced international negotiator in civil aviation, Shen Tu. Shen, who had been imprisoned for five years at the height of the Cultural Revolution was quickly made vice-director of the CAAC after his release, and with his and Premier Zhou's combined influence, considerable progress was made in developing international routes in the early 1970s. When the Gang of Four rose to power at the end of 1975, however, the 'flying forth' programme became an obvious target for the anti-Zhou/Deng clique and Shen Tu along with many of his colleagues in the CAAC were hounded and persecuted as part of a 'Criticize Deng' campaign in the CAAC between August and September 1976. In a reflection on the damage wrought by this campaign, Shen wrote that 'The impact and aftermath of Lin Biao and the Gang of Four cannot be underestimated' (Shen 1992: 7). Although the Gang of Four were arrested shortly after these 'Criticize Deng' meetings, the CAAC's status as a unit of the Air Force and the bureaucracy's key personnel remained intact into the beginning of the reform era. It is not hard to understand why Deng, as a newly minted leader still cementing his standing as first among equals, threw his weight behind a shakeup of this bureaucracy which had been so closely linked to his adversaries' efforts to undermine him.

From the very earliest days of the reform period, Shen Tu, who was appointed director of CAAC, along with top-level government elites, cobbled together an agenda for civil aviation reform premised on asserting government control over civil aviation, decentralization of power and government–enterprise separation. Though the scant historical record makes it difficult to draw firm conclusions about the precise divisions among elites at the time, it is clear that the Air Force was reluctant to relinquish control over the civil aviation bureaucracy to the State Council. In late February 1979, Vice-Premier Li Xiannian announced in a State Council meeting that CAAC would henceforth be removed from the Air Force system and placed under the oversight of the State Council. Shen (1992: 1) writes that because Air Force leaders held 'a different view' of matters, the State Council was forced to issue a moratorium on implementation of the shift in command in early March 1979; in fact, it remains unclear when exactly the Air Force finally did forfeit its ambiguous role as 'manager' (*daiguan* 代管) of CAAC on behalf of the State Council.[3] Although the State Council's 1979 declaration failed to decisively wrest control of civil aviation from the Air Force, it did strengthen Shen's hand in carrying out important internal reforms which served to reduce the influence of military leaders and increase the bureaucracy's autonomy in matters of economic decisionmaking.[4] The reform also significantly expanded the powers of the sub-national aviation bureaux.[5]

In the following year, plans for deeper decentralization and government–enterprise separation began to take shape. In early 1980, Deng Xiaoping summoned Shen Tu to his office for a rare one-on-one meeting to discuss what approach the government ought to take to civil aviation reform. Shen (1992: 4) notes that, regarding the Air Force's *daiguan* role, Deng was adamant that a 'change in leadership relations' be achieved quickly. Deng also declared that 'civil aviation must corporatize; this has already been decided'. Shortly after their meeting, the *People's Daily* ran an article entitled 'Civil Aviation Will Go the Route of Corporatization', a decisive signal from on high that the policy would go forward. Soon afterwards, Shen called a CAAC meeting where he outlined plans to, first, loosen ties with the sub-national bureaucracy by making the six regional CAAC bureaux independent economic units responsible for their own profits and losses and, second, establish bona fide airlines within two or three years. While Shen's ambitious time target for enterprises was ultimately not met, in January 1985 the State Council formally approved the CAAC's plan to establish airline and airport enterprises which were to be 'autonomous, self-financing, self-developing and self-restrained' (Liu 2007: 640–1). Thereafter, each of the six regional bureaux established its own airline, the largest of which, the 'Big Three'

---

[3] For example, in the official history, March 1980 is recorded as the date that the Air Force gave up its role as CAAC's *daiguan* (Liu 2007: 639). Most Western accounts put the date somewhat later. Dougan (2002: 153) claims that CAAC was only returned to State Council control in 1985. Jae-ho Chung (2003: 68) rightly points out that even after the CAAC came under the State Council system, the Air Force remained very influential in the sector: 'Only one of its three principal functions – airline management – became totally civilian (but still state-controlled). Air-traffic regulation has remained largely in the hands of the military and airport control has become increasingly demilitarized over the years.' See also Dougan (2003: 155–7).

[4] Crucially, the Planning and Finance Departments, in addition to other business departments, were restored while the Military Command and Logistics Departments were abolished.

[5] Under the Air Force, the CAAC was a four-level administrative system. Beneath the national bureau were six regional bureaux in Beijing, Guangzhou, Chengdu, Shenyang, Xi'an, and Shanghai, which had primary responsibility for managing aircraft flights and operating airports; twenty-three provincial/municipal department bureaux and finally seventy-eight civil aviation 'stations' (*hangkong zhan* 航空站).

airlines, were formed out of the CAAC bureaux in Beijing (Air China), Guangzhou (China Southern) and Shanghai (China Eastern).

Catching up: industrial policy and early encouragement for enterprise groups

In addition to the quick dismantling of the civil aviation monopoly, the central government employed various industrial policies to achieve rapid catch-up in this industry deemed vital to the overall success of China's reform and opening. First, two methods of profit retention were used to spur fixed-asset investment (see Table 3.1), but, in sharp contrast to the impact of telecommunications industrial policies discussed in the following chapter, the high degree of decentralization and early-stage corporatization in air services meant that rents accrued first to the largely financially independent regional bureaux of the CAAC and, from the mid 1980s, to the airline and airport enterprises themselves. In essence, the short-term winners in this partially reformed market were the regional bureaux and then newly formed enterprises and not the former monopolist in Beijing. In contrast to the central telecommunications bureaucracy which was a powerful opponent of ownership reform in the same time period, the wide dispersal of the early benefits of civil aviation reforms built a strong coalition in favour of marketization and liberalization. Airplane leasing was a popular method of increasing fleet size in the context of scarce investment funds. Former Minister Shen Tu described leveraged leasing as one of the key policy innovations of this period. While there was reportedly much resistance within the CAAC to 'renting' planes from abroad, partly because some felt this would cause China to lose face internationally, in the context of strict budget limitations there was no other way the government could afford to get access to planes in large numbers (Shen 1992: 10–12).

In addition, in recognition of the fact that retained revenues would not be adequate to power the physical development of a sector that was growing at an annual rate of 50 per cent in the early 1980s, the CAAC encouraged infrastructure investment from local governments, other central ministries and foreign investors (officially after a 1994 regulation authorized foreign investment in the sector). Indeed, while the central government shouldered most of the burden of constructing airports nationwide, local governments in addition to the military (principally the Air Force and Navy) also sponsored a number of major airport construction projects (Dougan 2002: 164–8).

The combined effect of these policies dramatically altered the face of the civil aviation sector. As Figure 3.1 shows, retained earnings combined with the popularization of plane leasing arrangements allowed airline enterprises to considerably expand their capacity over this time period. While the data show that the most astounding increases in airline passenger traffic have taken place

58   The state's advance in the air

Table 3.1: *Key industrial policies in airlines, 1980s and 1990s*

Year	Policy	Content and policy evolution
1980	Airplane leasing	With guarantees from Chinese state-owned financial institutions, typically the Bank of China, CAAC and later the airlines themselves arranged long-term leasing arrangements with foreign aircraft manufacturers via foreign lenders:
		• The method was first used to lease three Boeing 747s in 1980.
• Between 1980 and 1984, CAAC was granted extensive tax exemptions/reductions on these leasing arrangements.
• As recently as 2002, approximately 80 per cent of planes operated by Chinese airlines were leased.
1985	'Two 90 per cents'	Authorized civil aviation enterprises to retain 90 per cent of revenues derived from two sources:
		• *Profits*: to be used for expanding enterprise scale; plane purchase/leasing; and airport and other infrastructure construction.
• *Foreign currency earnings*: giving enterprises access to foreign currency reserves substantially increased enterprise autonomy with regard to investment decisions.
1993	Profit retention	Applied to CAAC-affiliated airlines between 1993 and 2000.
		• To promote the faster development of civil aviation, after civil aviation enterprises had paid 18 per cent tax to the central government and fulfilled obligations on their loans, they could retain the remaining profits.

Sources: Liu (2007): 706–8; Dougan (2002); Shen (1992)

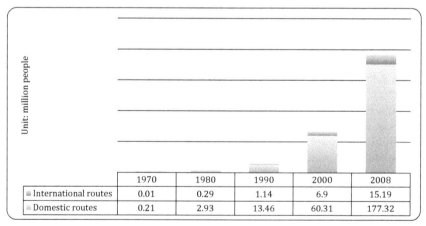

Figure 3.1 Airline passenger traffic, 1970–2008
Source: CTJKMH 2009: 169

since the late 1990s, after the loosening of government restrictions on ordinary citizens' flights, there was also rapid change in the early reform period. Passenger traffic had already surged by 456 per cent between 1978 and 1989 (ZGTJNJ 1990: 548). And between 1980 and 1995, the total number of planes in use increased fourfold, from 143 to 722 (ZGTJNJ 2007: 634). In the early 1990s, nodes on the domestic and international network considerably expanded with the construction of nineteen new airports and major upgrades of twenty-nine other airports. These investments brought the total number of Chinese airports capable of landing Boeing 747s to fourteen and those which could accommodate Boeing 737s to eighty-one (ZGTJNJ 1996: 266).

While the industrial policies outlined above had the shared aim of achieving a rapid increase in the aggregate supply of civil aviation services, other initiatives in the early reform period were oriented to increasing the competitiveness of the major airlines. Particularly significant was the inclusion of the 'Big Three' airline groups carved out of the command-era civil aviation system – Air China, China Eastern and China Southern – in the ranks of the 1991 trial group of large enterprises discussed in the previous chapter. The decision to extend the privilege of 'discrete planning unit' (计划单列 *jihua danlie*) status to the Big Three signified a considerable jump up the hierarchy of the planning system as the authority of the CAAC over their business was substantially curtailed – a bureaucracy described by a retired central government official as especially meddlesome in enterprise affairs (12BJ0522).

Analysis of the corporate structure of China's flagship carrier, Air China, sheds light on how the airline business groups have developed in accord with the large enterprise group strategy. Air China's core member, China National Aviation Holding Company (CNAHC), sits atop five wholly owned subsidiaries and acts as the controlling shareholder in two shareholding companies and one public company (the airline, Air China Company Limited). In accordance with policy pertaining to the large enterprise group trials, a fund management company, China National Aviation Finance Co. Ltd., was established in 1994. The company provides settlement services for companies within the group and offers a range of financial services including lending and underwriting for corporate bond issues. The group also includes an investment holding company, China National Aviation Corporation (Group) Ltd. (CNACG), set up in 1995. In addition to its equity holdings in three major airlines – Air China, China Eastern and Cathay Pacific – CNACG also has major holdings in many other segments of the mainland and Hong Kong civil aviation markets. CNACG holds 50 per cent of China National Aviation Fuel's shares and is a major shareholder in two domestic airports, several cargo terminals and seven catering companies. The Air China group also includes in its realm an advertising/media arm, a travel service company, a construction company and a highly successful delivery, cargo and logistics company, China Air Express. A later section of the chapter explores how the Big Three airline groups, together with the Hainan airline group, control the domestic market in air services.

Creating an airline market: liberalization and policy reversal

Along with various forms of industrial policy, civil aviation policymakers also saw market competition as another important driver of civil aviation development in China. The removal of administrative barriers to entry in the 1980s fed a dramatic upsurge in new entrants to the airline market. Initially, the scope of competition was limited by the existence of rigid rules on ticket pricing, but price liberalization later led to fierce competition on domestic routes. The new competitive environment paired with the occurrence of the Asian Financial Crisis in 1997–8 substantially eroded the revenue of Chinese airlines, above all those of the government-favoured Big Three carriers. In an atmosphere of crisis, members of China's civil aviation world examined the nature and causes of the crisis and considered the options before them. Both the problem definition as well as the policy solutions decided on by officialdom were deeply shaped by the set of ideas and institutions examined in previous chapters, which encouraged the development of large, state-controlled business groups with a commanding market share.

To meet growing demand for air services the central government opened the airline market to local governments and government departments. A 1984 State Council regulation calling for the establishment of new airlines set off a wave of small airline entry that began with the July 1984 establishment of Xiamen Airlines, a joint venture between the Shanghai Civil Aviation Authority, the Fujian Enterprise Investment Company, and the Xiamen Special Economic Zone Development Corporation. In the early years following market opening, local governments tended to seek out joint ventures with the six 'backbone' airlines under the direct authority of the CAAC – the Big Three along with China Southwest Airlines (based in Chengdu), China Northwest Airlines (based in Xi'an) and China Northern Airlines (based in Shenyang) (Dougan 2002: 159). In 1990, for example, the Zhejiang provincial government and China Eastern together established Zhejiang Airlines as a CAAC-affiliated enterprise. Gradually, provincial governments began to set up their own airlines independent of the CAAC, and by the mid 1990s, fifteen of China's thirty provinces had established their own airlines. Alongside local governments, a number of well-financed government ministries also entered the market. In 1996, a cargo airline, China Postal Airlines, was set up as a joint venture between the Ministry of Post and Telecommunications and the Tianjin city government. As a result of this loosening, the number of airlines swelled from eleven in 1987 to twenty-four in 1992 and to a peak of more than forty in 1995 before falling back to twenty-nine in 1996 and just seventeen in 2001.

The flood of new entrants placed considerable strain on the CAAC's capacity to monitor airline safety. Between July 1992 and December 1993 nine plane crashes occurred. The accidents were the deciding factor behind the CAAC's decision to impose a moratorium on the establishment of new airlines in 1993. The ban did not stick, however, likely due to strong lobbying from local governments (Chung 2003: 73). In fact, safety problems remained a grave problem in China's airline industry for several years after these tragic events. It was pressure from the US Federal Aviation Administration (FAA) that was, finally, the catalyst for an overhaul of safety standards in the Chinese airline industry in the late 1990s and early 2000s (Fallows 2012: 75–9). The FAA, working through the offices of US Department of Transportation, made it clear that they would no longer approve applications from Chinese airlines to operate flights to the US without evidence that airlines were adhering to global safety standards. This proved to be an effective incentive and subsequently 'an improbable alliance of Chinese, American and international businesses and organizations' took shape to respond to the challenge (ibid. 75). The group, in which Boeing's representatives in China played a leading role, ultimately succeeded in organizing an across-the-board review and upgrading of safety standards in Chinese airlines as well as deep reform of regulatory practice (ibid. 75).

Although regulatory barriers to entry had fallen away rapidly in the mid 1980s, the scope of competition in the airline industry remained quite narrow until pricing policies began to loosen in the early 1990s. In the 1980s, airline ticket prices were fixed by the State Price Control Bureau with input from the CAAC, and the airlines were required to sell tickets at a price set by the Price Bureau, meaning that there was no price competition between carriers. In 1992, some flexibility was introduced into the system when the pricing rules were amended to allow airlines to sell tickets at ±10 per cent of the state-fixed price. In 1994, the pricing system was further relaxed when the CAAC expanded the range to ±20 per cent of the published price and freed the airlines from having to register with the regulator when offering discounts. Passage of the Civil Aviation Law (1995) decisively transferred price-setting authority from the Price Bureau to the CAAC. In late November 1997 the airline regulator moved to further deregulate prices with the 'one kind of ticket, many kinds of discount' policy (*yi zhong piao duo zhong zhekou* 一种票多种折扣), which both unified the price of tickets for foreigners and Chinese alike and allowed airlines to charge varying ticket prices for the same seats on the basis of such factors as purchase timing, route and flight distance.[6] The rule change amounted to the de facto deregulation of ticket prices, and fierce price

---

[6] Between 1974 and 1997, foreigners (including citizens of Hong Kong and Macao) were charged a higher price for airline tickets than Chinese citizens (including Taiwanese). Cancellation of the two-ticket system coincided with the return of Hong Kong to the mainland.

wars set in which saw carriers selling tickets for as little as 50 per cent of the published price (Zhang 2007: 78).

The deregulation of ticket pricing and the resulting price war contributed to a collapse in industry revenue starting in 1997. In the years between 1980 and 1996, annual growth rates in the industry hovered around 20 per cent but shrank to just 7.5 per cent in 1997 before sinking to 3 per cent in 1998 (Dougan 2002: 172–3). As airlines struggled to recover their costs amid plummeting ticket prices, total losses in the industry were estimated to have topped 24 billion RMB in 1998 (Tai 2004: 82). The negative effects of this intensified competition were further compounded by the Asian Financial Crisis which resulted in a major contraction in demand for air travel. The crisis also brought to light the lingering problem of over-investment in civil aviation, which had created excess capacity in the late 1990s (Zhang 2007: 82). Between 1991 and 1994, fixed asset investment in the airline industry tripled from 4.2 billion to 12.5 billion RMB, and the number of airplanes in use more than tripled between 1990 and 1995, growing from 222 to 722 (ZGTJNJ 2007: 634). In the early years, this investment push was outpaced by booming demand, but signs that the market had become saturated were all around by the end of the 1990s. On the popular Beijing–Shenzhen route, for example, the nine airlines offering flights managed to fill just 30 per cent of their seats (Chung 2003: 76).

The crisis also brought to the fore endemic problems in China's developing airline industry. At the enterprise level, the most serious problem was the prevalence of the soft budget constraint. Because the majority of airlines were wholly state-owned, and all carriers had some large percentage of state ownership, manager-officials were typically more concerned with maximizing market share than they were with profitability; indeed, during the height of the late 1990s price wars, some flights operating at full capacity were still unable to turn a profit (Dougan 2002: 173). In addition, both the 'backbone' airlines and start-up airlines had become deeply indebted over the course of the 1990s, largely as the result of costly plane acquisitions and overly ambitious network expansion efforts. The state-owned airlines under the direct supervision of CAAC were especially burdened by having to purchase fuel at an inflated price from the China Aviation Oil Supply Corporation. Other factors which contributed to the weak profitability of airlines in this period, despite the industry's double-digit growth, included a CAAC rule requiring that airlines contribute 10 per cent of their annual sales to the CAAC's Civil Aviation Infrastructure Construction Fund as well as exorbitant fees charged by sales agents.[7]

---

[7] Although agent fees were officially not supposed to exceed 3 per cent of the ticket price, agents were known to levy fees as high as 20 per cent, thereby severely cutting into the airlines' profits.

As the dimensions of the crisis came into focus, CAAC began a strenuous effort to help the major airlines return to profitability. Jae-Ho Chung has argued that the government's statist response to the crisis is best explained by the ingrained planning instincts of policymakers faced with crisis: 'realizing the antinomies of efficiency embedded in excessive devolution, the government has sought both to re-centralize through conglomerations and to strengthen its regulatory power over sectors and localities' (Chung 2003: 62). The argument presented here posits that while disorder and crisis in the airline market indeed necessitated decisive action from industry regulators, the CAAC's particular policy choices in this period and in the years since have been strongly colored by the national champions blueprint outlined in the previous chapter.

The CAAC first tried to stifle the price wars through regulatory measures. In May 1998, the CAAC tried to set a floor on air ticket prices by banning the sale of discount tickets less than 20 per cent of the published price. The regulator also barred sales agents from charging fees in excess of 4 per cent of the ticket price. However, the regulations were widely flouted, and the price wars continued largely unabated until December 1998 when CAAC undertook a stringent inspection of airlines' pricing practices and imposed heavy fines on violators. Although the CAAC's hardened stance served to stifle price wars in the short term, in the low season that followed the Spring Festival in 1999, the airlines were once again in cutthroat competition, which prompted the regulator to seek out new means of supporting the airlines' revenue (Xuan 2003: 35–6).[8] Some of the regulator's wide-ranging efforts to rein in excess capacity in 1999 and 2000 included reducing the total number of domestic flights by 5 per cent; reasserting control over airlines' plane purchases from abroad; and urging airlines to offer jointly operated services (*lianying* 联营) on 108 of the most popular routes, which made up 50 per cent of all passenger air travel (Chung 2003: 77). None of these measures was judged a success, however, and the CAAC's failure to find a quick market fix prompted wide-ranging debate about the future course of airline reform.

To some observers, the crisis was not the result of a too-swift programme of marketization but instead a sign of government failure. In this view, industry crisis was the inevitable result of incomplete government–enterprise separation. This argument drew support from the broad-ranging powers of the

---

Between 1995 and 1997, for example, the Big Three airlines together spent a total of 4.25 billion RMB on sales fees (Tai 2004: 83).

[8] Officially, the industry returned to profitability in 1999, but industry insiders reported that the profits were largely engineered by a reduction in airlines' obligations to the CAAC's Civil Aviation Infrastructure Construction Fund (from 10 per cent to 5 per cent of annual sales) and a 15 per cent rise in the published price of tickets, nominally because of a spike in the price of jet fuel (Chung 2003: 77; Zhang 2007: 86).

CAAC in this airline market with Chinese characteristics. In this period, the CAAC remained responsible for the profits and losses of the backbone airlines under its direct supervision and had a say in many other aspects of the carriers' business all the way from investment to human resources. Since the CAAC-affiliated airlines faced a soft budget constraint, the argument was that they did not respond as market actors would have done after the switch from a seller's to a buyer's market, and thus they perpetuated the crisis long after a true market would have corrected itself. Critics also charged that the CAAC's dual role as market referee and 'boss' (*laoban* 老板) of the CAAC-affiliated airlines constituted a major conflict of interest, a problem which the regulator itself was well aware of. A 1998 editorial in the CAAC's journal put the matter bluntly:

> The CAAC must regulate enterprises and the market. At the same time, CAAC is also the 'boss' of the airlines under its direct supervision. These roles are contradictory. The inevitable result is difficulty in balancing the 'government functions' and 'boss functions'. For example: how should CAAC balance the aims of protecting enterprises and protecting consumers? And which should be the higher priority? Protecting competition or protecting profits? (*Minhang jingji yu jishu* 1998: 1).

From the perspective of those who saw the crisis as the result of excessive state intervention in the market, the only lasting solution was to decisively sever the ties between the CAAC and its affiliated airlines and establish a system of impartial market regulation. Unsurprisingly, this argument was favoured by many smaller airlines in competition with the large, backbone airlines under the CAAC. A Shenzhen Airlines manager published a sharp critique of the status quo which concluded that as long as the CAAC retained its dual role as referee and airline 'boss', any discussion of an 'air transport market' would be 'empty talk' (Han 1999: 11). A later article written by a Hainan Airline representative came to a similar conclusion (Miao 2000).

Others argued that the airline industry's fragmented market structure was the fundamental problem and advocated consolidation around the large carriers under CAAC. Just as some of the smaller airlines advanced arguments consistent with their particularist interests in further marketization, the CAAC-affiliated airlines tended to support reform proposals that would bring them the most benefit. An article written by a manager from China Southern Airlines drew on the writings of the nineteenth-century German economic nationalist, Friedrich List, in making the case that the only long-term fix for the airline industry in a globalizing world was the creation of an oligopolistic market with two or three large state-owned enterprises and three to five smaller enterprises to service regional routes (Zhou 2000: 13). Unlike many similar pieces written at the time which spoke of the need to increase industrial concentration in only vague terms, this article specified exactly how much market share should be held by the two or three largest players, namely 70–80 per cent. The author also reasoned that restructuring the market around the large carriers would

Creating an airline market 65

offer them some time to adapt to the demands of international competition: 'the protection of government policies would allow the industry to smoothly develop and buy them some time in order to increase their international competitiveness, easily enter the WTO and gather together strength to participate in international competition' (ibid.). Such arguments aligned well with the centre's emphasis on developing a national team of large, state-controlled enterprise groups to compete in global markets.

As the crisis wore on, expert opinion tilted in favour of proposals for consolidation around the big airlines. Interestingly, just as the large enterprise strategy was framed as a solution to a widening number of problems in the broader policy context outlined in the previous chapter, it was also perceived as something of a panacea within the airline industry during the crisis. A 1999 poll conducted by the Civil Aviation Association asked industry experts: 'What is the industry's best counter-measure against the effects of the Asian Financial Crisis and the depression in the air transport market?' to which the most popular response was: 'Implementation of the "large company, large enterprise strategy"'(Liu 1997: 14–16). A year later, a similar poll asked experts which counter-measures regulators should employ to ensure a smooth entry to the WTO (*Minhang jingji yu jishu* 2000: 27–30). Once again, the number one recommendation was 'implementation of the large enterprise strategy'. An accompanying discussion of the survey results presents the following rationale:

our airline industry is extremely weak, fragmented, lacking in scale and faced with serious safety problems. The way to solve these various problems is to establish a modern enterprise system and to implement the 'large company, large enterprise strategy'. In fragmented form, the industry is open to attack; ten fingers are not as good as a fist since only a fist can attack. Only when our industry has achieved scale and competitive advantages will it be able to compete with foreign airlines. (*Minhang jingji yu jishu* 2000: 27)

The market restructuring plan that the CAAC finally selected conceded something to the widespread complaints about the regulator's awkward dual role as market player and referee but sided more strongly with the proponents of oligopoly. In July 2000, the CAAC publicized its plan to consolidate the ten carriers under its direct supervision (*zhishu qiye* 直属企业) around the Big Three airline groups.[9] In April 2001, the CAAC unveiled its formal

---

[9] According to one insider, three other consolidation proposals were considered and ultimately rejected: (1) consolidate all thirty airlines in the industry (this was seen as too complicated since many airlines answered to local governments and not CAAC); (2) create a four-enterprise oligopoly from the airlines under CAAC control (his was seen as unworkable because Air China's heavy focus on international service was seen as difficult to balance out in a four-market structure; and (3) merge China Southern and Air China. (this was apparently vetoed by China

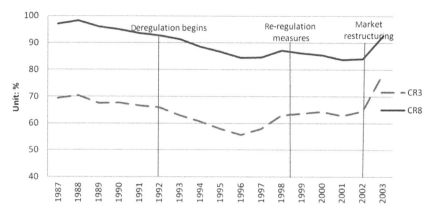

Figure 3.2 Market share of the three largest (CR3) and eight largest (CR8) airlines, 1987–2003
Source: Data from Tai (2004): 68

reform proposal which also included plans to overhaul the regulator (discussed below). The plan to create six large business groups gained swift approval, and the arduous process of 'voluntary' restructuring began the following year.[10] As Figure 3.2 shows, the administratively led consolidation succeeded in giving the Big Three a commanding share of the domestic market.

A sign of the significant influence of Air China on its home turf in Beijing, the consolidation was most advantageous to Air China and least welcomed by Shanghai-based China Eastern. Air China, arguably the weakest of the major airlines at the time, acquired both the well-run Southwest Airlines and CAAC's own holding company, China National Aviation Corporation, which owned Zhejiang Airlines and valuable equity in the greater China market (43 per cent of Hong Kong's Dragonair and 49 per cent of Air Macau). China Eastern, which was Asia's most profitable airline at the time, was saddled with the poorly run Northwest and Yunnan Airlines. Upon acquisition of Northwest, Eastern immediately lost 9 billion RMB because it was forced to pay off the airline's debts (08BJ1212). China Southern also fared relatively badly because it was merged with the weak China Northern and Xinjiang Airlines. For China Eastern and China Southern, these 'hard bones' became only harder to

---

Southern due to foreign shareholders' concerns about political interference from Beijing that might result from Air China's ties to officials in the capital) (Qiu 2002: 9).
[10] The three other big business groups to come out of the reorganization were: China Travel Sky, China National Aviation Fuel and China Aviation Equipment Import–Export Company.

digest when the CAAC subsequently opened up the Xinjiang and Yunnan route to rival airlines, effectively ending the airlines' regional monopolies and further squeezing their revenue streams (He 2002; 08BJ1212). This reorganization was an unambiguous signal of the government's intent to foster oligopolistic competition in airlines. As the chief of Air China during reorganization characterized the aims of this reform: 'The guidelines for the reorganization of China's civil aviation industry in 2002 were to "seize the big groups and ignore the small ones", as well as to create a favourable environment to help the core aviation companies to gain the upper hand in global competition' (Li 2008: 48).

How can we account for the central government's decision to replace an open market with a system of oligopoly? First, this move was deeply interwoven with the broader policy context trumpeting the value of large SOEs for Chinese development in the context of liberalizing markets. Indeed, a 1999 document by the State Planning Commission (SPC) hints that the crisis may only have hastened the implementation of a restructuring programme that central planners had already decided on for the tenth Five-Year Period (2001–5). Written by the SPC's Macroeconomic Research Group, the report outlined the planners' vision for transportation reform in the tenth FYP. Regarding the airline industry, the report notes as a top priority the need to: 'correct the current problem of many airlines of small size through increasing concentration and mergers and acquisition in order to improve the airlines' scale efficiency and competitive ability' (SPC Macroeconomic Research Group 1999: 30). In effect, the ideas and institutions that contributed to the advance of the state explored in previous chapters were crucial to engineering this policy reversal in the airline industry.

Second, as the discussion of airline preferences suggests, the move to oligopoly was also consistent with the particularist interests of the most powerful players in the airline industry, namely the CAAC-affiliated airlines. The opinion surveys cited above suggest that while many airline experts seem to have been convinced of the economic merits of the restructuring plan – indeed, airline authorities in many countries have experimented with re-regulation and consolidation in recent years – it stands to reason that a marriage of convenience between ideas and powerful interests also played a role in pushing policymakers towards the oligopoly model and away from the path of open competition favoured by smaller players. In addition, wearing its hat as the entity responsible for the profits and losses of the backbone airlines, the CAAC was also strongly incentivized by the 1997 'getting SOEs out of trouble in three years' campaign to intervene on behalf of the beleaguered large players for which it was responsible.

Post-reversal legacy: 2002–present

In the years since the reorganization of the airline market, the national champions blueprint has only become a more prominent feature of civil aviation policy and practice. Although a broad regulatory reform considerably altered the role of the CAAC vis-à-vis market players, the regulator, along with SASAC, retains wide formal and informal means of managing competition in support of the Big Three airline groups which, along with Hainan Airlines, the fourth-largest player, comfortably retain a commanding market share. The legacy of the Big Three airlines' inclusion in the large enterprise group trials is evident in the high degree of market power they wield in various segments of China's civil aviation sector. Most recently, the Global Financial Crisis prompted another round of asymmetric market interventions in support of the Big Three. Under the leadership of CAAC director Li Jiaxiang, a figure strongly in favour of SOE oligopoly, if not outright monopoly, the phrase 'advance of the state, retreat of the private sector' (*guojin mintui* 国进民退) has been widely applied to airline policy since 2008.

Regulatory reform

Over the past decade, CAAC's functions have been substantially narrowed. Following the market restructuring described above, the CAAC underwent a thoroughgoing reform based on three main goals: achieving decisive government–enterprise separation; streamlining the regulator's administrative structure; and narrowing the CAAC's regulatory ambit. After the creation of the six new business groups, CAAC's responsibility for asset management supervision of these groups was transferred first to the Ministry of Finance and then to SASAC in 2003. The regulator's former personnel management duties (e.g. the appointment of airline managers) became the joint responsibility of the Party's Central Organization Department in cooperation with SASAC. At the same time, CAAC transferred ownership rights for 129 airports under its direct control (*zhishu jichang* 直属机场) to local governments and kept only the Lhasa and Beijing Capital airports under its wing. The reform also significantly reduced the size of the CAAC bureaucracy as the three-level administrative structure (central, regional, provincial) was slimmed down to two levels comprising the central bureau and seven regional bureaux. The CAAC's regulatory ambit has been narrowed to safety administration, market regulation, air traffic management, macro-control and international cooperation.

Yet, while the 2002 reforms heralded a significant change in the relationship between regulator and regulated, central government agencies still retain considerable formal and informal levers of market control which are used to manage competition. Through its Planning, Development and Finance Department, the CAAC remains responsible for the overall 'development' of the industry and regulators use policy to guide the industry accordingly. Similarly, the government retains some hold on pricing authority. While a 2004 ticket pricing reform once again substantially loosened the ticket pricing system, domestic prices thereafter were still overseen by the National Development and Reform Commission (NDRC) with input from the CAAC. Finally, as an investor on behalf of the state for the Big Three airlines, SASAC plays a significant role in airline policy. As discussed below, the role of SASAC has become especially apparent since the Global Financial Crisis of 2008.

Recent appointments have also contributed to the advance of the state in this industry. In particular, the 2008 appointment of Li Jiaxiang as director of the CAAC made the national champions mandate an increasingly prominent aspect of airline policy. In a book and in various high-profile forums on civil aviation policy, Li has advocated increasing concentration in the airline market and has called for the establishment of a 'super carrier' (*chaoji chengyun ren* 超级承运人) to win market share in the global marketplace. Li has urged Chinese policymakers to adapt to the realities of the globalization of air services which, he argued, has mainly served the interests of the world's largest airlines in increasing their market share via industrial alliances. Echoing many of the ideas discussed in the previous chapter, Li has argued that fierce price competition in the domestic market has actually hindered Chinese airlines' ability to compete in the global marketplace and has advocates further concentration:

Another round of reorganization and integration among domestic airlines will most likely trigger off public concern about an 'industrial monopoly' ... Actually, there is no monopoly, just excessive competition in the current Chinese aviation market. (Li 2008: 209)

From his powerful perch, Li Jiaxiang has steadily guided civil aviation policy in the direction of further concentration and state advance. The CAAC's response to the 2008 Global Financial Crisis, discussed below, as well as the quickened pace of mergers under his leadership are two particularly significant recent developments.

The era of airline group competition

Since the 2002 consolidation, the three largest airlines have regained their commanding presence in the airline market, and a restructured version of Hainan Airlines has also steadily expanded its influence in the domestic market so that industry insiders now sometimes refer to the 'Big Four' airlines. Alone among the non-CAAC-linked airlines, Hainan Airlines has managed to secure

70 The state's advance in the air

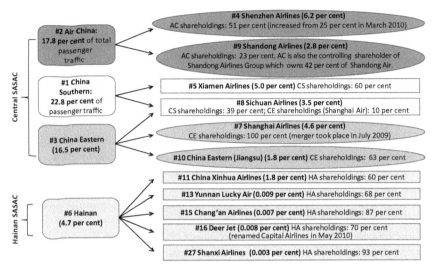

Figure 3.3 Big Four airline groups' shares of passenger traffic, 2008
Source: CTJKMH, 2009: 124–6; company annual reports

its place in the Chinese airline market by adopting the structure of the Big Three airline groups and emulating their business tactics. The business groups clustered around these airlines exercise immense and growing influence in all corners of the civil aviation market as major shareholders in smaller airlines, airports, aviation fuel companies and catering businesses. As Figure 3.3 shows, at least one member of the Big Four has a controlling stake in nearly all of the significant smaller airlines. Among the top fifteen airlines in 2008, only Spring Airlines (the twelfth-largest airline as measured by passenger traffic) remained non-aligned. Additionally, cross-holdings between the largest airlines also provide the major carriers with a measure of leverage over their rivals' business decisions, as will be discussed in more detail below.

Following the restructuring of the Air China group, formally completed in January 2003, the airline's strong profitability, the liberalization of domestic routes and strong policy backing from the central government all helped to propel its expanding presence in the domestic market via major equity investments in regional airlines. Shortly after the 2002 reorganization was complete, Air China began negotiations with Shandong Airlines, China's ninth-largest carrier, which operates lucrative routes around the Bohai Sea as well as in the Pearl and Yangtze river delta areas. In February 2004, Air China became Shandong's controlling shareholder with a share purchase of RMB 560 million (Li 2008: 48). With firm regional bases in the west and northeastern regions

following the Southwest and Shandong acquisitions, Air China's focus turned to establishing a foothold in the bustling southern market, the traditional stronghold of China's largest airline, China Southern Airlines. Air China made strenuous efforts to gain control of Shenzhen Airlines (China's fourth-largest in the passenger market) in which it has held a 25 per cent share since Shenzhen's establishment in 1993. In May 2005, Air China planned to purchase 65 per cent of the airline's stock rights when they came up for auction on the Shenzhen Assets and Equity Exchange Centre but the stock value was bid well beyond the airline's projections and two private investment companies controlled by businessman Li Zeyuan jointly purchased the rights for RMB 2.7 billion. Finally, in late 2009, an opportunity presented itself when Li Zeyuan and another Shenzhen executive, Li Kun, were investigated by the police for undisclosed economic crimes. Following Li's arrest in December 2009, Air China took control of Shenzhen's management and in March 2010 Air China made an RMB 682 million investment in the airline bringing its total equity holdings to 51 per cent, a move for control which Li's bankrupt company, Shenzhen Huirun Investment Company, was powerless to block.

While financial woes following the administrative reorganization have constrained China Southern's ability to meet the challenge for supremacy launched by Air China under Li Jiaxiang and his successor, Kong Dong, the Guangzhou-based airline has also extended its reach in the domestic market in recent years. In the midst of its own reorganization, China Southern acquired 39 per cent of Sichuan Airlines in a restructuring of the Chengdu-based airline which also saw China Eastern purchase 10 per cent of the airline's shares. The airline has also strengthened its bases in other regions of China through the ownership and operation of airline terminals in Beijing, Urumqi and Xi'an. In 2005, the airline announced its 'dual hub' strategy (in Guangzhou and Beijing) and established a subsidiary, China Southern (Beijing), to consolidate its presence in the Beijing market, Air China's home base.

A range of problems since the CAAC-led market consolidation have made China Eastern much less active than its primary competitors in establishing strategic partnerships with international companies and acquiring smaller airlines in the domestic market. In 2005, China Eastern began negotiations with Singapore International Airlines (SIA) about setting up a strategic partnership. By late summer 2007, the two sides had reached an agreement and China Eastern had all the necessary government approvals for a deal which would have seen SIA purchase a 15.7 per cent stake and Singapore's sovereign wealth fund, Temasek, a further 8.3 per cent. In a strange turn of events, however, Air China partnered with Cathay to block the deal by increasing their own holdings in China Eastern and voting down the takeover deal in a January 2008 shareholder's meeting. Later, central and Shanghai SASAC each pushed hard for China Eastern's merger with Shanghai Airlines, the seventh-largest domestic carrier. The primary aim of the merger, was to increase Eastern's market share in its hub, Shanghai, to a level similar to the percentage held by Air China and China Southern in their respective home bases. While the merger was reportedly unpopular with the top management of Shanghai Airlines, sustained pressure from central and Shanghai SASAC made the deal, finalized in July 2009, essentially a foregone conclusion.

To meet the challenge of survival in the post-2002 consolidated airline market, Hainan Airlines has built a group structure to rival the Big Three airlines' business empires. After the CAAC signalled that it would lead an administrative consolidation of the industry around its own carriers, in 1999 Hainan's CEO Chen Feng resolved to make Hainan (hereafter HNA) the centre of a consolidation drive among the independent airlines (Men and Sun 2007: 41).[11] In 2000, Chen announced HNA's '3-7-9 Strategy' signalling the airline's aspiration to become a well-known domestic brand within three years, a well-known Asian brand within seven years and a well-known global brand within nine years. In 2000 and 2001, HNA acquired controlling stakes of Xi'an-based Chang'an Airlines, China Xinhua Airlines and Shanxi Airlines. The acquisitions instantly made HNA China's fourth-largest airline group and significantly expanded its domestic network (especially its regional feeder routes) and padded HNA's fleet. Since then, HNA has become the major shareholder in two more airlines, Yunnan Lucky Air (a low-cost regional carrier) and Deer Jet/Capital Airlines, a Beijing-based charter airline focusing on business jet service. HNA's dogged market expansion against all odds, and its strong profitability prior to the financial crisis, has become a celebrated story of a non-state enterprise thriving in a SOE-dominated industry. HNA's rise has spawned dozens of books and academic studies and the venerable State Council Development Research Centre even established an 'HNA Development Strategy Research Group' which published a book entitled *HNA Phenomenon*, examining every aspect of the airline's development since its establishment in 1991 (State Council Development Research Centre 2005).

Yet, while HNA would have satisfied most definitions of a non-state enterprise in the 1990s, the company has undergone a partial nationalization, really 'provincialization', in recent years. As Figure 3.4 shows, in HNA's increasingly complex corporate structure, Hainan SASAC through its wholly owned holding company (Hainan Development Holding Company) has been the majority shareholder (40.65 per cent) in the Grand China Air Holding Company, the airline's parent company since 2004. Executives are said to

---

[11] In the late 1990s, the ten major independent airlines were (in decreasing order of market share): Shanghai Airlines, Hainan Airlines, Sichuan Airlines, China Xinhua Airlines, Shenzhen Airlines, Zhongyuan Airlines, Chang'an Airlines, Wuhan Airlines, China United Airlines and Shandong Airlines.

Guojin mintui 73

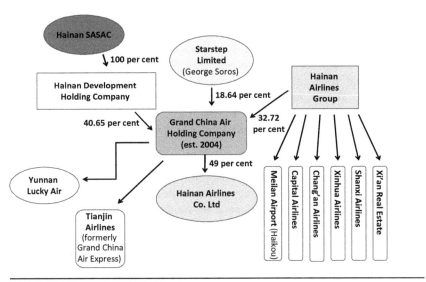

Figure 3.4 Corporate structure of Hainan Airlines Group (2005)
Source: Data primarily from HNA Annual Report (2008)

have appealed to the Hainan provincial government for help in 2005 when the company was struggling to meets its debt obligations and Hainan Province became Grand China Air's largest shareholder after a RMB 1.5 billion investment in October 2005 (*Zhengquan Ribao* 2007). The other major shareholders in the new group structure created in 2004 are a hedge fund controlled by American investor George Soros (18.64 per cent) and Hainan Airlines Group (32.72 per cent), which still controls most of HNA's ownership interests in civil aviation as well as the group's significant holdings in the travel, real estate and hotel industries.

Guojin mintui: advance of the state-owned airlines, retreat of the private carriers

The Global Financial Crisis prompted the CAAC to taken an interventionist stance reminiscent of the late 1990s re-regulation efforts. In December 2008, as concerns about the impact of the Global Financial Crisis were at their peak, the CAAC unveiled 'Ten Measures to Address the Financial Crisis' (*Zhongguo Xinwenwang* 2008). As in the late 1990s crisis, the CAAC measures aimed to bolster industry revenue through easing competitive pressures, reducing capacity in the industry, and promoting consolidation. Indeed, one of the key measures in the plan was 'regulation of market order', defined as the strict enforcement of the discount ticket price floor in order to 'prevent and avoid vicious competition'. Most importantly, the CAAC pledged to 'support the consolidation and reorganization' of the airline industry so that Chinese airlines could form a 'fist' (*quan tou* 拳头) in the arena of international competition. The response also involved a moratorium on the issuance of business licences to new airlines. Finally, the CAAC outlined a range of fee waivers and tax exemptions for all airlines and provided major capital injections for the Big Three airlines.

The crisis served to intensify the trend of consolidation around the Big Three airline groups. The central government's asymmetric interventions in the airline market after 2008 attracted intense media scrutiny of policies which many saw as propelling the 'advance of the state and retreat of the private sector'. In addition to the CAAC's ten-point plan for dampening 'vicious' (*exing* 恶性) competition in the airline market, the central government also organized massive bailouts and indirect subsidies for the Big Three airlines, preferential treatments which were generally not provided to smaller airlines.[12] Besides these direct measures, the Big Three were also reported to be receiving other indirect forms of assistance from government authorities. A senior airport executive reported that during the crisis, the Big Three received 80,000 RMB for each airport 'movement' (a landing or takeoff) in certain locales which were paid for by provincial governments and disbursed through the airports. These subsidies which, prior to the financial crisis, had only been issued for every tenth movement, were reportedly not extended to smaller carriers except those which were able to finagle codeshare arrangements with one of the Big Three airlines (10XI0525).

Alongside CAAC, SASAC also played a very assertive role in shaping the Big Three's response to the crisis. SASAC's first move came in late 2008 when it orchestrated a management shuffle among the Big Three carriers in an effort to revitalize China Eastern's management and turn the airline's fortunes around.[13] And even though SASAC was a central player in the design and implementation of the airline bailouts, the bureaucracy also applied an increasing amount of pressure on state-owned carriers to make profitability their top priority. SASAC's '2008 Report on Central SOEs' Operations', which compares the performance of enterprises in nine key

---

[12] First, China Southern received an RMB 3 billion capital injection via its parent company in November 2008. Later, China Eastern received two successive bailouts, totalling RMB 7 billion. Eastern's funds came by way of a private issue of shares to its parent company which raised the group company's share of the airline's shares from 60 per cent to 75 per cent.

[13] At the height of the crisis, in December 2008, Eastern's CEO, Li Fenghua, was replaced by China Southern's chair, Liu Shaoyong, and the deputy general manager of Air China's parent company, Ma Xulun, swapped positions with Eastern's deputy Party secretary, Cao Jianxiong.

industries, notes that among them 'only airlines have not maintained the value of state assets'. And yet other aspects of SASAC's response to the crisis give the impression of a less stern, more protective parent. In August 2009, for example, SASAC instructed six of its SOEs that had bought fuel-hedging derivative products from international investment banks to write letters to the banks to terminate these contracts ahead of the date of expiry (Zhang and Wu 2009). Unfavourable fuel hedging contracts had contributed greatly to China Eastern's and Air China's losses in the financial crisis, and it was widely suspected, though not confirmed, that both carriers were among these six enterprises.

With the exception of Spring Airlines, a private carrier which claimed to be the only Chinese airline to turn a profit in 2008, smaller carriers were ravaged by the crisis, and a number found themselves taken over by larger airlines in sometimes murky circumstances. Media scrutiny of the 'advance of the state, retreat of the private sector' in the airline industry focused especially on the controversial collapse of a small carrier based in Wuhan, East Star Airlines. Prior to the crisis, Air China's parent company, China National Aviation Holding Company (CNAHC), expressed interest in purchasing the airline, which would have helped it establish a stronger footing in central China, a weak point in its domestic network. Air China's eagerness also expressed itself in efforts to build closer relationships with the Hubei government, culminating in a March 2010 agreement officially designating Wuhan a regional hub for the airline. Yet, despite Air China's success in wooing the province, CNAHC's overtures were reported to have been continually rebuffed by East Star's mercurial chair, Lan Shili.

Given the context of Air China's expressed interest in acquiring the airline and its cosy relationship with the Wuhan government, there was widespread media speculation that political forces had been in play when CAAC, with support from the Wuhan government, abruptly suspended East Star's operations in March 2009, citing safety concerns. East Star subsequently went into bankruptcy, paving the way for Air China's acquisition of most of its assets at auction. Suspicions that strong-arm tactics had been used to force East Star out of the market were subsequently fuelled by reports that Lan Shili had gone missing in March 2009. East Star employees alleged he had been taken into custody after steadfastly rejecting Air China's takeover bid. The employees also reported that Wuhan officials had interfered in the negotiations, tapped East Star's communications and controlled the movements of its executives (Anderlini 2009).[14] Subsequent events only fed these suspicions of political

---

[14] One interviewee, an Air China executive close to the episode, offered a different version of events. He claimed that East Star had actually been in protracted negotiations with Air China. In a weakening bargaining position – East Star had fallen months behind on its aircraft leasing

interference, though the true course of events remains unclear. After resurfacing, Lan Shili was imprisoned, convicted of tax evasion and sentenced to four years in prison. In September 2011, Lan's niece read a statement by her imprisoned uncle at a Beijing news conference accusing Wuhan's deputy mayor, Yuan Shanla, of destroying the company out of spite and engaging in a number of crimes including embezzling public money and money laundering.

In the years since the restructuring of the airline market around the Big Three airlines, state agencies have used a variety of different tactics to aid the advance of state-owned carriers. First, traditional industrial policy levers such as subsidies and administrative limits on market entry have been used to manage competition in favour of the airlines under SASAC authority. Government agencies at various levels have also used indirect and informal market interventions to come to the aid of the Big Three. The influence exerted by the Wuhan government in support of Air China in the East Star case is one such example. Likewise, SASAC's role in the industry has notably broadened since the Global Financial Crisis, as it has employed various measures to boost industry performance, including exerting pressure on other market players such as investment banks to reduce the airlines' losses.

Conclusion

This chapter has shown that inclusion of the airline industry in the ranks of China's strategic sectors was far from inevitable. Driven by an elite push to draw power away from CAAC headquarters, in the early years after 1978 policymakers plunged ahead with a bold slate of liberalization and deregulation measures. A very different policy climate fed the abrupt reversal of policy after the industry crisis of the late 1990s. In the context of increasingly broad support for the idea that the state ought to support the development of state-controlled large enterprise groups and the creation of institutions to achieve that end, the move to restructure the airline market around the Big Three state-owned airlines was wholly consistent with the centre's new stated priorities. Indeed, the reversal in airline policy cannot be understood without reference to that policy backdrop. Likewise, the continuing industrial policy and regulatory privileges of the Big Three in the post-restructuring airline market draw legitimacy from the centre's emphasis on developing a national team to compete with established players

---

obligations – Lan baulked at Air China's hard negotiating tactics and abruptly withdrew from negotiations because he felt he had lost face (09BJ0709).

Conclusion 77

in global markets. The appointment of the pro-oligopoly figure of Li Jiaxiang to the position of CAAC director is a strong indicator of how leading officials wish to see this market develop.

Of course, interests have not been absent from the story of China's national champions push. Yet, as discussed in Chapter 1, the perspective taken in this analysis perceives interests and ideas as 'cluster concepts' and not as explanatory rivals. While interests have played a role in shaping policy outcomes in China's civil aviation sector, interested behaviour has itself been deeply informed by ideas. In the late 1990s crisis period, when many ideas about the possible future of aviation in China were on offer, debate about the way forward was certainly not academic; different players in the airline market cleaved to the ideas that suggested the most benefit for their business. But in this process, ideas functioned not simply as cloaks for interests, the view to which some rational choice scholars are inclined. Instead, ideas about states and markets helped to furnish actors' understandings of their interests. In the chaotic circumstances of a punishing regional financial crisis and plummeting airline revenues, the particular interests of market players were themselves something to discern in the *Sturm und Drang*.[15] The argument favoured by smaller airlines that the path of marketization and liberalization ought to be deepened was grounded in classical liberal views of the benefits of a market operating free of government interference. The liberal view offered both a way to explain the industry crisis – namely, too much state and not enough market – and an interpretation of where the interests of small airlines lay, i.e. in an open market structure in which competitiveness and not government favour would decide firms' fortunes.

A more heterodox, economically nationalist outlook informed the arguments of the larger players as well as like-minded government officials and industry experts. To these proponents of industry consolidation, the sectoral characteristics of the airline industry as well as the existence of a global marketplace populated by airlines many times larger than the Big Three were the most salient factors to consider in piecing together a reform agenda. This set of ideas, which ultimately won the day and remains the foundation of much present-day airline policy in China, offered an alternative, statist, conception of interests. From this perspective, the foremost interests to be considered were not those of individual firm or even those of the consumer. Instead, the salient interests were those of the *nation*. To be

---

[15] As Daniel Béland (2009: 708) has described the interplay between ideas and interests in such conditions: 'During periods of high uncertainty and beyond, ideational processes help actors to define their interests.'

sure, the Big Three airlines may well have seen an opportunity to dress up their particularist interests in continuing government support with this line of economic nationalist argumentation but it does not explain why policy-makers as far removed as the State Planning Commission were persuaded of this view. These pro-consolidation arguments drew support from officials and industry, and eventually became policy, principally because the prevailing ideas and institutions in this time period supported the conclusion that China's best interests were best served by forming a tight oligopoly around the Big Three airlines.

4 Advance of the state in telecommunications: the bricolage of managed competition

Like airlines, the place of telecommunications services among China's strategic sectors is a rather curious development and one that previous generations of PRC leaders would not have foreseen. In the Maoist period, telecommunications held on to the fringes of the command economy and claimed just a tiny fraction of resources from a state investment regime that leaned towards heavy industry development. Today, by contrast, China's highly profitable state-owned telecommunications service enterprises are nothing less than the crown jewels of state capitalism with Chinese characteristics. Why, then, has telecommunications come in from the cold?

Interests and institutions provide only a partial answer to the question. In her comparative work, Roselyn Hsueh (2012, 2011) presents the case that the state has retained a high degree of ownership and control in the telecommunications basic services market because, in contrast to industries such as textiles which the state liberalized and deregulated from early on in the reform process, telecommunications is an industry with high 'strategic value' that sits close to core national interests. But, seen against the marked shift over time in the policy status of telecommunications, the salient question is: why does the state *now* view telecommunications as a strategic sector? And why did it not previously? And while a number of rich empirical analyses have provided a valuable record of the institutional twists and turns that have shaped the status quo in China's telecommunications industry (e.g. Wu 2008; Harwit 2008; Laperrouza 2006), further analysis is needed to address the question of why and how the state's stance towards this industry has shifted so fundamentally.

This chapter draws attention to the role of ideas in shaping policy outcomes. It shows that every major turn in Chinese telecommunications policy over the past half-century has been preceded and shaped by vigorous debate about the role of telecommunications in China's rapidly changing economic and social structures. In these moments of uncertainty, different visions of the possible future of Chinese telecommunications emerged, the merits of which were widely debated among academics, officials, and occasionally even the wider public. As new institutionalist scholars would expect, such debates were not far removed from questions of material benefit; in a manner similar to the process of the airline

80 Advance of the state in telecommunications

policy reversal of the late 1990s, short-term winners in the telecommunications industry argued powerfully for the ideas that they perceived to be beneficial to their interests. It is this incremental process of arguing leading to institutionalization that has led telecommunications from the margins of the Chinese economy into the protected, strategic core of Chinese state capitalism.

Mere letter carriers: dominant ideas about telecommunications in the Maoist period

China's reform-era leaders inherited a telecommunications sector left in disarray by the ideological campaigns of the Maoist era when telecommunications was decried as a 'tool of autocracy' (*youdian shi zhuanzheng gongju* 邮电是专政工具).[1] After the Great Leap Forward, the bureaucracy of the Ministry of Post and Telecommunications (MPT) was left severely weakened by a disastrous round of localization (*xiafang* 下放) of SOE control rights between 1958 and 1961 in which the provision of telecoms services was left to local governments. During the Cultural Revolution, leftists launched attacks on officials in the telecoms bureaucracy as well as on telecommunications infrastructure. In Chongqing, for example, the destruction of communication cables left the Sichuan provincial network so crippled that 91 per cent of the wired communications infrastructure was unusable. In Fujian Province, employees simply stopped reporting to work at the local Telecoms Bureau in Ningde county and telecommunications ceased to function entirely for more than half a year (Wang 2001: 18).

Telecoms investment and bureaucracy were left deeply frayed by the years of chaos. Between 1950 and 1978, investment in telecoms accounted for just 0.86 per cent of total investment and dipped as low 0.41 per cent in 1962 (Wang 2001: 23). For comparison, the International Telecommunications Union recommended at the time that Asian countries allocate at least 2.5 per cent of total investment to telecoms development and many countries met or exceeded this target. Not only was the physical infrastructure badly underdeveloped, the telecoms bureaucracy was left in tatters after a series of politically driven bureaucratic reorganizations. In 1967, the MPT was placed under the control of the People's Liberation Army (PLA) – likely so as to protect the infrastructure from further damage by the Red Guards – and then altogether abolished in 1970 before being finally reinstated in 1973 (Harwit 2008: 33). In the waning years of the Cultural Revolution prior to Mao's death, the MPT was said to have

---

[1] This paragraph draws on Wang's (2001) superb economic history of telecoms reform. Though there are now a large number of Chinese-language studies tracing telecoms reforms post-1978, Wang's is one of the few to look in detail at Maoist-era processes and this work points up some continuities in the Maoist and post-1978 eras, particularly the pronounced 'fragmented authoritarianism' in this sector then and now (Lieberthal and Oksenberg 1988).

been all but excluded from decisionmaking on important telecoms policies. Instead, decisions about technical issues such as tariff-setting and the allocation of resources were made by top-level generalist officials in government (Wang 2001: 28). A retired senior telecommunications policymaker claimed that one reason for the relative neglect of telecommunications in the Maoist years was that, historically, telecommunications work had been regarded as unimportant in the army – in sharp contrast to the prestige accorded to oil and heavy industry bureaucracy – and workers therein were seen as mere letter carriers and answerers of telephones. This bias towards heavy industry was carried forward after the establishment of the People's Republic of China when many PLA generals headed off to lead heavy industry ministries (09BJ0323).

From messengers to vanguards: policy entrepreneurship in the early reform period

In the early reform period, the top leadership showed a new openness to ideas about the contribution of telecommunications to economic growth. After the start of the period of 'reform and opening' in December 1978, telecoms development quickly earned a place on the national agenda thanks to interventions from top leaders.[2] One important early signal from the new leadership came just a month after the historic Third Plenary Session of the Eleventh Central Committee of the CCP, when Deng Xiaoping declared that 'investment focus should fall on electricity, coal, petroleum, transportation and telecommunications' (Wang 2001: 31). In the first year of reform, telecommunications policymakers focused on identifying the errors that had been made in the past and starting to devise policies that would spur fast-paced development (Wu et al. 2008: 15–17). The Seventeenth National Post and Telecommunications Work Meeting, held in April 1979, was a crucial first step to that end. This gathering, which ordinarily did not attract attention from the top leadership, was attended by three vice-premiers – Yu Qiuli, Wang Zhen and Gu Mu. At the meeting, MPT Minister and Party Secretary Wang Zigang presented a report of more than forty pages detailing the serious damage that been wrought during the 'ten years of chaos' (1966–76) and emphasizing the importance of making telecoms development a high priority.

---

[2] This section draws especially from former Ministry of Post and Telecommunications (MPT) and Ministry of Information Industry (MII) Minister Wu Jichuan's (1997) personal account of telecoms reform as well as a recent (Wu et al. 2008) official history of telecom reform, *The Great Leap: Thirty Years of Reform China's Telecommunications Sector* published in commemoration of thirty years of 'reform and opening'. (Wu was the director of the editorial team on this second book and much of the book's contents seems to reflect his input.) Together, these two accounts, especially the latter, provide a rich insight into policymaking at the highest levels at various critical junctures.

Shortly after the conclusion of the work meeting, the MPT presented a report based on Minister Wang's analysis and recommendations to the State Council. This report subsequently became the basis for the State Council Document No. 165 issued in June 1979 (see Table 4.1). 'No. 165' designated telecoms as a 'leading-edge sector' which would drive the development of other sectors (*youdian tongxin shi guomin jingji de xianxing bumen* 邮电通信是国民经济的先行部门). Crucially, the policy also directed city-level officials to include the construction of urban telephone networks in cities' construction plans. The policy also approved the collection of telephone installation fees to subsidize network construction. Following this decisive policy breakthrough, the Party's propaganda apparatus went to work on dispelling telecoms' ideological stain left over from the Cultural Revolution. On 17 October 1979, *The People's Daily* ran an article entitled 'Strengthen the Building of Post and Telecommunications', which cited Marx's discussion of the contribution of the telegram to the enormous productivity of capitalism in support of the argument that telecommunications is a productive sector. *The People's Daily* editorial, in turn, led to a number of academic articles advocating the importance of telecommunications to a communist economy.

In 1980, the high priority of telecoms development was further cemented following a high-level meeting held to set priorities in the upcoming planning period. Chaired by Premier Zhao Ziyang and attended by eight vice-premiers in addition to the Central Finance Leadership Small Group, the purpose of the June meeting was to hear reports from the railroad, transport and post and telecommunications ministers. The inclusion of the MPT in the discussion was seen to be highly symbolic: 'For MPT, having eight vice-premiers listen to their work report was without precedent' (Wu *et al.* 2008: 19). Minister Wang's report to the leadership detailed telecoms' woes and his comments were said to have been warmly received by the leaders, especially by Vice-Premiers Gu Mu and Bo Yibo, each of whom had been previously responsible for telecoms policy. Wang also presented the results of an empirical research project examining the relationship between the expansion of industrial output and the rate of increase in the number of telephones. The report concluded that in most countries with fast-growing economies expansion in the number of telephones was 1.5 times greater than the rate of industrial expansion. He pointed out that in China the rate of increase in telephones had always lagged behind industrial output.

Bo Yibo was said to have been particularly impressed by Wang's report and, with Gu Mu, became a vocal advocate for telecommunications development in the three-day planning meeting and at high-level forums thereafter (Wu *et al.* 2008: 19–22). At the June planning meeting, Central Committee member Wan

From messengers to vanguards 83

Table 4.1: *Key industrial policies in telecommunications, 1980s and 1990s*

Policy type, name	Content and policy evolution
Installation fees ('No. 165')	Authorized the collection of initial installation fees to subsidize city telephone construction. Also permitted formerly within-government private networks to expand into the provision of services to households. • In 1985, the installation fee was set at 2,000 RMB for businesses and 1,500 RMB for households. • In 1990, the MPT and the State Price Bureau jointly issued a notice stipulating that fees should be set on a capital-cost recovery basis such that each new telephone number should recover the construction costs of one telephone (including telephone line construction, machinery and equipment investment costs, etc.). Local authorities were given discretion over how to set the fees. In Beijing, installation fees reached as high as 5,000 RMB.
Local revenue funding (*yi hua yanghua;*以话养话)	Authorized local authorities to use revenue earned at local level to finance city telephone construction. • In 1981, the MPT issued a regulation stipulating that provincial-level MPTs could use revenue from three earmarked funds for city telephone construction. • In 1982, the Ministry of Finance issued a notice to the MPT stating that, between 1982 and 1985, the MPT could retain all the profits derived for reinvestment, i.e. rather than turning it over to state coffers.
Profit, foreign exchange retention and soft loans 'Three 90 per cents' (*san get dao yi jiu*; 三个倒一九)	Authorized the MPT to retain revenue derived from three sources. • In 1982, the State Council announced that the MPT need only turn over 10 per cent of its profits to the central government; the remainder could be reinvested. • Later, the MPT was authorized to retain 90 per cent of non-trade foreign currency revenue (the bulk of which accrued from international calling). • In 1986, the central government decreed that the MPT could be relieved of paying up to 90 per cent of the principal and interest on central government loans.

84   Advance of the state in telecommunications

Table 4.1: *(cont.)*

Policy type, name	Content and policy evolution
Postal, telecoms tariffs	• In 1992, the State Council authorized the continuance of the 'three 90 per cents' in order to spur investment in telecoms to meet ballooning demand. • Finally cancelled in 1995. Authorized the charging of special tariffs in order to promote construction of local postal and telecommunications facilities.
Import tariff reduction	• In 1986, the former State Economic and Trade Commission issued a policy authorizing the charging of postal and telecoms tariffs. Thereafter, local authorities began collecting surcharges on long-distance telephone calls, telegraph and postal business. Authorized the reduction and cancellation of tariffs charged on the import of telecoms technologies. • In 1986, the State Council decreed that import tariffs applied to the purchase of foreign communications equipments could be cancelled entirely.

Sources: Wang (2001: 34–6); Wu *et al.* (2008); Harwit (2008: 36)

Li expressed scepticism and pointed out that telephones at the central headquarters in Zhongnanhai worked quite well. In response, Bo Yibo joked that:

The work of the Zhongnanhai Telephone Bureau is indeed MPT's greatest achievement but this very achievement is one of the main reasons that China's telecommunication is now so backward. Since all of us use the central government's telephone network (*hongjizi* 红机子) and all our calls go through as they should, we're not very upset. If the *hongjizi* worked like the phones used by everyone else, we'd also see the problem! MPT's current hardships are precisely the result of having done a good job with *hongjizi*. (Wu *et al.* 2008: 20)

While this early policy entrepreneurship helped to forge a consensus around the urgency of telecoms development, in the first three years it remained unclear just where such large-scale investment would come from. Though policy 'No. 165' had given the MPT a revenue stream for investment, the installation fees fell well short of what was envisioned when policymakers spoke about making telecoms into a vanguard sector. The key obstacle was that, in the first years of reform, investment decisions were still decided by the centralized planning bureaucracy, which allocated funds to different industrial ministries on the basis of stated planning priorities. In vying for a larger slice of what was a small pie of budgetary funds, the MPT found itself in zero-sum competition with politically more powerful industrial ministries that had long drawn a much larger portion of central government funds. In a meeting in April 1980 with the new MPT Minister, Wang Minsheng, Bo Yibo conceded that: 'regarding future investment, it probably won't be less than today's, but an increase would be very difficult to achieve. My guess is that the state will not be able to increase investment for two or three years' (Wu *et al.* 2008: 24).

The critical breakthrough came at a large meeting in February 1982 held to discuss how to clear the telecoms bottleneck. The meeting was chaired by Bo Yibo and attended by leaders from seventeen central government authorities with a stake in telecoms development including all the most powerful economic ministries: the State Planning Commission, the Ministry of Finance, the State Economic Commission, the State Import and Export Committee and the People's Bank of China. The very act of bringing together all these bodies to discuss telecommunications development was in itself a matter of key significance. Former MPT Minister Wu Jichuan (Wu *et al.* 2008: 24) writes:

The true meaning of this meeting was not in its size or scale; rather it meant that telecommunications development had truly become a part of national economic planning. In the giant chess game of national economic development planning, the meeting established the coordination relationships (*xietiao guanxi* 协调关系) that would link together post and telecommunications and other interested parties and decided how policies affecting multiple parties would be decided.

The meeting also laid the groundwork for the slate of industrial policies that would substantially increase the MPT's access to investment funds. Bo Yibo was said to have criticized officials from the Ministry of Finance for 'taking good care' of the transportation sector but neglecting telecoms. He also appealed to the State Import and Export Committee (SIEC) to allow the MPT to retain the foreign exchange which had been earned primarily from international calls. The SIEC representatives are said to have protested, claiming that there was no precedent for such a measure and complaining that granting the MPT special treatment would lead to endless demands for the same treatment from other ministries. Bo Yibo is said to have responded sharply with the invocation to 'seek truth from facts' (*shishi qiushi* 实事求是) and to be nimble in addressing any such problems. These exchanges paved the way for the passage of two of the 'three 90 per cents' policies (Table 4.1). In 1982, the State Council ruled that the MPT could retain 90 per cent of its profits for reinvestment. The position of the SIEC later softened and permitted the telecoms authorities to keep 90 per cent of non-trade foreign currency revenue.

Legacies of the telecommunications 'big push': infrastructure and vested interests

The effect of these industrial policies on telecoms sector investment was tremendous. The MPT's self-raised funds pot grew exponentially between 1981 and 1995 and especially so from the early 1990s. In 1981, the budget supplied 50 per cent of fixed asset investment in post and telecommunications, whereas in 1995 this figure had shrunk to 0.5 per cent. Over the same period, the percentage of fixed asset investment provided from MPT funds grew steadily from 49.6 per cent to 76.5 per cent (Wang 2001: 37). This slate of industrial policies afforded the MPT considerable flexibility in meeting booming household and business demand for telephones and stimulated an unprecedented expansion of telecoms services. Figure 4.1 shows the increase in rural and urban telephone subcriptions and reflects the changing proportions of rural and urban subscriptions between 1980 and 2005. Over the 1980s, the number of urban fixed-line subscriptions in cities quadrupled and rural subscriptions nearly doubled. The data from the 1990s show that in the second decade of reform, fixed-line services became much more accessible to businesses and residents in rural areas. In the 1990s, the number of rural subscribers grew thirty-five times while urban telephone subscriptions increased only seventeen times between 1990 and 2000. To put these numbers in comparative perspective, in 2005, 57 out of 100 Chinese citizens had a telephone, a figure roughly equivalent to the situation in Japan and Australia of the early 1990s (Harwit 2008: 38). The 1994 market entry of a rival to the MPT in basic services, China Unicom, helped to promote the wildfire spread of

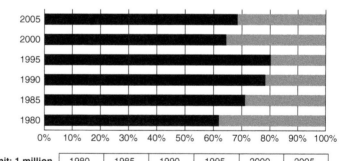

Figure 4.1 Increase in fixed-line subscriptions, 1980–2005
Source: Data from China Statistical Yearbook database (2008)

mobile services. In 2003, mobile phone subscriptions overtook fixed-line telephones as the primary means of communication.

The MPT's 'self-raised' investment funds fuelled this incredible expansion of telecommunications services by providing a revenue stream adequate for financing a huge expansion and technological upgrading of China's telecommunications infrastructure. In 1985, the MPT announced its goal of increasing the number of telephone lines nationwide five-fold by the year 2000 (from 6 million to 30 million). By 1993, the goal had already been met and in 1996, 93 million lines had been laid (Wu *et al.* 2008: 36–7).

The particular nature of these industrial policies also provided the MPT with the incentive to jealously guard its turf from would-be entrants to the telecommunications service business. Within the MPT's pot of self-raised investment funds, the contribution of installation fees increased steadily as the fee schedules were ticked upward twice, first in 1985 and then again in 1990 (see Table 5.1). Between 1986 and 1990, the installation fee revenue collected by the MPT contributed 33 per cent of total investment in the post and telecoms sector. And between 1991 and 1995, installation fees accounted for 46 per cent of total investment in the sector (Wang 2001: 39). Given that China's per capita GDP in 1990 was 1,644 RMB, the cost of installing a telephone, which reached as high as 5,000 RMB in Beijing, was priced well out of reach of ordinary citizens. Although this method of subsidizing network expansion has been utilized in many parts of the world, the astronomic expense of telephone installation fees became a matter of widespread resentment in this period and has fed public dissatisfaction with the telecoms 'monopoly' down to the present day.

Informatization and the technocrats: ideas about telecommunications in the early 1990s

In the late 1980s and early 1990s, telecommunications acquired a new significance in connection with the leadership's efforts to reinvent the mode of state control of the economy. Two streams of thought converged in shifting telecommunications from its marginal position on the outskirts of the Chinese economy to one situated close to core national interests. First, scholarly interest in 'informatization' (*xinxihua* 信息化) from the mid 1980s had the effect of popularizing the notion that China's telecommunications capacity would be a determining factor in the country's ability to face up to the challenges of the global IT revolution (Mueller and Tan 1997: 13–17). Second, officials' efforts to shift the planning system towards 'macro control and micro flexibility', an idea discussed in Chapter 2, brought them to thinking about the benefits of a robust telecommunications system in providing a channel of information needed by national planners to effectively exercise macro control.

The term 'informatization', which remains in wide use in China, refers to the economic implications of rapid advances in information technology. To some scholars, informatization amounts to a profound break in the course of world economic development such that IT sectors will gradually come to displace industry as the economic base of wealthy countries. To China's technocrats in Zhongnanhai, this was an immensely appealing message because it implied that massive investment in new technologies, and not necessarily rolling back state intervention in markets, offered a path to national wellbeing and power (Mueller and Tan 1997: 23). And for telecommunications policymakers, this discussion supplied a rallying cry as influential contributions to debate in the late 1980s emphasized China's 'backwardness' (*luohou* 落后) in comparison to other states on key measures of informatization – above all, telecommunications capacity (Jie and Chen 1987; Qiu 1988; Jia 1984).

The perceived value of new telecommunications technologies for strengthening the centre's macro control capacity comprised the ideational backdrop to the 'Golden Bridge' (*jinqiao gongcheng* 金桥工程) initiatives of the early 1990s (Mueller and Tan 1997: 56–7), described in contemporary accounts as the state's initial response to the challenge of realizing the 'information society' (*xinxi shehui* 信息社会) (Chen and Zhu 1994). A vice-minister, Zhu Rongji, was the primary patron of the 'Golden Bridge' projects, which began to take shape in early 1993. Having been tasked with solving a crippling triangular debt crisis in the state sector, Zhu found information bottlenecks a significant barrier to carrying out reform and spoke of the need to establish a 'state channel' (*guodao* 国道) of economic information to assist leaders with policymaking and regulation (Li and Bo 1994: 3; Mueller and Tan 1997: 57).[3] Developed under the auspices of the State Planning Commission, the various Golden Bridge projects (see Table 4.2 below) reflected central officials' aspirations to draw on new technologies to coordinate more closely with key economic units (large enterprise groups), exercise firm guidance of the process of informatization in key sectors (especially finance) and establish a robust and steady flow of reliable data to enhance technocratic control of the economy. Two close observers of the Golden Bridge projects found that the macro control objective was everywhere to be found in policy discussion:

---

[3] This image of Zhu Rongji as a centralizing technocrat is at odds with his characterization by some observers as a market reformer stymied by vested interests. One retired central government official said that Zhu Rongji was actually seen by many within the central government as more of a dyed-in-the-wool planner than a market reformer (12BJ0520). Regarding this perception gap, a respected Chinese political journalist related the following about Zhu Rongji: 'Foreigners view him more positively than Chinese people; lower levels see him more positively than upper levels; and outsiders like him more than insiders' (12BJ0518).

Informatization and the technocrats 89

Table 4.2: *Golden projects, 1993–2000*

Project Name	Goal	Specifics
Golden Bridge project (*jinqiao gongcheng* 金桥工程)	To establish a nationwide special-purpose network connecting government agencies with key state-owned enterprises and projects.	To link together all provinces and autonomous regions, 12,000 large and medium-sized enterprises, 100 *jihua danlie* large enterprise groups as well as large infrastructure projects (e.g. Three Gorges).
Golden Card project (*jinka gongcheng* 金卡工程)	To promote the informatization and development of finance and business through the adoption of new information technologies; upgrading legal and regulatory structure; and knowledge dissemination initiatives.	To establish a modern and practical electronic currency system within ten years; to improve the credit card management system; to increase the use of credit cards; to establish and improve the associated laws and regulations; to disseminate knowledge about and ethical use of credit cards.
Golden Customs project (*jinguan gongcheng* 金关工程)	To promote the informatization of foreign trade activities.	To establish a nationwide information network for the management of foreign trade, achieve the automation of customs clearance and reach harmonization with international trade business practice.
Golden Tax project (*jinshui gongcheng* 金税工程)	To employ information technology to combat tax evasion.	To establish a national integrated tax management information system in order to eliminate tax evasion through computerization of the tax collecting and auditing system.
Golden Agriculture project (*jinnong gongcheng* 金农工程)	To use information technologies to aid agricultural policymaking and achieve poverty alleviation goals in rural areas.	To set up a database providing information about agriculture collected from county seats with the intent of aiding national macro control and regulation by providing information about total demand for agricultural products. The project also involves the establishment of a market intelligence information system to guide agricultural production, aid disaster prevention, increase

90   Advance of the state in telecommunications

Table 4.2: *(cont.)*

Project Name	Goal	Specifics
		agricultural incomes and provide information to support poverty alleviation.
Golden Enterprise project (*jinqi gongcheng* 金企工程)	To set up an information system about enterprises that will provide a scientific basis for national macro control.	To link together a group of large and medium-sized enterprises and provide information about market entry, restructuring and technology upgrading, and provide guidance for these enterprises.
Golden Wisdom project (*jinzhi gongcheng* 金智工程)	To promote informatization in research centres and upgrade the general public's knowledge about informatization and information technology.	To establish a collection of technological texts, scientific databases and education and research management databases for use by universities, colleges and science and research *danwei*. The project also aims to link up with the global internet, establish a system for the cultivation of specialized personnel with information technology skills to implement information technology projects and spread knowledge about informatization and information technology to the general public.
Golden Macro project (*jinhong gongcheng* 金宏工程)	To upgrade economic information sources in order to support national leaders in macroeconomic policymaking.	To establish a national database for use by central organizations (and, gradually, the public) comprised of comprehensive statistics on the industrial economy, taxation, prices, investment, resources, assets, energy and transportation.

Source: *Quanguo jianshe shichang xinxi*, 1997; Mueller and Tan, 1997: 57–8

One Chinese participant in the project concluded, 'Therefore the economic information can be collected and sent to the State Council, and used to make scientific macro control decisions.' A clearer expression of the technocratic view of informatization could not be imagined. In essence, China's planners see information networks – technology – as the equivalent of price signals, profit incentives and legal structures that promote coordinaton in a market economy. (Mueller and Tan 1997: 58)

Where are the wolves? 91

The association of the telecommunications industry with the macro control agenda in the post-Tiananmen period had the effect of demarcating it as an industry closely related to core state interests: in other words, as something resembling a strategic sector. It is thus somewhat ironic that the national security tint that the telecommunications industry acquired in the post-Tiananmen period, a result in part of Zhu Rongji's efforts to strengthen the centre's macro control capacity, was subsequently used against him in pitched battles within the central government over the liberalization of the telecommunications sector in the late 1990s.

Where are the wolves? Arguing about market liberalization

As in China's airline industry, the late 1990s was a period of protracted debate in the telecommunications industry about what kind of market structure was most beneficial to China's national conditions (*guoqing* 国情). The catalysts were also similar. After a measure of competition was introduced to the telecommunications basic services market in the mid 1990s, demands were made for deeper marketization of the industry. China's impending WTO entry was another source of contention that generated open fissures within the central government over the question of market access for foreign capital. The outcome of this debate was also similar to that of airlines as proponents of a highly regulated, oligopolistic market carried the day and laid the institutional groundwork of the present market.

Debate background: limited domestic liberalization

In the late 1990s, limited competition and high prices for consumers in China's partially reformed market in telecommunications services informed discussion about what to do with telecommunications, seen by some as the 'last dinosaur' among China's industries (Li 2000). Against the dogged resistance of the incumbent monopolist, the MPT, the State Council granted approval for the establishment of a new fully licenced telecommunications service provider, Unicom, in July 1994. As part of the reform, the MPT was formally hived off from its telecommunications services arm, China Telecom, and reinvented as an arm's-length industry regulator. In practice, the MPT retained very close ties to Telecom and used the regulatory tools at its disposal to stymie Unicom's development.[4] In view of these problems, in 1997, three high-ranking

---

[4] The most important aspect of telecommunications regulation is the administration of an interconnection regime to facilitate the smooth flow of communications between different telecoms service providers on the backbone network. This is typically the most challenging aspect of telecommunications regulation and has been especially thorny in China, in large part because of

commissions jointly issued a report reviewing the competition that had emerged between Unicom and China Telecom and considering the arguments for and against the further liberalization of the telecoms market. Although the report did not side clearly with either China Telecom's or Unicom's positions, it did call for a decisive severing of the link between the MPT and Telecom and for the establishment of a system of impartial regulation (Harwit 2008: 59). Ultimately a new regulator, the Ministry of Information Industry (MII) was established as part of a 1998 administrative overhaul of the central government. The creation of the MII entailed the merger of the MPT with the Ministry of Electronics Industry (MEI) – the ministry that had lobbied for Unicom's creation.[5]

Shortly after the establishment of the MII in 1998, a major restructuring of the telecoms market began to take shape. The government began formally vetting proposals for a structural separation of China Telecom's businesses. Although bringing Unicom under the MII umbrella did much to improve the terms of competition between the two major enterprises, even in the mobile phone market, in which Unicom had become relatively competitive, Telecom still commanded 91 per cent of the market share in 1999 (Harwit 2008: 65). With considerable pressure from the media, which regularly derided China Telecom's poor customer service, high installation fees and reputation for wasteful expenditure on extravagant office buildings, top policymakers began to consider various options for dismantling the former monopolist in order to increase competition and bring down prices (Wu 2008: 47).

Debate background: hidden foreign liberalization and crackdown

For foreign companies hoping to gain access to the telecommunications basic services industry, the foggy policy environment of the early 1990s offered

---

the MPT's rocky transition from monopolist service provider to referee. After Unicom's establishment in 1993, an interconnection regime had to be built *de novo* in China in the 1990s because previously the majority of connections ran through the MPT system. In addition to the technical difficulties involved in setting prices and collecting interconnection charges, establishing an impartial regulator to police the practice of interconnection proved difficult and the MPT, and to lesser extent its successor, MII, showed pronounced favouritism towards the former monopolist China Telecom. Although Unicom had been granted a general licence entitling it to sell all the same telecommunications services as had been offered by China Telecom, the MPT, to which Unicom had to apply before opening any new service in any specific location, effectively blocked it from operating wireline services in all but a few cities and strongly curtailed the development of its mobile network in the early years.

[5] Unsurprisingly, the process of combining the former adversaries involved pitched political battles over leadership positions in the new ministry. Following rumours that an MEI vice-minister would lead the new MII, the MPT's Wu Jichuan was finally given the post (Wu 2008: 31). Under Wu's leadership, many of the highest-ranking MEI figures in the new MII were pushed out of their vice-ministerial posts within months (Harwit 2008: 63).

hidden opportunities (Hsueh 2011: 64–6). In 1993, during the pitched battles over Unicom, the State Council issued the industry's first ruling on foreign investment, Policy No. 55, which stated flatly that 'foreign businesses are not allowed to run or participate in the telecommunications service business in China'. Mueller and Lovelock (2000: 736) suggest that the timing of this foreign investment ban was not in the least coincidental. They argue that the rule, which had been drawn up by the MPT, was primarily intended to stifle Unicom's development by depriving the new company of much-needed capital and cooperative opportunities with foreign telecoms service providers. The rule was also consistent with the State Council's interests in breaking the MPT's monopoly but retaining a strong hand in the development of telecommunications. In sum, 'coupling competition with a ban on FDI was the bargain that reconciled these concerns' (Mueller and Lovelock 2000: 737). Yet after its establishment, Unicom flouted the FDI ban by exploiting a loophole in the regulation that allowed Unicom, operating through satellite companies, to set up joint ventures with foreign companies. These 'China–China–foreign' (*zhong zhong wai* 中中外) arrangements allowed Unicom to set up lucrative joint ventures with a legion of foreign companies including Ameritech (USA), Bell Canada and Deutsche Telecom before the MPT closed the loophole in a 1998 ruling that forced Unicom to terminate its forty-six CCF agreements (Wu 2008: 70). Angered by the MPT's unilateralism as well as the poor compensation they received from Unicom in the process of dissolving the CCF joint ventures, foreign telcos noisily lobbied their home governments to make majority foreign investment in telecommunications a condition of China's WTO entry. The concrete policy question in 1998–9 was whether to allow majority foreign ownership, a condition which Premier Zhu Rongji was pushing for against resistance from the telecoms bureaucracy and a rising tide of nationalist sentiment.

Against this background, a wide-ranging debate about the possible futures of Chinese telecommunications took place in 1998 and 1999. The following pages analyse the ideas which informed influential views about three central points of contention: (1) whose interests come first – the nation's or consumers'? (2) how will prices be reduced? and (3) by what means could Chinese telecommunications enterprises ready themselves for global competition?

The question of interests: consumers vs. the nation

Policymakers and scholars debated, often quite fiercely, the question of whether the putative interests of consumers ought to trump those of the country (*guojia* 国家) or vice versa. The first missive from the nationalist side was an article by Zhi Bi and Wang Xiaoqiang (1998) one of the most influential contributions to the telecoms debates of 1998 and 1999 (Chen 1999). In a passionate section recalling the traumatic events of China's century of humiliation, the authors invoked *The Art of War* in support of their argument that China Telecom and Unicom ought to first shore up their position in the domestic market to ward off foreign encroachment:

> Security against defeat implies defensive tactics; ability to defeat the enemy means taking the offensive. In the current situation of global competition in the telecommunications industry, the main battlefields are in Europe and North America. As a developing country, China's telecommunications industry does not possess dominating world power. Relying on China's broad market depth to deal with multinational companies and focusing on carrying out the fight on 'interior lines' (*neixian zuozhan* 内线作战) is a strategic policy of the Chinese telecommunications industry. (Zhi and Wang 1998: 19)

While this analysis framed telecommunications policy first and foremost as a matter of China's rejuvenation (*zhenxing zhonghua* 振兴中华), there were other influential types of national interest arguments in circulation. Writing in the top Party journal, *Qiushi*, Minister Wu Jichuan (1999: 21) made the case for a cautious approach to external liberalization by highlighting the strategic aspects of the sector: 'The telecommunications industry is a "lifeline industry" (*mingmai hangye* 命脉行业) with strong system and network properties that has a significant impact on national economic development. Telecommunications resources are scarce resources that belong to the country. The security of the telecommunications network and information security are related to national sovereignty and economic security' (Wu 1999: 21).[6]

Zhou Qiren, a well-known economist from the Chinese Economy Research Centre at Peking University, offered the most spirited rebuttal to nationalist claims in a widely read piece that captured the sentiments of many liberalization advocates. Zhou argued that framing telecommunications liberalization as an issue of national rejuvenation would lead to grave policy mistakes that were harmful, above all, to consumers. He attacked Zhi's and Wang's nationalist claims as a cynical sleight of hand:

---

[6] While not a focal point in this debate, official views on the salience of telecommunications for social stability were developing, somewhat belatedly, in this period. Lynch's (1999: 194) research on the evolution of Party 'thought work' in the 1990s shows that despite the role of fax machines in helping organizers to relay messages during the Tiananmen protests 'only in early 1996 did the Chinese authorities finally seem to grasp the significance of the Internet and to target telecommunications services' in a series of regulations limiting the provision of internet services and requiring value-added service (VAS) providers to register with the MPT. Lynch's work also points out that largely because telecommunications and propaganda fall under different policy systems (*xitong* 系统), telcos in the 1990s were far removed from the business of thought work: 'individuals working in the telecommunications industry do not see it as their responsibility to manage the content of telecommunications networks, while individuals working in the party's propaganda apparatus do not see it as their responsibility to concern themselves with what passes through the nation's telecommunications networks'(Lynch 1999: 190–1).

In fact, the main problems we Chinese face today are the departments, 'companies' and organizations created by 'our people' (*ziji ren* 自己人) which use all kinds of great names to carry out administrative monopolies ... If 'foreign wolves' were to monopolize the Chinese market and bully Chinese consumers, that would be altogether different. But do 'our' administrative monopolies benefit our market, customers, enterprises and modernization projects? The common sense of ordinary people has been able to judge matters: once the words 'national interest' are 'introduced', the truth has to be reversed.

In telecommunications, for example, to make a phone call, consumers must pay an 'installation fee' of more than 5,000 RMB and are charged for international long-distance calls at five times the rate in the United State and receive poor service. With this price base, what wolf in the world could Chinese consumers possibly fear? (Zhou 1998: 36–7)

Several articles written by researchers from the Ministry of Commerce's Foreign Investment Department, Ma Yu and Xu Dansong, shared Zhou's disdain for what they perceived as playing the national security card in defence of what were actually the particularist interests of industry. They argued that China's national interests were, in fact, compromised by monopoly since stifling the competition that drives innovation made China's telecommunications system vulnerable to outside threats (Ma and Xu 1999a; Ma and Xu 1999b; *Lingdao juece xinxi* 1999).

Unsurprisingly, such calls to liberalize telecommunications in the name of consumer and (true) national interests drew their own vitriolic rebuttals. Popular New Left economist, Han Deqiang, concluded his sharp critique of Zhou Qiren's article with this passage: 'Could Mr Zhou not change the name of [Peking University's] Chinese Economy Research Centre? How about Auctioning the Chinese Economy Research Centre? Or a US Takeover of the Chinese Economy Research Centre?' (Han 1999).

Making telecommunications cheaper: more competition or more scale?

Astronomical installation fees and long-distance charges that the MPT was only slowly regulating downwards led many, including a large proportion of the general public, to the view that thoroughgoing liberalization of the telecommunications market was in order. A 1999 survey of consumers in Beijing, Shanghai and Guangzhou found that 72 per cent believed there was a need for reform, specifically for breaking up monopoly and increasing competition (Chen 1999: 7). At a March 1999 press conference on the sidelines of a gathering of the National People's Congress, a reporter from Hong Kong asked Premier Zhu Rongji about the state's plan for making telecommunications services more affordable for consumers:

[I]f I were to call US President Clinton from Hong Kong, it would cost me 0.98 Hong Kong dollars/minute; if I were to call you [in Beijing], it would cost 9.8 Hong Kong dollars/minute – 10 times the price. On this visit, I discovered that the cost of calling Hong Kong from Beijing has dropped from 8.1 RMB to 5 RMB. We know that competition can bring down calling charges and raise service quality. What methods would you use to quicken the pace of competition in China's telecommunications market?

Zhu's widely quoted reply quickly became a shibboleth for proponents of liberalization and deregulation:

> China's telecommunications service prices are currently falling, but they haven't fallen far enough and must continue to come down. *The method is introducing competition.* First and foremost, we are currently reforming China's telecommunications system, an important principle of which is breaking monopoly and encouraging competition. Secondly, we will open the telecommunications market step-by-step to let foreign capital enter China's telecommunications market. (Zhu 1999: 21, emphasis added)

The Premier was not speaking for all of government, however. In the context of difficult negotiations with the US over China's WTO entry, in which market access in telecommunications services had become a particular sticking point, Zhu's vision of a more open telecommunications market was unpopular in the telecommunications bureaucracy, and met with particularly staunch resistance from Minister Wu Jichuan. The acrimony between the two was driven by more than differences in economic belief, however; Wu and Zhu were at odds over the Premier's unpopular efforts to streamline central government.[7]

Minister Wu's own plan for making telecommunications services affordable was based on a very different understanding of what was wrong with telecoms. In a striking parallel to the arguments then being made in the civil aviation bureaucracy, claiming a need to nurture large enterprise groups and manage competition, Wu's view was that the basic problem facing telecommunications was that neither China Telecom nor Unicom was yet sufficiently large to reap economies of scale. In response to a reporter's query about his response to Zhu's clarion call for more competition, Wu replied: 'Premier Zhu said

---

[7] At the time, leaders of the former industrial line ministries were incensed by Zhu's upending of government–business relations in the 1998 administrative reforms. In the wake of these reforms, Wu Jichuan emerged as one of the most outspoken opponents of Premier Zhu and he used his post as head of the restructured telecoms regulator to frustrate Zhu's efforts to conclude the most difficult part of WTO negotiations, the US agreement. In April 1999, after a failed round of talks, Zhu came under intense pressure domestically after the Clinton administration unilaterally publicized concessions that had supposedly been made by Chinese negotiators at the meetings, including an agreement in principle to allow 51 per cent foreign equity investment in telecommunications service enterprises (Fewsmith, 1999). Upon Zhu's return to Beijing, Wu was rumoured to have tendered his resignation in protest, a defiant gesture which the leadership rejected (Johnson 1999). In the months following Zhu's disastrous visit to Washington, MII Minister Wu worked assiduously to undermine the premier's public assurances that China's telecommunications industry was gradually opening to foreign investment.

telecommunications prices must gradually come down and this is quite right. As the scale of telecommunications operations expands and technology improves, prices will gradually adjust' (*Youdian Shangqing* 1999: 10). As we will see below, Wu's thinking in this period was heavily influenced by the large enterprise group strategy discussed in previous chapters.

How should enterprises prepare for global competition?

Proponents of opening China's telecommunications basic services to foreign capital participation argued that opening to global markets was the best medicine for China's inefficient and uncompetitive telecommunications enterprises. Some analyses emphasized the benefits that foreign investors would bring to Chinese telcos in the form of know-how about global standards of service and other 'software' issues that were seen to be the biggest deficiencies of Chinese telcos at the time (Li 2000: 17). Leading telecoms expert and former senior MPT official, Kan Kaili, argued that the main benefits of opening to global markets lay in introducing new rules that would themselves provide incentives for enterprises to adapt and innovate:

> Liberalization of the telecommunications services market will greatly promote the reform of the telecommunications system in China and further promote the separation of enterprise as well as the transformation from a planned economy to a market economy. The government regulates the market, the market guides business. The government is to supervise fair competition in the telecommunications market, while companies' management and ownership is separate. In our current situation, the mechanisms of fair market competition have not been established and business operations do not comply with market rules such that government–enterprise separation has not yet been realized. With the liberalization of the telecommunications market, China's telecommunications market will be integrated into the international telecommunications market. Our telecommunications businesses must rely on the market competition mechanism of survival of the fittest to ensure the rapid, healthy and sustainable development of our telecommunications businesses. (Yu 2000: 7)

Not all experts were so sanguine about the benefits of exposing China's comparatively young and inexperienced telcos to international competition, however.

Minister Wu Jichuan, in particular, was a vocal and powerful proponent of the view that the large enterprise strategy ought to be employed in order to first groom China's telecommunications service providers at home before opening China's doors to the world market. This was necessary, he argued, in view of increasing levels of concentration in the global telecommunications industry:

> The changing structure of international telecommunications competition brings pressures and challenges to the development of China's telecommunications

industry. In the assault of globalization and technological advancement, liberalization and competition in telecommunications markets has become a trend. Some of the world's leading telecommunications and information companies are making use of modern economic means to seize the international market, such as alliance formation, merger, or reorganization to form cross-industry, cross-border 'combined fleets' (*lianhe jiandui* 联合舰队). Moreover, their use of technological and service penetration constitutes a threat to developing countries. (Wu 1999: 19)

Wu saw a need to employ the tools of administrative guidance to replicate these processes of increasing concentration in the home market:

In our information industry, a prominent problem is its weak and fragmented foundation, excessively small scale and low technology level. It is imperative to carry out a trans-regional, cross-sectoral strategic industrial restructuring in order build an elite and strong army of national enterprises. (Wu 1998: 8)

In a later piece written shortly after China's entry into the WTO, Wu stated that development and training of this 'army' was the very centrepiece of China's telecommunications policy: 'Reform is a means, development is the end. Through competition and opening up, [we will] gradually develop a few large enterprises with advanced management, first rate service and economies of scale' (*Tongxin xinxi bao* 2002: A01) .

Debate conclusion: the choice for managed competition

This wide-ranging debate about the future of Chinese telecommunications was resolved much as the concurrent deliberations in airlines had been, namely for the proponents of managed competition in an oligopolistic, state-controlled market and against the advocates of liberalization and deregulation. In April 1999, Minister Wu Jichuan announced that China Telecom would be 'vertically' separated such that its wireline businesses would go to the new China Telecom (which also kept internet services); its wireless services would go to a new company, China Mobile, and; its paging business to Unicom; while its satellite operations were hived off in a new enterprise, China Satellite (see Figure 4.1).[8] While the 1999 restructuring and later iterations have been designed to foster a more balanced competition in telecommunications basic services and to bring down prices for consumers, advocates of deregulation argue that prices remain

---

[8] It is likely that the MII favoured the vertical option because it would ensure a higher stock valuation and allow China Telecom to hold its place as one of the world's largest telecoms operators (Wu 2008: 49).

artificially high and claim, with reference to recent corruption scandals (discussed below), that rent-seeking continues unabated in the protected market.

On the question of foreign participation, insiders described Premier Zhu's weakened political position (see note 7) combined with the heightened popular appeal of nationalist forms of argument following NATO's bombing of the Chinese embassy in Belgrade in May 1999 as the factors which turned the tide against the majority foreign ownership proposal (09BJ0924). In China's agreement with the US on the terms of WTO entry, reached in November 1999, foreign equity investment in telecommunications basic services joint ventures was limited to 49 per cent (after 2004 for mobile and after 2006 for fixed line services) and 50 per cent in value-added services. In practice, because all applications for telecommunications joint ventures in basic services are vetted by the regulator, the market remains effectively closed to prospective foreign and private service providers in the basic services market segment (08BJ1201).[9]

The nationalists' triumph at this critical juncture also moved telecommunications decisively, if not quite formally, in the direction of strategic sectorhood. The Fifteenth Party Congress Report (1997) marked an important first step in the leadership's efforts to differentiate industries – so-called 'lifeline industries' – in which a high degree of state control and a high proportion of ownership would develop, from those that would be more lightly regulated and open, in varying degrees, to private and foreign capital. Crucially, the exact membership of the lifeline industries was left undefined, leading to protracted debate about how 'adjusting the layout of the state sector' (*guoyou jingji buju tiaozheng* 国有经济布局调整), should be carried out (Eaton 2011: 86–96). It is this policy context that makes Minister Wu Jichuan's pointed characterization of telecommunications as a lifeline industry during the 1998–9 debates significant. In fact, the central government has as yet declined to publicly name China's strategic sectors (see Chapter 1, note 2), yet various documents from the bureaucracy with the primary mandate for managing strategic sector SOEs, SASAC, show that telecommunications is, for all intents and purposes, a 'lifeline industry', along with the defence industry, the power grid, petroleum and petrochemicals, coal, civil aviation and shipping

---

[9] The WTO's 2012 Trade Policy Review of China described the 'foreign presence in the telecommunications services sector' as 'extremely marginal' (WTO 2012: 145). The report noted that while twenty-five licences to foreign companies had been granted in the VAS market (of sixty applications received), this number was dwarfed by the 23,259 VAS licences that have been granted to applicants from Chinese citizens and companies. In the basic telecommunications services, no applications from foreign companies had been received given the restrictive environment.

100 Advance of the state in telecommunications

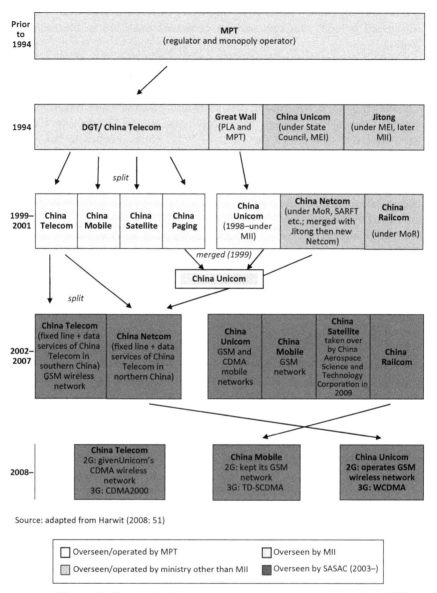

Figure 4.2 Competition in telecommunications basic services, 1994–2009

(SASAC 2007: 176–7). Had Zhou Qiren and the advocates of an open regime carried the day, telecommunications may well not have taken its place on this list.

The managed competition legacy

The outcome of the 1998–9 telecommunications debates secured the institutional foundations of 'managed competition' (*youxu jingzheng* 有序竞争). In the years since, Wu Jichuan's vision of developing China's telecommunications industry by increasing the scale of the telecommunications national champions in a highly regulated, semi-competitive marketplace has coloured all aspects of telecommunications policy. As Pearson (2005) has argued, in telecommunications, as in all of China's lifeline industries, calibrating a state of managed competition is a bedrock norm of state regulation. The following pages examine, first, the particular conceptualization of 'managed competition', a phrase encountered most often in reference to the telecommunications industry, before turning to the analysis of how this concept has become embedded in telecommunications policy in the past fifteen years.

To some degree, managed competition is defined by its antonyms, 'disorderly competition' (*wuxu jingzheng* 无序竞争) and 'vicious competition' (*exing jinzheng* 恶性竞争). To proponents of managed competition, the most common symptom of a state of disorderly or excessive competition is a price war between telcos on service packages. What differentiates such activities from beneficial forms of competition in the eyes of these analysts is that China's telcos – which remain creatures of government to some degree, and thus prone to moral hazard – continue to prioritize market share over profitability, and thus will continue the fight long after cost considerations dictate a laying down of arms (Nong 2004; Fan 2008). Analysts worry that in the absence of a strong regulator to manage competition between the telcos, such price wars will ultimately undermine the state's efforts to develop telecommunications enterprises to international standards:

One side cuts prices, then the other, resulting in repeated seesaw-style price reductions. The frequency of price cuts gets faster with each party wanting more market share, but revenue and profits are reduced. Ultimately the result is a lose–lose situation which makes it difficult for enterprises to achieve stable and sustainable development and reduces the value of the enterprise. (Fan 2008: 24)

In this vein, in 2003, the vice-governor of Yunnan Province, Li Xinhua, called on the provincial branches of the telecommunications service providers to put an end to price wars as they contravened the policy of telecoms enterprises 'going big and going strong' (*zuo da zuo qiang* 做大做强) (Peng 2003: 2). Others argue that consumers are also ultimately not served well by price wars, since shrinking revenues lead to lower standards of service as telcos seek to reduce costs elsewhere in their operations (Yao 2004). (These analyses are generally rather unclear about which aspects of firms' behaviour are affected by moral hazard and which are not.) Other afflictions seen as stemming from disorderly and excessive states of competition, and therefore demanding of regulation, are continuing interconnection problems as well as wasteful, duplicate investments in infrastructure (Yao 2004; Gao 2001).

Whereas excessive competition is seen to ultimately erode enterprise competitiveness, orderly competition is thought to serve industry development by creating a market environment of relative calm in which the telcos have the freedom to focus on developing their capabilities in preparation for dancing with wolves in global markets. One widely cited piece outlining the principles of managed competition urged Chinese enterprises to make use of the tools of competition *and* cooperation and identified increasing industrial concentration as an area of shared national interest:

> In our efforts to deepen enterprise reform, one very important policy is 'encouraging mergers' (*guli jianbing* 鼓励兼并) which encourages the use of capital as the link to conduct cross-regional, cross-industry, cross-ownership and cross-border restructuring and transformation operations aimed at the formation of large enterprise groups with strong competitiveness. Because the globalization of markets has led to global competition, any powerful enterprises or enterprise groups seeking to maintain competitive advantage in the international market will be weakened if they rely just on themselves. Only strengthening cooperation, especially encouraging alliances between strong companies (*qiangqiang lianhe* 强强联合) will lead to winning greater competitive advantage internationally. In recent years, alliances and mergers between large enterprises is a wind that has swept across the world; this is a reflection of the trend from competition to cooperation. (Cao and Han 1999: 70)

Minister Wu's statements on orderly competition reflect a similar view of what the challenges of the globalization of telecommunications imply for appropriate methods of regulation in the domestic market. During a study trip in Fujian Province in 2001, Wu explained that China's telecommunications reform and development strategy was formulated with an eye to international developments. He characterized introducing competition and enhancing cooperation as two important methods of telecommunications policy, the ultimate aim of which is to develop the industry as a whole (Sun *et al.* 2001).

In the context of strong official encouragement for national champions in target industries to 'go big and go strong' in the home market in order to 'go forth' (*zouchuqu* 走出去) into global markets, managing competition is ultimately a matter of industrial policy. One intriguing excerpt from the official *Annual Report on the Development of China's Large Groups* illustrates how industry regulators are tacitly and sometimes overtly encouraged to consider the impact of rules on the revenue intake of the national team SOEs:

In order to create large-scale operations in a short period of time, the state must aggregate its resources and make large-scale investments in priority industries. At the same time, the state should limit the entry of foreign enterprises for a period of time, in order to provide domestic enterprises with a protective buffer zone behind which they can develop. The state should also limit market entry in the domestic market so as to prevent excessive competition; this will allow enterprises to make profits. In the process of expanding into the international market, Chinese enterprises will be able to use these super-profits earned in the domestic market to subsidize losses abroad. In this way, Chinese enterprises will be able to establish a base in international markets. (ZGDQYJTNDFZBG 2007: 73)

The following section examines how this strategy has been applied to telecommunications.

The new policy framework of managed competition

Towards the end of the 1990s, telecommunications policy reflected a new emphasis on moulding internationally competitive national champions. In the process of creating these national champions, overseas capital markets played a pivotal role. A wave of overseas IPOs by large SOEs began with the listing of Brilliance China Automotive on the New York Stock Exchange in October 1992 and was followed by a series of 'red chip' offerings of municipal assets repackaged as corporations in the Hong Kong market (Walter and Howie 2010: 96–106).[10] The October 1997 listing of China Telecom in Hong Kong marked a new phase of SOEs tapping global capital markets because it was the first time almost the entirety of an industry had gone public.[11] The IPO raised a record US $4 billion and demonstrated the considerable confidence foreign investors had in the future prospects of an incumbent monopolist in a booming growth market (Walter and Howie 2010: 105). The China Telecom offering was the model for the subsequent listing of oil and gas giants PetroChina and Sinopec in 2000. In that same year, China Telecom's rival, China Unicom, went public and raised US $5 billion by selling a mere 5 per cent of the company's shares. To China's policymakers, these overseas IPOs were attractive because they considerably strengthened the financial position of SOEs at minimal cost in terms of loss of influence, since only a small fraction of the companies' total equity was offered for sale to foreign investors. By virtue of

---

[10] The decisions about which companies would go public were heavily political, as the securities regulator, the China Securities Regulatory Commission, had responsibility for vetting domestic companies' IPO applications on the domestic as well as the overseas market. The CSRC's decisions were made in consultation with the top leadership in Beijing. The record of Chinese companies' IPOs shows the strong preference given to state-owned companies.

[11] At the time, China Unicom commanded a small fraction of the market in mobile services, and fixed-line services were entirely monopolized by Telecom.

majority equity holdings often exceeding 75 per cent, the mainland group companies at the helm of these national champions continue to exercise unrivalled control over decisionmaking in the listed companies.

While 'going forth' is a term most often associated with China's energy giants, the country's largest telecoms operators have begun expanding into overseas markets focusing on the South and Central Asian regions. In 2007, China Mobile made its first venture into overseas markets with the purchase of 89 per cent of the shares of Paktel, a small mobile operator in Pakistan. China Mobile subsequently purchased Paktel's remaining shares and established China Mobile Pakistan (CMPak) as a 100 per cent subsidiary of the Chinese parent company. In addition to Pakistan's market of more than 165 million people and strong GDP growth prior to the onset of the global recession, China Mobile was said to have been lured by the opportunities among the 66 per cent of the Pakistani population living in rural areas where the company had hoped to replicate its successes in expanding coverage to the Chinese countryside (Lee 2007). As yet, though, China Mobile's Zong brand has struggled to take market share from Pakistan's four established larger telcos, in part because the rural strategy successfully employed in China has proven difficult to transplant to Pakistan where rural land prices are higher, making the provision of telecoms bases and equipment more expensive (Zhao 2011). After a seven-year lull in overseas investment acivities, China Mobile purchased an 18 per cent stake in the Thai telecommunciations group, True Corp, and is rumoured to be considering investments in a further five countries (Clover and Peel 2014; Huang 2013).

The establishment of SASAC in 2003 has served to strengthen the role of managed competition in telecommunications. SASAC exercises considerable influence over the SOEs in its charge through high-level management appointments, the dispatch of supervisory panels to SOEs and, most importantly, through annual performance reviews, the results of which are published in industry-specific rankings and SASAC-wide enterprise rankings. Consistent with SASAC's responsibility for 'maintaining and increasing the value of state assets' (*baozhi zengzhi* 保值增值), the main criterion in the annual performance reviews is profitability, and the salaries of SOE managers are tied to the outcome of these reviews. China Mobile's extremely high profit margins have consistently landed it top marks in both the industry and the SASAC-wide rankings. Indeed, for several years, China Mobile ranked first overall in the cross-industry rankings.

In its role as coach of the national team, SASAC has come to play a leading role in telecommunications policymaking. Yukyung Yeo (2009) has argued that the most important role played by SASAC in the telecoms industry is not actually as the acting owner of the telecommunications enterprise but instead as the industry regulator. She finds that SASAC's mandate to increase the value of state assets has led to conflicts with the telecoms regulator over rule changes that would threaten telcos' profitability. For instance, SASAC was said to have intervened after the MII tabled a proposal to introduce a caller-pay system which might have reduced fees paid by consumers by as much 30 percent (Yeo 2009: 1020). SASAC is also reported to have been a main protagonist in the government's effort to suppress a 2004 price war between mobile operators in Guangzhou, labelling the competition between Guangzhou Mobile and Guangzhou Unicom 'vicious' (Yeo 2009: 1030). SASAC was also the main architect of the 2008 reshuffling of the telecoms industry which saw the creation of a three-firm oligopoly (China Mobile, China Telecom and China Mobile).[12] Similarly, Roselyn Hsueh (2011: 94) suggests that one of SASAC's aims in carrying out the periodic rotation of the major telco executives is dampening price wars between the major players in the interests of maximizing total revenue intake. In response to such actions, telecoms expert Kan Kaili has argued that SASAC's mandate to 'maintain and increase the value of state assets', combined with its regulatory functions, place it in a deep conflict of interest with Chinese consumers, since its primary interests are in the maximization of SOE revenue or in the promotion of competition. In a speech at a forum on 'The Price System and Monopoly Sector Reform' held at Peking University in September 2008, Kan called, on these grounds, for SASAC's immediate dissolution.

Exogenous shock or mere shake? Scandals and the mounting pressure for change

In recent years, voices critical of the managed competition modus operandi have grown into a chorus as a succession of high-level corruption scandals have generated renewed calls for liberalization and deregulation. Between 2009 and 2013 a total of twelve senior officials from China Mobile were removed from office for corruption, including former vice-chair, Zhang

---

[12] In 2008, a '3+1' restructuring plan was adopted which divided up mobile networks and mobile telecommunication standards between the three firms. China Mobile would absorb China Railcom and operate a TD-SCDMA network; China Telecom would take over Unicom's CDMA network and run a 3G CDMA2000 network; and China Unicom would absorb Netcom, keep its GSM network and be licenced for a WCDMA 3G network. In deciding the terms of restructuring, SASAC's telecommunications performance ranking was apparently a critical factor in the decision for Netcom to be taken over by Unicom because Netcom had consistently finished behind its competitors Unicom, Telecom and Mobile (08BJ1107). While China Mobile is seen to be at a disadvantage in the 3G market, since the company kept its most lucrative business line, the 2G GSM wireless network, it is likely that Mobile will retain its commanding market position in the immediate future. According to one interviewee, at no point in the process was a structural separation of China Mobile's businesses given serious consideration because policymakers were committed to preserving the company's market capitalization and growing international presence (09BJ0323).

Chunjiang, who has charged with accepting 7.5 million RMB in bribes and handed a suspended death sentence in July 2011 (*The Economic Observer* 2013). The National Auditing Office has reportedly discovered evidence of widespread corruption in examinations of the accounts of all three of the major telecoms service providers (China Mobile, China Unicom and China Telecom). Much of the corruption is related to 'power-for-money' deals involving Chinese service providers, a segment of the telecommunications market that is particularly attractive to foreign companies since investment rules are comparatively lax. In 2009, the Australian company Telstra Corp. successfully navigated the regulatory thicket to purchase controlling stakes in two privately owned China Mobile service providers, China M and Sharp Point, which provided music platforms and other content to Mobile's mobile phone customers (Qin *et al.* 2014). A later investigation of the deal by the Communist Party's Central Commission for Discipline Inspection resulted in charges being laid against two China Mobile managers, Ye Bing and Ma Li, who had reportedly accepted bribes of US $17 million and US $50 million respectively from a senior executive of service provider Tom.com, Wang Leilei, in exchange for China Mobile's grant of approval for the Telstra deal.

The scandals have, inevitably, reawakened debate about the costs and benefits of the managed competition model. In an exhaustively researched book on China's telecommunications scandals, *Caixin* investigative journalist, Zhao Hejuan, argues that market conditions are largely to blame for what she characterizes as an entrenched culture of corruption in the industry:

> The title of the book《天下有贼》, in English, *The Invisible Thief*, is to tell the reader that, today, when there are more than 1 billion mobile phone users, when there is no place that telecommunications services are not present, when it has become an essential part of life for you and me, in circumstances of monopoly and the absence of effective regulation, as soon as one enters the area of grey deals, invisible thiefs who, at any time, can take illegitimate profits (*bu zhengdang liyi* 不正当利益) from customers' wallets are also everywhere to be found. (Zhao 2012: 10)

Such analyses of the root causes of endemic corruption in telecommunications has generated some enthusiasm about the leadership's call for a turn to 'mixed ownership' (*hunhe suoyouzhi* 混合所有制) made at the Third Plenum of the Eighteenth Party Congress in November 2013. One expert argues that diversifying the ownership of China's telcos would improve internal supervision and stem corruption, since new shareholders would bring with them demands for transparency and accountability (Wang 2014).

Recent policies by the Ministry of Industry and Information Technology (MIIT), the successor to MII, suggest that a less-managed form of competition may be ahead for China's telecommunications industry. The current minister, Miao Wei, dubbed by *Caixin* 'China's Minister of Reform', has identified telecommunications as one of two 'lifeline' industries (the other is defence) that will be gradually opening to private capital (Hu and Wang 2014). Miao declared in an interview that nineteen licences have already been granted to private enterprises active in the telecoms services resale business. In addition, in the Shanghai Free Trade Zone established in September 2013, seen as a pilot for testing China's next round of economic reforms, the value-added services market has been further opened to foreign enterprises.

Conclusion

The process through which telecommunications acquired the mantle of strategic sector presents both similarities and contrasts with the airline case. Telecommunications, like airlines, had been of comparatively marginal importance to the Mao-era command economy. But whereas Deng Xiaoping supported, partly for political reasons, the early dismantling of the airline monopoly and the establishment of a (partial) separation between government and enterprises, the dismantling of command-era institutions in telecommunications took place much more gradually. This protracted period of 'partial reform' had the effect of nurturing an especially powerful 'short-term winner' in the MPT, and indeed the incumbent monopolist behaved much as Hellman's (1998) model would predict.

The nature and pace of institutional change also differed between the two industries. In airlines, the proximate cause of broad industry debate in the late 1990s leading ultimately to re-regulation and consolidation was an exogenous shock – the plummeting revenues of all the Big Three airlines under CAAC supervision. The perceived severity of this crisis contributed to a rapid policy reversal and the establishment of a new equilibrium of managed competition. Telecommunications was, as we have seen, host to debate fuelled by similar ideas in the same time frame, but the absence of any comparable crisis made for a smoother process of institutional change, one characterized by bricolage rather than rupture, in which the institutional foundations of the market order were laid gradually drawing on a variety of ideational sources.

In both industries, ideas provided the motive force behind institutional change. To be sure, particularist interests in both airlines and telecommunications have made effective use of ideas as weapons at critical junctures – they aligned themselves behind the ideas that they believed would preserve their benefits in partially reformed markets. But the weapons preceded the warriors. In the case of telecommunications, a sequence of ideas emphasizing the contribution of telecommunications to reform-era China gradually transformed common perceptions of this once peripheral industry. In the late 1970s, the Deng Xiaoping-era leadership proved open to arguments advanced by telecommunications insiders about the vanguard role telecommunications could play in boosting China's economic growth. The subsequent informatization discourse reinforced this perception and also dovetailed with the contemporaneous efforts of central planners to create a new mode of economic guidance based on 'macro control and micro flexibility'. The idea that telecommunications is a sensitive industry close to core national interests, and thus in need of both protection from foreign competition and a high degree of regulatory control, gained ground in industry debate inspired by China's looming WTO entry in the late 1990s.

In both airlines and telecommunications, ideas about the importance of large enterprise groups for a China on the cusp of full-scale entry into global markets were especially salient to debate in the critical period of the late 1990s, when the institutions of managed competition were laid. While the phraseology has changed over time, the basic aspiration – to nurture globally competitive national champions in a market in which competition is managed by the state – remains deeply embedded in market institutions and practice to the present day. But the spate of recent corruption scandals in telecommunications and other strategic sectors have, to some eyes, laid bare the pitfalls of managed competition. These revelations of widespread graft in the lifeline industries have been a key factor in reigniting debate about China's economic future since Xi Jinping's accession after the Eighteenth Party Congress (2012), a topic to which we return in the following chapter.

5   Is the state's advance coming to a halt?

The advance of the state in China long predates the Global Financial Crisis of 2008–9. To be sure, the reversal of fortunes in the state sector and the rapid ascent of the SASAC national champions up the ranks of the Global 500 has taken many by surprise, including policymakers in Beijing. But these outcomes were, in fact, envisioned, if perhaps not wholly expected, by the architects of the large enterprise strategy and successive industrial policies. This manuscript has narrated the incremental process through which this vision was assembled and has detailed its far-reaching impact on the pathway of two unlikely entrants into the ranks of the lifeline industries, airlines and telecommunications. While the two big 'I's' of comparative political economy scholarship – institutions and interests – give us some insight into the causes behind this development, the focus on ideas presented here helps to unravel some of the more puzzling aspects of state advance in China.

Institutions are the rails upon which the state has advanced. As previous works have shown (Nolan 2001; Sutherland 2001, 2003; Fischer 1998; Keister 2000), industrial policies that took shape from the mid 1980s in support of large enterprise groups provided the first loose outlines of China's 'refurbished' state capitalism (McNally 2013). Later refinements under SASAC's tutelage employed the tools of managed competition to support the national team 'going big and going strong'. In markets gated with high regulatory barriers to entry and with ready access to both soft loans from state-owned banks and scarce state-controlled resources including land, many SASAC enterprises have enjoyed booming profits over the last decade and a half. When the Global Financial Crisis of 2008–9 descended, bringing crisis to non-state enterprises accustomed to thinner margins, the opportunity for central SOEs to take over struggling private enterprises was ripe.

Interests have also supplied momentum. As the case studies of telecommunications and airlines have shown, particularist interests opposed to liberalization and increased competition in the state sector have definitively shaped state sector policy at key junctures. In the manner of Hellman's (1999) short-term winners, during crucial reform debates in the late 1990s, state-owned enterprises and their patrons in government pushed for policies that would minimize competitive pressures and maximize their intake of monopoly profits. As the recent corruption scandals in telecommunications have revealed, many an illicit fortune has been made in the lifeline industries under these conditions.

The case that has been presented here is that a focus on a third 'I' long neglected by comparativists – ideas – sheds light on the puzzling issue of institutional origins. Why did China first develop an industrial policy regime for large SOEs so at odds with both Maoist orthodoxy and the Washington Consensus? The answer provided in Chapter 2 is that this policy line developed incrementally as the solution to various problems identified by policymakers in the 1980s and 1990s. In the early reform period, prominent policy economists argued that China's fragmented industrial structure was irrational and would hinder the development of industry to global standards. This argument, which made frequent reference to the contributions of large enterprise groups to rapid economic development in other East Asian states, provided a powerful justification for the use of industrial policy in the effort to raise industrial concentration levels in key sectors. Ideas about how best to adapt the planning apparatus to the new demands of reform and opening also informed these institutions. Planners, often looking towards the example set by Singapore, argued that grabbing firm hold of large state-owned enterprises in key sectors would anchor the state's capacity to guide China's rapidly changing economy. In the anxious political climate after the events of 4 June 1989, this argument was recast in the terms of authoritarian resilience as neoconservatives argued that the Party must control not only the gun but also key assets in the economy in order to shore up authoritarian rule.

A focus on ideas also helps us to understand the process through which China's strategic sectors have come to be defined as such. In sharp contrast to the image of Chinese state capitalism as a meticulously designed and executed top-down affair popularized in recent bestsellers (McGregor 2012; Bremmer 2010), the overriding impression to emerge from this analysis is one of 'muddling through' (cf. Lindblom 1959). While the institutions may have declared the state's intent to exert a 'controlling force' of the 'lifeline industries', down to the present day the central government has declined to provide an unambiguous list of these sectors. This reticence has provided a space in which industry leaders themselves could present their case for inclusion. In both of the industries examined here, this moment presented itself in uncertain times at the end of the 1990s. These were turning points, or critical junctures, when debate participants argued for starkly differing possible futures. With the balance of political influence on their side, advocates of SOE oligopoly and non-retreat of the state were triumphant in both instances. The ideas embraced by the victors informed their de facto entry into the lifeline industries and also underpinned the institutions of managed competition in the SASAC era.

The effort has also been made to describe the dissenting opinions in these debates not just for the sake of historical accuracy but also because these ideas continue to inform critiques of the status quo in the state-owned economy. Condemnation of the policies protecting SOEs in the 'monopoly sectors' is a mainstay of liberal-leaning news media outlets like *Caixin, The Economic Observer, FT.com* and *Southern Weekend*. The accession of a new leadership under Xi Jinping and the central government's pledges to renew reform of the state sector have given these critiques a new importance in current debate about China's economic future.

Current debate: China's possible economic futures

Among experts on the Chinese economy, the Global Financial Crisis served to widen and deepen a long-standing divide between so-called 'experimentalists' and 'convergence' theorists (Woo 1999). The 'E-school' contend that China's 'experimentation has fostered the emergence of new, non-capitalist institutions that have promoted growth; and that other countries would do well to study these "lessons from China"' (Woo 1999: 116). The 'C-school' counter that China's development is a process of convergence with the world economy fuelled by liberalization, internationalization and privatization (ibid.). The world since Lehman Brothers' collapse has provided grist for both mills.

The experimentalist-cum-China Model view of SOEs

Tsinghua professor and director of the Centre for China Studies, Hu Angang, whose ideas regarding SOE reform were introduced in Chapter 1, has become one the most vocal and influential proponents of the China Model (Li 2012). While Joshua Cooper Ramo's 2004 book *The Beijing Consensus* made the China Model a hot topic overseas before it was ever taken up by Chinese intellectuals, within China, Hu's name is now closely associated with this perspective. His arguments have attracted a wide readership particularly in the crisis period and afterwards, when the Chinese economy stayed afloat while Western economies sunk into the worst economic crisis since the Great Depression. Against the convergence school's insistence that there is nothing new under the sun in matters of economic development, Hu argues that the Chinese economy has blazed a new trail:

China's model of reform differs from those of other countries and cannot be interpreted using existing economic growth theories or models. The Chinese refer to their model as the mind emancipation model. I refer to it as *mind emancipation* and *concept innovation-based economic reform*. (Hu 2011: 30, emphasis added).

And unlike most economists, who credit Deng Xiaoping's reform and opening policies for China's roaring growth since 1978, Hu argues that this model had already taken its nascent form in the Maoist period (ibid. 32). The other attributes of the China Model in Hu's rendering are the 'cat theory' which prioritized economic results above ideological conformity ('it doesn't matter whether a cat is white or black, as long as it catches mice') and the 'theory of exploration', or a commitment to pragmatic policy experimentation ('crossing the river by feeling the stones'). Hu characterizes these 'conceptual innovations' as having been effectively institutionalized in the reform period under Deng but actually first developed in the Maoist period by other senior leaders, Chen Yun in particular (ibid. 32). In contrast to much Western discussion of the China Model as an alternative to the Washington Consensus but one that sits comfortably in a capitalist world economy, Hu's vision is ultimately starkly socialist in outline and entails a rejection of the liberal claim that economies function best in the circumstance of a clear divide between state and market.

This state socialist orientation is much in evidence in China Model arguments for preserving SOEs. From this perspective, China's SOEs are not a problem to be solved but instead one of the great success stories of China's distinctive approach to economic development. In his book, *The China Model*, Singapore-based political scientist Zheng Yongnian (2010: 103) argues that SOEs served a key role in the post-crisis period as recipients of the state's stimulus package. Hu (2013) sees SOEs as crucial elements of the Chinese economy not just in times of crisis. He argues that SOEs, which he defines as both 'modern' and 'socialist' enterprises, possess four primary advantages over private firms that help to explain their recent successes alongside those of the country as a whole. First, in contrast to firms subject to the whims of the capital market, SOEs with steady access to China's 'abundant' (*xionghou* 雄厚) state capital enjoy a 'state-owned capital advantage', which has allowed for their rapid expansion and powered their ascent up the ranks of the Fortune 500. Second, SOEs' 'state-supporting advantage' has provided the positive externality of stability during China's many years of rapid growth. With special responsibility for implementation of national initiatives, particularly poverty alleviation measures, SOEs have played an indispensable role as providers of employment and business opportunity in China's less-developed regions. Third, Hu argues, SOEs enjoy a 'political advantage'. He claims that they are better run than public companies in which decisionmaking power is divided between managers and owners because the supervisory and coordinating function of SOE Party Committees ensure that the enterprise speaks with one voice. Finally, they have an 'organizational advantage', by which he means more harmonious industrial relations thanks to organizationally closer ties between management and labour.

Leading scholars on the so-called 'New Left' have also argued the merits of preserving a high degree of state ownership and securing strong state control of the economy, though for somewhat different reasons.[1] Prior to Bo Xilai's abrupt fall from grace in 2012, both Wang Shaoguang (2011) and Cui Zhiyuan (2011) offered praise for the 'Chonqing Model' developed under Bo's leadership in his term as Party Secretary of Chongqing (2007–12). In a widely commented-upon piece, Wang argued that Chongqing was an exemplar of 'socialism 3.0' and a model for the central government to follow. In Chongqing, Wang argued, the overarching concern with maximizing economic growth (the hallmark of 'socialism 2.0' in his rendering) had been replaced by the aim of building a Galbraithian affluent society in which massive public investment in housing, transport, health and education had begun to narrow the yawning gap between the haves and have-nots. And key to the model's success, in Wang's eyes, was the city government's strong support for development of the state sector alongside a rapidly growing non-state sector. He approvingly quotes Bo Xilai on the matter of ownership:

> If our reform, in the end, means a complete denial of the past and simply bringing in the set of originals from the West, I think this is not reform ... We should have state ownership and we should learn the essence of the system and realize its advantages ... I think this is our superiority, this is the impressive system of socialism with Chinese characteristics.

Many on the left now see China's economy as 'two-legged', as supported by increasingly robust state and private sectors. Hu Angang has argued that the 'core mission' of China's large and globally competitive SOEs in resource-, capital- and technology intensive industries is 'to engage in fierce competition with the world's top 500 companies and Global 2000 enterprises' and become 'industry leaders' therein. Meanwhile, the primary task of the 'job-creating,

---

[1] It is typical among scholars writing about contemporary economic debate in China to treat China Model advocates and New Leftists as essentially one and the same group. And there is certainly considerable overlap in both the policy leanings and the people linked to the two. Indeed, Hu Angang and Wang Shaoguang were co-authors of two books in the 1990s, *The Political Economy of Uneven Development* (1999) and *The Chinese Economy in Crisis* (2001), that stand as two of the most influential statements of the New Left view of the dilemmas of the Chinese approach to reform. Nevertheless, this author perceives a subtle but significant divergence in views in recent years, which arguably warrants treating them as allied but distinct perspectives. Prominent voices of the New Left, among them Wang Shaoguang, Cui Zhiyuan and Wang Hui, share a concern with the perils and pitfalls of neoliberalism, which, to varying degrees, they see as having shaped China's economic reform pathway since 1978. They are especially troubled by the problems of growing inequality and corruption in China that have attended marketization, and they caution against a wholesale transition to a society organized around the self-regulating market, what Karl Polanyi (2001) famously called the 'satanic mill'. Scholars linked to the China Model, including Hu Angang, Pan Wei and Zheng Yongnian, are also sceptical of neoliberal universalism but premise their arguments against the latter on the basis of China's unprecedented record of economic success. As discussed above, they see this success as a consequence *not* of neoliberal policy choices but instead of judicious experimentation and 'seeking truth from facts' – in short, the China Model.

labour-intensive and employment-intensive' private enterprises, is to focus on local development with a few larger enterprises entering the fray of global competition (Hu 2012). In his writing, Hu's most often-cited evidence of the strong performance of these two legs, especially that of the state's, is the Fortune Global 500 list, a ranking based on firms' gross revenue intake. An editorial in the *Beijing Daily* commented gleefully that while a total of 51 American companies dropped off the Fortune 500 list between 2000 and 2014 (taking the total down from 179 to 128) the number of Chinese companies has jumped from 11 to 100 in the same period and now account for one-fifth of the entire list. Given that a large proportion of these firms are state-owned, Hu argues that this amounts to a powerful affirmation of the China Model:

[On] September 19, 2000, then-US President Bill Clinton's televised speech to the US Senate ahead of the final vote on Permanent Normal Trade Relations (PNTR) with China included this prophecy: 'If China can join the WTO, external competition will accelerate the demise of Chinese state-owned enterprises.' State-owned enterprises have experienced painful and difficult reforms, but not only did they not die, in the transition from old SOEs to new SOEs, they have been renewed and strengthened and have become the main force in 'China's corps' in the Global 500 as well as the aircraft carriers in China's 'going out' strategy.

This proves once again that China, as the 'Giant of the East' with 'two legs' – SOEs and private enterprises, state-owned economy and the non-state economy – goes faster and better than America's one leg (the private sector). We can predict that it won't be long before China surpasses the United States on the Global 500 list ... Whether China's state-owned enterprises or private enterprises, they are shouldering the historical mission of 'enterprises rejuvenating the country, enterprises strengthening the country' (*qiye xingguo qiye qiangguo* 企业兴国 企业强国) [Hu 2014].

The mood is not as triumphant everywhere, however.

Converge or stagnate: the liberal critique

Economic liberals tend to see the China Model as a dangerous illusion that masks deep problems, the root causes of which have been known since Adam Smith's time: excessive government intervention in the economy. Liberals have framed a number of current problems in these terms. First, China's fiscal stimulus proved very difficult to unwind as China's local state corporatist system (Oi 1992) generated a vast volume of local government debt. With a green light from Beijing to ramp up investment but with little share in the central government's US $586 billion fiscal stimulus plan which tilted heavily towards large SOEs, local governments turned en masse to off-budget spending. The magnitude of the resulting debt has proven difficult to estimate with any accuracy, but moderate estimates put the fiscal debt at about 45 per cent of GDP in 2012 (Zhang and Barnett 2014). The worry is that much of this debt will go bad when the returns on buildings and infrastructure projects fail to materialize and may lead to financial crisis. Second, China's extraordinarily high investment and flagging consumption levels are seen as adverse consequences of state capitalism with Chinese characteristics. IMF researchers have argued that China has been 'over-investing' – defined as investments that do not contribute to the capital stock – by about 10 per cent of GDP and as much as 20 per cent between 2007 and 2011 (Lee et al. 2012). Previous work suggests that the privileges of state ownership in the financial system have contributed significantly to this imbalance. Dollar and Wei (2007) estimate that China's investment rate would fall by as much as 8 percentage points if banks' lending bias towards SOEs were erased. Third, and relatedly, liberals argue that the state's costly SOE-directed industrial policy regime has not, in fact, picked winners. While improvements over time in return on equity (ROE) among SOEs – up from 2.2 per cent in 1996 to 15.7 per cent in 2007 – are evidence of efficiency gains, non-state firms have consistently outperformed SOEs on this measure. In 2009, for example, non-state firms had an average ROE 9.9 percentage points above that of state firms (World Bank and Development Research Centre of the State Council 2012: 111).

Where Hu Angang and others see innovation and bold experimentation in breaking away from the strictures of the Washington Consensus, liberals perceive stagnation and perilous straying from the path of reform and opening. Zhang Weiying, former head of Peking University's Guanghua School of Management and a well-known proponent of the Austrian School of economics, has argued this point vigorously, apparently at considerable cost to his academic career.[2] Zhang sees the growing appeal and policy influence of both New Left and China Model thought as stemming from popular concern about corruption and wastage of state assets in the process of privatizing local state-owned enterprises, a problem which economist Larry Lang drew attention to in 2004 (Zhang 2012: V–VIII). The consequences, he argues, have been far-reaching:

> over the past decade, our ideas have experienced a major setback. We have gone from believing in the market to believing more in government, from believing in entrepreneurship to believing in the dominance of SOEs. This has led to the 'advance of the state, retreat of the private sector'. But since China's economic growth has been very good, we have seen the emergence of a China Model of guidance by the state and state enterprises. But I think this China Model is completely wrong. The reason China has

---

[2] Zhang was fired by Peking University in 2010. Although the university never disclosed an official reason for his dismissal, a widely held view in the Chinese media and among foreign China watchers was that his insistent criticisms of government policy had simply ruffled too many feathers in Beijing (Johnson 2012). When this author interviewed Zhang in the spring of 2012, he had set up temporary shop in an ersatz old-style tea room in the middle of Beijing's bustling Zhongguancun shopping area where he patiently received a steady stream of visits from students, journalists and colleagues.

made such big achievements is that state intervention was less and less and the scale of SOEs was smaller and smaller. And the reason there are still so many problems is that there are still many SOEs in existence and their scale is still very large! Our next step is to solve this significant problem. (Zhang 2013: 15)

Referencing the famous closing lines of Keynes' *General Theory*, Zhang argues that these wrong-headed ideas are in fact more pernicious than the interests which now buttress state capitalist policies.[3] To unseat these mistaken beliefs, Zhang calls on liberal economists to present their own case effectively to the public: 'I believe that if these ideas can become the ideas of the general public, if they can become policymakers' ideas, Chinese reform will not be reversed and our society will have a glorious future!' (Zhang 2012: XII).

Liberal economists also reject the China Model school's claims of development exceptionalism. Wu Jinglian, a participant in much reform policymaking since 1978, argues that reformers were not 'thinking without banisters', to borrow Hannah Arendt's (1981) felicitous phrase:

At present, the press has popularized a saying that is not very precise. They say that China's thirty years of reform never had a clear goal and overall plan and until now is still 'feeling the stones'. In fact, when Chen Yun and Deng Xiaoping put forward 'feeling the stones', it was as a method for the early stages of reform when traditional ideas did not provide a basis, and when there was no existing experience to draw from – it was a no-other-way way (*meiyou banfa de banfa* 没有办法的办法), or a suboptimal choice. Later, the situation changed a lot ... Back in the late 1980s, the State Commission for Restructuring of the Economy, with the participation of many scholars, developed an overall design for China's socialist commodity economy in China (i.e. the market economy). In 1993, the Third Plenum of the Fourteenth Party Congress 'Decision on the Establishment of a Socialist Market Economy' was an economic system reform programme that was received with praise by insightful people in China and abroad. In 1997, the Fifteenth Party Congress also produced a master plan for adjusting and improving the ownership structure. The implementation of these plans brought the rapid development of China's economy and prosperity in the 1990s. Unfortunately, in recent years, the implementation of these overall plans has slowed down, leading to a series of problems. (Wu 2011b)

In the context of what they interpret as wayward drift, Wu and other liberals have called for the design and execution of a new grand reform plan, or a 'top-level design' (*dingceng sheji* 顶层设计), a phrase first used in the Twelfth Five-Year Plan (FYP) (2011–15). Wu's own preferred phase is 'top top-level design' (*ding ding ceng sheji* 顶顶层设计):

---

[3] 'I am sure that the power of vested interests is vastly exaggerated compared with the gradual encroachment of ideas. Not, indeed, immediately, but after a certain interval; for in the field of economic and political philosophy there are not many who are influenced by new theories after they are twenty-five or thirty years of age, so that the ideas which civil servants and politicians and even agitators apply to current events are not likely to be the newest. But, soon or late, it is ideas, not vested interests, which are dangerous for good or evil' (Keynes 1997 [1936]: 383–4).

After the Central Committee put forward suggestions for the Twelfth FYP, academic discussion was a lot about finance, banking, social security, housing and other aspects of top-level design of the economic system. Of course, this sort of discussion is necessary, essential even. However, in my opinion, even more important is a 'top top-level design', above these sectors. In other words, this [discussion should be about] what kind of society China actually wants to create.

[Following] the ideological liberation movement around the Third Plenary Session in December 1978, when insightful people in government, industry and academia were working together, this kind of top top-level design became increasingly clear. In my understanding, the plan was to build a prosperous, civilized, democratic and harmonious China through the market, the rule of law and democratic reform.

However, in recent years, some top top-level designs have appeared in society that are inconsistent with, or even diametrically opposed to the [original design]. For example, some people insist on 'holding high the great banner of continuing the revolution under the dictatorship of the proletariat' ... Others have advocated the establishment of a strong government in order to manage and control the national economy and society as a whole as the main characteristics of the 'China Model'. Regarding these claims, they should not be suppressed, rather we should try to clarify thinking and form a consensus through free and earnest discussion. So, I think a top top-level design is key. [Do we want] a market economy governed by the rule of law which can achieve social justice and common prosperity? Or do we want a strong government controlling the national economy and society as a whole in a state capitalist, even crony capitalist, system? This is a critical issue we face. (Wu 2011b)

Some elements of the mainland media have provided an enthusiastic platform for spreading liberal views on this point. Both the Phoenix news website (ifeng.com) and *Sina.com* have set up special pages to gather commentary and news relating to the topic of 'top level reform design'.

On the question of SOE reform, liberal designs envision a rationalization of the state sector in line with liberal theory going back to Adam Smith's 'three duties of the sovereign'. A 2013 report co-authored by the World Bank and the Development Research Centre of the State Council (DRC), *China 2030: Building a Modern, Harmonious and Creative Society*, has given voice to this view. The report calls for a broad shift in the role of the state in the economy, for a 'more limited direct (more arm's-length) role in resource allocation and an enhanced role in delivering public goods and services and ensuring equality of opportunity' (World Bank and Development Research Centre of the State Council 2013: 86). The report appeals for a 'review' of existing state ownership and industrial and competition policies and an increased role for government in the areas of health, education and social security (ibid.). DRC researcher, Xia Bin, argues in line with the sentiments of China's mainstream liberals, for a 'top-level plan' for strategic adjustment of the state sector. He advocates the 'advance' of state capital in the provision of public goods and for doing away with the current focus on expanding the scale of SOEs and maximizing the value of state assets. Zhang Weiying (2013) called for bringing the proportion of state-owned and state-controlled SOEs in China's GDP down to 10 per cent. In his view, any country with a proportion of state ownership above 10 per cent cannot really be considered a market economy, 'so China now cannot be called a complete market economy' (Zhang 2013: 15).

Something resembling a liberal 'top top-level design' was released just prior to the highly anticipated Third Plenum of the Eighteenth Party Congress in November 2013 in the form of a reform proposal drafted by the DRC for the Central Committee. Dubbed the '383 Plan', this document emphasized the need for an overhaul of the role of government in the economy. In even stronger terms than their earlier *China 2030* document, the DRC Plan calls for 'breaking monopoly and promoting competition' on the grounds that the state monopolies' 'corrupt practices' (*biduan* 弊端) were 'having a negative impact on overall economic and social development that is increasingly obvious' (*Caixin* 2013).

State advance or retreat? The direction of state sector policy in the Xi Jinping era

What are the guiding ideas and institutions of the Xi Jinping–Li Keqiang administration that came to power at the Eighteenth Party Congress? How deeply has the liberal critique penetrated officialdom? Will the China Model stride forward on its 'two legs'? Since the Third Plenum, these questions have been widely debated in China and abroad. At present, the reforms taking shape are suggestive of a 'grab the large, let go the small 2.0' in which local governments struggling under the weight of debts accumulated since 2008 are now trying to sell off state assets. Central SOEs in the lifeline industries, meanwhile, are also offering stakes to investors but, outside a few stragglers on SASAC's list, these share sales will likely be small in size and, in line with past policy and practice, aimed not at transferring ownership and control of the national champions away from the state but rather increasing their competitiveness and efficiency (Walter and Howie 2010).

Liberals hoped that the Third Plenum of the Eighteenth Party Congress would deliver a 'top top-level design' that would signal the new leadership's decisive rejection of the China Model and New Left versions of China's economic future. The release of an important post-Plenum document on 15 November 2013, 'The Decision on Major Issues Concerning the Comprehensive Deepening of Reform', revealed that while liberals have made some impression on the new leadership, this is a partial victory at best. Barry Naughton has argued that, taken together, various components of the Third Plenum resolution do suggest a purpose broadly in line with the principles of the *China 2030* and the 383 Plan:

State advance or retreat? 119

The resolution emphasizes, and returns repeatedly to, the need to redefine the relationship between government and market, and to reduce direct government intervention in the economy. 'Economic system reform is the crux of comprehensively deepening reform, and the core question is the relationship between government and market, allowing the market to play the decisive role in resource allocation, and to better bring into play government's role' (3.1). In order for this to happen, 'government will greatly reduce its direct allocation of resources' (3.3), reversing the current situation of government that 'intervenes too much, and doesn't regulate effectively' (3.2). This 'vision' informs the entire resolution. (Naughton 2014a: 3–4)

But this may be overstating the case somewhat; some of the specific sections of the document present a more murky vision that attempts to strike an awkward compromise between the liberal and leftist perspectives. For instance, liberals were pleased to find this statement in a section on 'adhering to and improving the basic economic system': 'We must unwaveringly encourage, support and guide the development of the non-public sector, and stimulate its dynamism and creativity.' But, no less significantly, it comes on the heels of this sentence: 'We must unswervingly consolidate and develop the public economy, persist in the dominant position of public ownership, give full play to the leading role of the state-owned sector, and continuously increase its vitality, controlling force and influence.'

The twain shall meet, it seems, in a system of mixed ownership characterized by 'cross holding by and mutual fusion between state-owned capital, collective capital and non-public capital' ('The Decision on Major Issues', 15 November 2013). The Decision calls for an enhanced role for non-state capital in public enterprises in monopoly sectors and for allowing more SOEs to become mixed enterprises. While the emphasis placed on mixed ownership in this document is perhaps new, the concepts are not. The State Council's '36 Clauses for the Non-State-Owned Economy' (2005) and '36 New Clauses for the Non-State-Owned Economy' (2010) documents, widely seen as dead letters, promised to 'implement equal access and fair treatment' for non-state enterprises in monopoly sectors (*Caixin* 2010). Collating various conservative commentaries since the Third Plenum, the editors of the Party journal *Qiushi* (2014) argue that the mixed ownership system already has a firm hold in the Chinese economy. They point out that 90 per cent of SOEs have now implemented shareholding reforms and 70 per cent of central SOE net assets are with listed companies. Of course, they point out, the state maintains firm control of the listed companies through controlling interests as well as enterprise Party Committees and SASAC oversight. But the Third Plenum resolution is seen as quite consistent with past practice in this respect:

Development of a mixed ownership economy has a unique role in the amplification function of state capital and improving the competitiveness of SOEs. According to statistics, in 2010, 2011, 2012 for 'industrial enterprises above designated size' (*guimo yishang gongye qiye* 规模以上工业企业), state-owned and state holding enterprises had returns on assets (ROA) of 4.9 per cent, 5.4 per cent, 4.6 per cent while joint-stock enterprises had ROA of 6.6 per cent, 8.4 per cent, 7.6 per cent. These three years show that the benefits of mixed ownership economy are relatively high …

In his description of the Plenary Session's decision, Xi Jinping pointed out that upholding and improving the basic economic system in which public ownership plays the dominant role and develops alongside multiple forms of ownership is an important pillar of consolidating and developing the socialist system with Chinese characteristics. And the development of a mixed-ownership economy in which state capital, collective capital, and private capital are mutually integrated is important to realizing the form of the basic economic system and will benefit the amplification function of state capital, increase the value of state assets and improve competitiveness. In order to uphold the dominant position of public ownership under the new situation and enhance the vitality, controlling force and influence of the state economy, this is an effective means as well as an inevitable choice.

It is thus clear that the aim of the pledge to develop a mixed ownership economy put forward at the Third Plenum is to consolidate the dominant position of public ownership, and strengthen the leading role of the state economy. Clarifying this point provides a clear direction for the future development of mixed ownership economy: China is developing a mixed ownership economy in order to do a better job of building socialism with Chinese characteristics. (*Qiushi* 2014).

While this author is inclined to the same interpretation of the Third Plenum pronouncements, it remains a matter of current debate. The Central Party School's Zhao Zhenhua, among others, has parsed the meaning of Third Plenum pronouncements on the mixed economy differently (Salidjanova and Koch-Weser 2013: 6). Along with Naughton, he argues that the wording encouraging development of the non-state sector is far stronger than in past documents. Others insist that trying to discern the government's direction is premature. Experts gathered at a meeting in Beijing on SOE reform in early 2014 were reported to be mostly in agreement that no such direction existed, with one participant claiming that the leadership had adopted a position of 'strategic ambiguity; given the intense debate the subject provokes, the leadership does not to come down on either side of the debate clearly' (Green and Shen 2014: 5). In late summer 2014, Xinhua reported that such direction would become clear after the release of 'systematic guidelines on SOE reforms', perhaps in autumn 2014 (*Xinhua* 2014c). Yet very little in the way of concrete reforms has actually come to pass. Instead, it now seems that, in the context of weak economic performance among many central SOEs, SASAC is intent on doubling down on its time-worn strategy of increasing the scale of central SOEs via mergers and consolidation within the state sector. State media is currently reporting that the central government will reduce the current 112 state-owned business groups under SASAC's watch to 40 through mergers (Reuters 2015). A spokesperson for SASAC insists that the core principles of

SOE reform since 2003 remain unchanged, that is to improve the vitality, competitiveness, controlling force and influence of targeted enterprises (*Jingji Guancha Bao* 2015). Some speculate that SASAC will launch a broad culling of the herd such that the number of central SOEs under its authority could fall from the current 112 to somewhere between 30 and 50. Yet a spokesperson for SASAC insists that the core principles of SOE reform have remained unchanged since 2003: that is to improve the vitality, competitiveness, 'controlling force' and influence of targeted enterprises (ibid.).

The state's approach to implementation of Third Plenum reforms has so far employed the experimentalist methods extolled by the China Model school. To the surprise of many close observers of Chinese economic policy anticipating a top-down approach to reform, it is 'instead progressing through a broad mobilization of agencies and local governments throughout China' (Naughton 2014b: 2). 'Deep reform' groups at all levels of government and state organizations – Barry Naughton estimates there may be as many as 800 throughout China – bear primary responsibility for developing specific reform measures in different issue areas. On the implementation of a mixed economy, sub-national administrative units have taken the boldest steps to date. Shanghai, Chongqing and the provinces of Anhui and Guangdong have each rolled out plans for the implementation of a mixed economy, which typically centre on offering SOE stakes to private investors (Naughton 2014b). Shaky government finance has made mixing ownership an appealing prospect to officials in many localities, but private investors have not always reciprocated this enthusiasm. This is partly due to the fact that local SOEs, which extend into all corners of industry, are much less profitable on average than central SOEs concentrated in the protected lifeline industries (Wildau 2014b). Others suggest that private investors are hesitant because they carry the memory of the backlash after the last round of local SOE restructuring and, circa 2004, charged debate about the 'advance of the private sector, retreat of the state'.[4]

Central SASAC has also initiated a pilot scheme to improve corporate governance and attract private capital. The plans are seen by most as fairly tepid, since none of the six central SOEs involved is a star performer, and

---

[4] Zhang Wenkui, an influential economist at DRC who played a lead role in both the *China 2030* and the *Plan 383* documents, has argued that an exoneration of Gu Chujun could help to ease private investors' fears (Green and Shen 2014: 4). After buying a loss-making state-owned electronics firm from a local government in Guangdong, Gu found himself at the centre of debate over 'retreat of the private sector, advance of the state' stirred up particularly by Larry Lang who publicly accused Gu of the theft of state assets. A Guangdong court later convicted Gu of economic crimes for which he served seven years of a ten-year prison term before receiving a commutation of his sentence in 2012. Gu protested his innocence throughout his imprisonment, and and in May 2013 the Guangdong Higher People's Court accepted his application to appeal his conviction.

partial privatization is just one of the items on the reform agenda (Wildau 2014a). Just two enterprises, China National Building Material Group (CNBM) and China National Pharmaceutical Group Corporation (Sinopharm), will undergo experimentation in a pilot reform on mixed ownership. Two other enterprises, State Development and Investment Corporation (SDIC) and China National Cereals, Oils and Foodstuffs Corporation (COFCO), will join a pilot aimed at increasing efficiency without any change in ownership. A third pilot group will experiment with enhanced autonomy for the board of directors and will include Sinopharm and CNBM as well as Xinxing Cathay International Group (XXCIG) and China Energy Conservation and Environmental Protection Group (CECEP).

SASAC's pilots follow mixed economy initiatives generated by the national champions themselves. Much media coverage was given to energy giant Sinopec's decision to sell off 30 per cent of its marketing and distribution business, but the sales are seen by some as something of a token gesture since they pertain to a peripheral business area – gas station convenience stores (Hsu 2014). China Telecom is also looking for private investors to improve emerging businesses, including social networking and online payments, and has recently partnered with Amazon and Infiniti on sixty-eight innovative projects (Gao 2014; Xinhua 2014a). There may well be political considerations behind their readiness to reform. Since both enterprises have been high-profile targets in Xi Jinping's anti-corruption drive, senior managers are likely now eager to create an impression of moving with the new reform tide.

In parallel to the above measures aimed at improving the efficiency of the state sector, the Communist Party has also leveraged its formidable organizational power to stem widespread corruption and bring down SOE managers' salaries by administrative fiat. The new leadership is now carrying out an unprecedented crackdown on corruption aimed at both 'tigers' (senior leaders) and 'flies' (low-ranking officials). Since 2012, the campaign has ensnared a total of 182,000 Party officials nationwide and led to the arrest of thirty-two leaders at the rank of vice-minister or above (Li and McElveen 2014). The high-profile takedowns in telecommunications, described in the previous chapter, comprise just one front in Xi Jinping's war against corruption in SOEs. The biggest 'tiger' to have fallen to date is Zhou Yongkang, a former member of the Politburo Standing Committee with a long history in the oil and gas sector, including a stint as head of China National Petroleum Corporation. Before the announcement on 29 July 2014 that Zhou had been place under investigation for 'serious disciplinary violations', the most high-profile corruption case in the state sector was against Jiang Jiemin, former head of both Petrochina and SASAC. The CPC Central Commission for Discipline Inspection found Jiang guilty of corruption and expelled him from the Communist

Party in June 2014. To date, the crackdown on graft has resulted in the punishment of more than fifty senior SOE executives (*Xinhua* 2014b).

The government has also pledged to reduce the salaries of central SOE executives. While not exorbitant by international standards – SOE executives earned between 650,000 RMB (US $105,691) and 700,000 RMB in 2010–11 (*Xinhua* 2014c) – these salaries are significantly above the average in the non-state sector, an issue that has long fuelled public rancor towards the 'monopoly sectors'. But one wonders about the possible unanticipated consequences of imposing limits on managers' *legitimate* salaries in an opaque environment with unlimited opportunities for corruption. Indeed, this populist initiative could work at cross-purposes to anti-corruption efforts, since the experience of countries such as Singapore suggests that providing attractive salaries to state officials is an effective deterrent against corruption.

Conclusion

Economic life in China, like economic life everywhere, is deeply shaped by ideas about the nature of the economy, polity and society. Ideas that gain the support of policymakers and which thus come to shape state institutions – what we might call prevailing ideas– are extremely powerful. This book has followed the trail of one such prevailing idea about the importance for China of having a group of large and globally competitive state-owned business groups. This idea developed and gathered momentum over time as a solution to a series of successive problems – relating to industrial fragmentation, the Communist Party's anxiety about the private sector and the myriad challenges of globalization. Indeed, it is an idea that has proven remarkably adaptable to China's constantly changing reality. Beginning in the mid 1980s with experimentation with the large enterprise strategy in the auto sector, this idea has provided the rationale for a series of industrial policies and regulatory practices that have had a profound impact on China's evolving market order.

Prevailing ideas are powerful but not immutable. The remarkable scene of Alan Greenspan's admission to Congress that the whole 'intellectual edifice' which had shaped his policy choices as head of the US Federal Reserve had 'collapsed' in the summer of 2008 is a reminder that crises can serve to unseat reigning economic beliefs almost overnight. If the collapse is dramatic enough, intellectual edifices radically different from the incumbent paradigm may draw support and inspire a new set of institutions. As we have seen, the ideas behind the state's advance have had their critics since day one. When the idea of creating large enterprise groups by administrative fiat was first floated in the 1980s by the 'structural ' camp, the 'system' camp, among them a young Zhang Weiying, argued for focusing on establishing the institutions of a market system instead, and expressed misgivings about an industrial policy approach to addressing the burdensome legacies of the command economy. Liberals continue to argue the case, and their arguments have gained a measure of popular appeal in the context of abiding public anger over pervasive corruption in the lifeline industries.

Paired with this growing resentment of official corruption among ordinary Chinese, liberal arguments about the costs of state capitalism have in recent years shaken prevailing ideas and institutions. But reform measures since the Third Plenum of the Eighteenth Party Congress suggest that this is not an exogenous shock forceful enough to unseat prevailing ideas that, appropriately or not, continue to reap the benefits of performance legitimacy. While growth in China has slowed in recent years, and policymakers now worry about heading off the so-called middle-income trap, China in 2015 is hardly a parallel to the United States in October 2008. China's incredible record of economic growth since 1978 served first as a warm incubator and later as a protective shelter for state capitalist ideas. In these felicitous circumstances, liberal critiques of state policy towards the lifeline industries have not made significant headway. Indeed, given how deeply embedded state capitalist ideas are in China's political economy, and in view of past examples of paradigm change, it is likely that only something as forceful as a deep and prolonged economic crisis could unseat them.

Bibliography

Adler, Emanuel and Peter M. Haas (1992) 'Conclusion: Epistemic Communities, World Order and the Creation of a Reflective Research Program', *International Organization* 46(1): 367–90.
Anderlini, Jamil (2009) 'East Star Chief Missing After Talks Collapse', *Financial Times*, 18 March.
Arendt, Hannah (1981) *The Life of the Mind*, New York: Harcourt Brace Jovanovich.
Barboza, David (2009) 'China's Mr. Wu Keeps Talking', *New York Times*, 26 September.
Baum, Richard (1996) *Burying Mao: Chinese Politics in the Age of Deng Xiaoping*, Princeton University Press.
Béland, Daniel (2009) 'Ideas, Institutions and Policy Change', *Journal of European Public Policy* 16(5): 701–18.
Béland, Daniel and Robert H. Cox (2011) 'Introduction: Ideas and Politics', in Daniel Béland and Robert H. Cox, eds. *Ideas and Politics in Social Science Research*, Oxford University Press.
Berman, Sheri (2013) 'Ideational Theorizing in the Social Sciences since "Policy Paradigms, Social Learning and the State"', *Governance* 26(2): 217–37.
Blyth, Mark (2002) *Great Transformations : Economic Ideas and Institutional Change in the Twentieth Century*, Cambridge University Press.
  (2007) 'Powering, Puzzling or Persuading? The Mechanisms of Building Institutional Orders', *International Studies Quarterly* 51: 761–77.
Bremmer, Ian (2010) *The End of the Free Market: Who Wins the War Between States and Corporations?* New York: Portfolio.
Broadman, Harry G. (2001) 'Business(es) of the Chinese State', *The World Economy* 24(7): 849–75.
Brødsgaard, Kjeld Erik (2012) 'Politics and Business Group Formation in China: The Party in Control?' *China Quarterly* 211: 624–48.
Caixin (2010) 'China's 36 Reasons for Private Sector Support', 24 May.
  (2013) 'Guoyan zhongxin gaige luxiantu' [DRC's Reform Roadmap], 27 October.
Campbell, John L. (2002) 'Ideas, Politics, and Public Policy', *Annual Review of Sociology* 28: 21–38.
  (2004) *Institutional Change and Globalization*, Princeton University Press.
  (2005) 'Where Do We Stand? Common Mechanisms in Organizations and Social Movements', in G. F. Davis *et al.*, eds. *Social Movements and Organization Theory*, Cambridge University Press.

Cao, Mengqin and Han Xiujing (1999) 'Lun qiyejian de jingzheng yu hezuo' [On Competition and Cooperation Between Enterprises] *Shehui Kexue Luntuan [Tribune of Social Sciences]* nos. 9–10: 70–1.

Capoccia, Giovanni and Daniel R. Kelemen (2007) 'The Study of Critical Junctures: Theory, Narrative, and Counterfactuals in Historical Institutionalism', *World Politics* 59(3): 341–69.

Carstensen, Martin B. (2011) 'Paradigm Man vs. the Bricoleur: Bricolage as an Alternative Vision of Agency in Ideational Change', *European Political Science Review* 3(1): 147–67.

Communisty Party of China Central Commission for Discipline Inspection (2014) Presentation by Senior CCDI Officials to Overseas Scholars, 4 September, Beijing, China.

Chang, Gordon (2012) 'Why China Wants to Break its State Bank Monopoly', *Forbes*, 8 April.

Chen, Qun (1999) '1998–1999 zhongguo dianxin gaige da tiaowang' [1998–1999 China's Telecommunications Reform Takes a Big Look into the Distance], *Hulianwang Zhoukan* [Internet Weekly], 7 June, 6–7, 60.

Chen, Yangyong (2009) 'Jiang zemin "zou chu qu" zhanlue de xingcheng jiqi zhongyao yiyi' [On the Development and Importance of Jiang Zemin's 'Going Forth' Strategy], *Dang de Wenxian* [Party Literature] no. 1: 63–9.

Chen, Zhengqing and Zhu Pengju (1994) 'Guojia xinxihua he xinxi chanye' [National Informatization and Information Industries], *Xinxi Jingji yu Jishu* [Information Economics and Technology] no. 11: 11–13.

Chen qingtai zai guojia shidian qiye jituan gongzuo huiyi shang de jianghua [Chen Qingtai's Speech to the Conference on National Pilot Enterprises] (1995) *Jingji yanjiu cankao ziliao* [Reference Materials for Economic Research] no. 83: 2–10.

Cheng, Hao *et al.* (2003) 'Zhongguo shehui liyi jituan yanjiu' [Research on Social Interest Groups in China], *Zhanlüe yu Guanli* [Strategy and Management] no. 4: 63–74.

Cheng, Xiaonong (2013) '*The Self-Empowered New Master at the Workplace: Privatization in Russia and China*', unpublished Ph.D. thesis submitted to Princeton University, Department of Sociology.

China Economic Review (2013) 'Businessmen in Line for Policy Posts in Beijing Hinder Reform', 11 July.

Chung, Jae Ho (2003) 'The Political Economy of Industrial Restructuring in China: The Case of Civil Aviation', *China Journal* 50: 61–82.

Clover, Charles and Michael Peel (2014) 'China Mobile's Thai Deal Highlights Competition Impact', *FT.com*, 20 June.

CNN (2008) Interview with Premier Wen Jiabao, 29 September. Available at: http://edition.cnn.com/2008/WORLD/asiapcf/09/29/chinese.premier.transcript/.

Colpan, Asli M. *et al.* (2010) 'Introduction', in Asli Colpan *et al.* eds. *The Oxford Handbook of Business Groups*, Oxford University Press.

Cui, Zhiyuan (2011) 'Partial Intimations of the Coming Whole: The Chongqing Experiment in Light of the Theories of Henry George, James Meade, and Antonio Gramsci', *Modern China* 37(6): 646–60.

Deng, Guosheng and Scott Kennedy (2010) 'Big Business and Industry Association Lobbying in China: The Paradox of Contrasting Styles', *China Journal* 63: 101–25.

Deng, Yong and Thomas G. Moore (2004) 'China Views Globalization: Toward a New Great-Power Politics?' *Washington Quarterly* 27(3): 117–36.

Deng, Yongheng *et al.* (2011) 'Monetary and Fiscal Stimuli, Ownership Structure, and China's Housing Market', working paper. Available at: www.ires.nus.edu.sg/workingpapers/IRES2011-004.pdf.

Dollar, David and S. J. Wei (2007) 'Das (Wasted) Capital: Firm Ownership and Investment Efficiency in China', IMF Working Paper 07/9.

Dougan, Mark (2002) *A Political Economy Analysis of China's Civil Aviation Industry*, New York: Routledge.

Downs, Erica (2008) 'Business Interest Groups in Chinese Politics: The Case of the Oil Companies', in Cheng Li, ed. *China's Changing Political Landscape: Prospects for Democracy*, Washington, DC: Brookings Institution Press.

Eaton, Sarah (2011) 'China's State Capitalist Turn: Political Economy of the Advancing State', dissertation submitted to University of Toronto, Department of Political Science.

Economic Observer (2013) 'China Mobile Corruption Scandal Continues to Unfold', 26 April.

Economist Intelligence Unit (2009) *China's Stimulus Package: A Six-Month Report Card*, Corporate Network Special Report, London: The Economist.

Fallows, James (2012) *China Airborne*, New York: Pantheon Books.

Fan, Pengfei (2008) 'Youxu jingzheng yingzao hexie dianxin shichang' [Managed Competition Constructs a Harmonious Telecommunications Market], *Xi'an Youdian Xueyuan Xuebao* [Xi'an Post and Telecommunications College Journal] 3(2): 24.

Ferchen, Matt (2013) 'Whose China Model Is It Anyway? The Contentious Search for Consensus', *Review of International Political Economy* 20(2): 390–420.

Fewsmith, Joseph (1999) 'China and the WTO: The Politics Behind the Agreement', *NBR Analysis* 10(5).

(2008) *China Since Tiananmen: From Deng Xiaoping to Hu Jintao*, 2nd edn, Cambridge University Press.

Fischer, Doris (1998) 'Chinesische Unternehmungsgruppen: Status und Genes Eines Reformkonzepts', *Duisburger Arbeitspapire zur Ostasienwissenschaft* 40: 1–39.

Gao, Haorong (2001) 'Gongping, touming, youxu: cong SK dianxin jianbing xin shiji tongxin kan hanguo yidong tongxin hangye de guanli yuanze' [Fair, Transparent, Managed: Learning about the Management Principles of South Korea's Mobile Telecommunications Industry from SK's Acquisition of New Century Communications], *Guoji Jingmao Xiaoxi* [International Trade News], 9 August, 1.

Gao, Yuan (2014) 'China Telecom Calls for Investors', *China Daily*, 14 May.

Garrett, Banning (2001) 'China Faces, Debates the Contradictions of Globalization', *Asian Survey* 41(3): 409–27.

Gerth, Karl (2012) 'A New Brand of Chinese Economic Nationalism: From China Made to China Managed', in Anthony P. D'Costa, ed. *Globalization and Economic Nationalism in Asia*, Oxford University Press.

Granovetter, Mark (1995) 'Coase Revisited: Business Groups in the Modern Economy', *Industrial and Corporate Change* 4(1): 93–130.
Green, Stephen and Lan Shen (2014) 'China – The Long, Long March to SOE Reform', *Standard Chartered on the Ground*, 24 March.
Gu, Xin and David Kelly (1994) 'New Conservatism: Intermediate Ideology of a New Elite', in David S. G. Goodman and Beverly Hooper, eds. *China's Quiet Revolution: New Interactions Between State and Society*, Melbourne: Longman Cheshire; New York: St Martin's Press.
Guest, Paul and Dylan Sutherland (2010) 'The Impact of Business Group Formation on Performance: Evidence from China's National Champions', *Cambridge Journal of Economics* 34: 617–31.
Guowuyuan Yanjiushi Ketizu [State Council Research Office Research Group] (1994) 'Wo guo suoyouzhi jiegou bianqe de qushi he duice yanjiu zong baogao' [Research Report on Trends in Ownership Change and Countermeasures], *Jingji yanjiu cankao ziliao* [Reference Materials for Economic Research] 43 (16 March): 1–35.
Haggard, Stephan and Yasheng Huang (2008) 'The Political Economy of Private Sector Development in China', in Loren Brandt and Thomas G. Rawski, eds. *China's Great Economic Transformation*, Cambridge University Press.
Haggard, Stephan and Robert R. Kaufman, eds. (1992) *The Politics of Economic Adjustment: International Constraints, Distributive Conflicts, and the State*, Princeton University Press.
Hall, Peter A. (1993) 'Policy Paradigms, Social Learning and the State: The Case of Economic Policymaking in Britain', *Comparative Politics* 25(3): 275–96.
Hall, Peter A. and Rosemary C. R. Taylor (1996) 'Political Science and the Three New Institutionalisms', *Political Studies* 44(5): 936–57.
Halper, Stefan (2009) 'The World of Market Authoritarianism', *The American Spectator*. Available at: http://specttor.org/articles/40803/world-market-authoritarianism.
  (2010) *The Beijing Consensus: How China's Authoritarian Model Will Dominate the Twenty-First Century*, New York: Basic Books.
Han, Deqiang (1999) 'Zhou Qiren zhengzhong shei de xiahuai?' [Whose Heart's Desire Does Zhou Qiren Represent?]. Available at http://blog.ifeng.com/article/2096452.html.
Han, Yushi (1999) 'Shichang shiluo haishi zhengfu shiling?' [Out of Order: The Government or the Market?), *Minhang jingji yu jishu* [Civil Aviation Economics and Technology] 206: 9–11.
Harwit, Eric (2008) *China's Telecommunications Revolution*, Oxford University Press.
Hay, Colin (2011) 'Ideas and the Construction of Interests', in Daniel Béland and Robert Henry Cox, eds. *Ideas and Politics in Social Science Research*, Oxford University Press.
He, Jun (2002) 'Minhang chonzu dailai xin longduan?' [Will Civil Aviation Restructuring Bring a New Monopoly?], *Nanfang Zhoumo* [Southern Weekend], 11 October.
He, Wei Ping (2013) 'Regulatory Capture in China's Banking Sector', *Journal of Banking Regulation* 14(1): 80–90.

Bibliography

Heilmann, Sebastian (2005) 'Regulatory Innovation by Leninist Means: Communist Party Supervision in China's Financial Industry', *China Quarterly* 181: 1–21.

Heilmann, Sebastian and Lea Shih (2013) 'The Rise of Industrial Policy in China', *Harvard-Yenching Institute Working Paper Series*. Available at www.harvardyenching.org.

Hellman, Joel S. (1998) 'Winners Take All: The Politics of Partial Reform in Postcommunist Transitions', *World Politics* 50(2): 203–34.

Helmke, Gretchen and Steven Levitsky (2004) 'Informal Institutions and Comparative Politics: A Research Agenda', *Perspectives on Politics* 2(4): 725–40.

Hogan, John W. (2006) 'Remoulding the Critical Junctures Approach', *Canadian Journal of Political Science* 39(3): 657–79.

Hsu, Robert C. (1986) 'The Political Economy of Guidance Planning in Post-Mao China', *Weltwirtschaftliches Archiv* 122: 382–94.

(1991) *Economic Theories in China, 1979–1988*, Cambridge University Press.

Hsu, Sara (2014) 'China's Changing State-Owned Landscape', *The Diplomat*, 25 June.

Hsueh, Roselyn (2011) *China's New Regulatory State: A New Strategy for Globalization*, Ithaca, NY: Cornell University Press.

(2012) 'China and India in the Age of Globalization: Sectoral Variation in Post-Liberalization Reregulation', *Comparative Political Studies* 45(1): 32–62.

Hu, Angang (2011) *China in 2020: A New Type of Superpower*, Washington, DC: Brookings Institution.

(2012) '"Guojin mintui" shuo zhengwei' ['The Advance of the State, Retreat of the Private Sector' is a Falsification], *Beijing ribao* [Beijing Daily], 7 May.

(2013) 'Guoyou qiye de neihan' [The Meaning of State Enterprise], *Zhongguo Zhiliang* [China Quality] 12: 38–9.

(2014) '"Liang tiao tui" de zhongguo bi meiguo pao de kuai' [China's 'Two Legs' Run Faster than America's], *Zhongguo ribao* [China Daily], 15 July.

Hu, Shuli and Wang Liwei (2014) 'Miao Wei: China's Minister of Market Reform', *Caixin*, 11 April.

Huang, Ryan (2013) 'China Mobile Eyeing Investment in Five Countries', *ZDNet*, 28 January. Available at www.zdnet.com/cn/china-mobile-eyeing-investment-in-five-countries-7000010390/.

Huang, Yasheng (2008) *Capitalism with Chinese Characteristics: Entrepreneurship and the State*, Cambridge University Press.

Jacques, Martin (2009) *When China Rules the World*, London: Penguin.

Jia, Suying (1984) 'Xinxi, "xinxi geming" yu "xinxi shehui"' [Information, 'Information Revolution' and 'Information Society'] *Xuexi yu Yanjiu* [Study and Research] 3: 27.

Jie Shulin and Chen Dong (1987) 'Zhongguo de xinxihua' [China's Informatization], *Qiushi* [Seek Truth] 3: 40–6.

Jingji Guancha Bao (2015) 'Guoqi gaige fangan jiang zai 2015 nian chutai buru "luoshi nian"' [SOE Reform Programme To Be Introduced in 2015, the 'Implementation Year'], 5 January.

Jituan jingji yanjiu [Enterprise Group Economic Research] (1997) 'Jin yi bu guanche da gongsi, da jituan zhanlüe' [Further Implement the Large Company, Large Enterprise Strategy] 8: 1.

Johnson, Ian (1999) 'Top Minister Offers his Resignation – Telecom Official Wu Opposed Concessions in WTO Entry Bid', *Asian Wall Street Journal*, 3 May.

—— (2012) 'China Closes Window on Economic Debate, Protecting Dominance of State', New York Times, 26 June.

Kang, Huijin (1989) 'Longduan wei bi dailai tingzhi he fuxiu' [Monopoly Need Not Bring Stagnation and Decadence], *Jingji yanjiu cankao ziliao* [Reference Materials for Economic Research] 36 (7 March): 2–15.

Keister, Lisa A. (1998) 'Engineering Growth: Business Group Structure and Firm Performance in China's Transition Economy', *American Journal of Sociology* 104(2): 404–40.

—— (2000) *Chinese Business Groups: The Structure and Impact of Interfirm Relations During Economic Development*, Oxford University Press.

—— (2009) 'Interfirm Relations in China: Group Structure and Firm Performance in Business Groups', *American Behavioral Scientist* 52(12):1709–30.

Kennedy, Scott (2003) 'The Price of Competition: Pricing Policies and the Struggle to Define China's Economic System', *China Journal* 49: 1–30.

—— (2005a) *The Business of Lobbying in China*, Cambridge, MA: Harvard University Press.

—— (2005b) 'China's Porous Protectionism: The Changing Political Economy of Trade Policy', *Political Science Quarterly* 120(3): 407–32.

—— (2010) 'The Myth of the Beijing Consensus', *Journal of Contemporary China* 19 (65): 461–77.

—— (2011) 'Overcoming our Middle Kingdom Complex: Finding China's Place in Comparative Politics', in Scott Kennedy, ed. *Beyond the Middle Kingdom: Comparative Perspectives on China's Capitalist Transformation*, Stanford University Press.

Keynes, J. M. (1997 [1936]) *The General Theory of Employment, Interest, and Money*, Amherst, NY: Prometheus Books.

Khanna, Tarun and Yishay Yafeh (2007) 'Business Groups in Emerging Markets: Paragons or Parasites?' *Journal of Economic Literature* 45: 331–72.

Kingdon, John W. (1984) *Agendas, Alternatives and Public Policies*, New York: Longman.

Kirby, Richard J. R. (1985) *Urbanisation in China: Town and Country in a Developing Economy, 1949–2000 AD*, New York: Columbia University Press.

Koch-Weser, Jacob (2013) 'The Reliability of China's Economic Data: An Analysis of National Output', US–China Economic and Security Review Commission Staff Research Project. Available at: www.uscc.gov/sites/default/files/Research/TheReliabilityofChina'sEconomicData.pdf.

Kroeber, Arthur (2011) 'Developmental Dreams: Policy and Reality in China's Economic Reforms', in Scott Kennedy, ed. *Beyond the Middle Kingdom: Comparative Perspectives on China's Capitalist Transformation*, Stanford University Press.

Lam, Willy Wo-Lap (1995) *China After Deng Xiaoping: The Power Struggle in Beijing Since Tiananmen*, Singapore: John Wiley & Sons.

—— (1999) *The Era of Jiang Zemin*, New York: Prentice Hall.

Lardy, Nicholas (2014) *Markets Over Mao: The Rise of Private Business in China*, Washington, DC: Institute for International Economics.

Bibliography

Lapperouza, Marc (2006) *'China's Telecommunications Policy-Making in the Context of Trade and Economic Reforms'*, dissertation submitted to the London School of Economics, Department of Information Systems.

Lee, Il Houng, Murtaza Syed and Liu Xueyan (2012) 'Is China Over-Investing and Does It Matter?' IMF Working Paper WP/12/277.

Lee, Keun and Young-Sam Kang (2010) 'Business Groups in China', in Asli M. Colpan *et al.*, eds. *The Oxford Handbook of Business Groups*, Oxford University Press.

Lee, Kevin (2007) 'China Mobile Invests in PakTel', *Telecomasia.net*, 23 January. Available at: www.telecomasia.net/content/fasttakes-sony-docomo-sri-lanka-telecom.

Leonard, Mark (2008) *What Does China Think?* New York: Public Affairs.

Li, Cheng (2012) 'Introduction: A Champion for Chinese Optimism and Exceptionalism', in Hu Angang, *China in 2020: A New Type of Superpower*, Washington, DC: Brookings Institution.

Li, Cheng and Ryan McElveen (2014) 'Debunking Misconceptions About Xi Jinping's Anti-Corruption Campaign', *China–US Focus*, 17 July.

Li, Jiaxiang (2008) *My Way: The Eight Strategies of Air China Towards Success*, Singapore: Cengage Asia Publishers.

Li, Min and Bo Yinhua (1994) '"Jinzi gongcheng" tuoqi zhongguo de xinxi xiandaihua' [Golden Projects Support China's Information Modernization], *Jiangsu Keji Xinxi* [Jiangsu Science and Technology Information] 12: 2–3.

Li, Peiyu (1989) 'Guowai chanye zhengce de bijiao yanjiu' [A Comparative Study of Industrial Policy in Other Countries], *Jingji yanjiu cankao ziliao* [Reference Materials for Economic Research] 166 (29 October): 1–15.

Li, Peng (2007) *Shichang yu Tiakong: Li Peng Jingji Riji* [Markets and Regulation: Li Peng's Economic Diary], 3 vols., Beijing: Xinhua Publishers.

Li, Rongrong, ed. (2004) *Binggou Chongzu: Qiye Fazhan de Biyou Zhilu* [Mergers and Acquisitions: The Only Way for Enterprise Development], Beijing: China Finance and Economic Publishers.

Li, Xiaodong (2000) 'Zhongguo dianxin: zuihou de konglong' [Chinese Telecommunications: The Last Dinosaur], *Gaige yu Lilun* [Reform and Theory] August: 13–18.

Li, Yue and Chen Shengchang (1981) 'Shilun gongye qiye de guimo jiegou' [On the Scale of Industrial Enterprises], *Zhongguo Shehui Kexue* [China Social Sciences] 1: 65–76.

Li, Zheng (2010) 'Guojin mintui zhizheng de huigu yu chengqing?' [Advance of the State, Retreat of the Private Sector – Review and Clarification of the Debate], *Shehui Kexue Qikan* [Social Science Journal] 5(190): 98–102.

Lieberthal, Kenneth and Michel Oksenberg (1988) *Policymaking in China: Leaders, Structures and Processes*, Princeton University Press.

Lin, Gang and Zhang Chen (2013) 'Guanyu jin yi bu tuijin guoyou jingji gaige fazhan de yixie yijian' [Some Ideas Regarding Advancing Reform of the State Economy], *Jingji lilun yu jingji guanli* [Economic Theory and Management] 2: 5–15.

Lin, Kun-Chin (2003) 'Corporatizing China: Reinventing State Control for the Market', Ph.D. dissertation submitted to University of California, Berkeley, Department of Political Science.

132 Bibliography

(2013) 'Review of *China's Regulatory State: A New Strategy for Globalization*, by Roselyn Hsueh', *China Journal* 69: 180–3.

Lindblom, Charles E. (1959) 'The Science of "Muddling Through"', *Public Administration Review* 19(2): 79–88.

Lingdao juece xinxi [Information for Deciders] (1999) 'Dianxin shichang fazhan de liang zhong bu tong kanfa' [Two Different Views on Telecommunications Development] 7: 13.

Liu, Dawei (1996) 'Guanyu qiye jituanhua zhanlüe de sikao' [Thoughts on the Enterprise Group Strategy], *Jingji yanjiu cankao ziliao* [Reference Materials for Economic Research] 58 (12 April): 2–10.

Liu, Ping (1997) 'Zhongguo minhang fazhan redian wenti diaocha yu fenxi' [A Poll on the Hot Topics in Developing China's Air Transport Industry], *Minhang jingji yu jishu* [Civil Aviation Economics and Technology] 211: 14–16.

Liu, Yazhou (2007) *Zhongguo hangkong shi (di er ban)* [A History of China's Aviation], 2nd edn, Changsha: Hunan Science and Technology Press.

Lynch, Daniel C. (1999) 'Dilemmas of "Thought Work" in Fin-de-Siecle China', *China Quarterly* 157: 173–201.

Ma, Jun (2010) 'Wo guo zongti qushi bu cunzai "guojin mintui"' [Overall 'The Advance of the State and Retreat of the Private Sector' Does Not Exist in China], *Hongqi Wengao* [Red Flag Manuscript] 2: 15–17.

Ma, Ning and Xu Dansong (1999a) 'Zahongguo dianxin: kaifang yu fazhan' [Chinese Telecommunications: Liberalization and Development (Part Two)], *Zhongguo Waizi* [China Foreign Investment] 3: 9–13.

Ma, Ning (1999b) 'Nengfou kaifang dianxin fuwu shichang' [Can the Telecommunications Market be Liberalized?], *Sichuan Jiancha* [Supervision of Sichuan] 4: 30–2.

Ma, Xufei and Jane Wenzhen Lu (2005)'The Critical Role of Business Groups in China', *Ivey Business Journal* 69(5): 1–12.

Marukawa, Tomoo (1995) 'Industrial Groups and Division of Labour in China's Automobile Industry', *Developing Economies* 33(3): 330–55.

(2001) 'WTO, Industrial Policy and China's Industrial Development', in Ippei Yamazawa and Ken-ichi Imai, eds. *China Enters WTO: Pursuing Symbiosis with the Global Economy*, IDE-JETRO Symposium Proceedings No. 21, Tokyo: IDE-JETRO.

Mattlin, Mikael (2009) 'China's Strategic State-Owned Enterprises and Ownership Control', Brussels Institute of Contemporary China Studies, Asia Paper.

McGregor, Richard (2012) *The Party: The Secret World of China's Communist Rulers*, New York: HarperCollins.

McNally, Christopher A. (2013) 'How Emerging Forms of Capitalism are Changing the Global Order', *Analysis from the East–West Center* 107: 1–8.

Mehta, Jal (2011) 'The Varied Role of Ideas in Politics: From "Whether" to "How"', in Daniel Béland and Robert H. Cox, eds. *Ideas and Politics in Social Science Research*, Oxford University Press.

Men, Honghua and Sun Yingchun (2007) *Haihang ruan shili* [Soft Power of Hainan Airlines], Beijing: Qinghua University Press.

Miao, Weisheng (2000) 'Shichanghua shi zhongguo minhangye fazhan de biyou zhi lu' [Marketization: The Only Path for Chinese Airline Industry Development], *Minhang jingji yu jishu* [Civil Aviation Economics and Technology] 219: 20–1.

Minhang jingji yu jishu [Civil Aviation Economics and Technology] (1998) 'Gan wen lu zai hefang' [Where Is the Way Out?] 198: 1.

(2000) '1999 Zhongguo minhang fazhan redian wenti diaocha yu fenxi' [A Poll on China Civil Aviation Hot Topics in 1999] 223: 27–30.

Misra, Kalpana (2003) 'Neo-Left and Neo-Right in Post-Tiananmen China', *Asian Survey* 43(5): 717–44.

Morck, Randall (2010) 'The Riddle of the Great Pyramids', in Asli M. Colpan *et al.*, eds. *The Oxford Handbook of Business Groups*, Oxford University Press.

Mueller, Milton and Zixiang Tan (1997) *China in the Information Age: Telecommunications and the Dilemmas of Reform*, Westport, CT: Praeger.

Mueller, Milton and Peter Lovelock (2000) 'The WTO and China's Ban on Foreign Investment in Telecommunications Services: A Game-Theoretic Analysis', *Telecommunications Policy* 24: 731–59.

Nathan, Andrew (2003) 'Authoritarian Resilience', *Journal of Democracy* 14(1): 6–17.

Naughton, Barry (1990) 'China's Experience with Guidance Planning', *Journal of Comparative Economics* 14: 743–67.

(1995) *Growing out of the Plan: Chinese Economic Reform, 1978–1993*, Cambridge University Press.

(2008) 'SASAC and Rising Corporate Power in China', *China Leadership Monitor* 24: 1–9.

(2010) 'China's Distinctive System: Can it be a Model for Others?' *Journal of Contemporary China* 19(65): 437–60.

(2014a) '"Deepening Reform": The Organization and the Emerging Strategy', *China Leadership Monitor* 44: 1–14.

(2014b) 'After the Third Plenum: Economic Reform Revival Moves Toward Implementation', *China Leadership Monitor* 43: 1–14.

Nolan, Peter (2001) *China and the Global Economy: National Champions, Industrial Policy and the Big Business Revolution*. Houndmills: Palgrave Macmillan.

Nolan, Peter and Wang Xiaoqiang (1999) 'Beyond Privatization: Institutional Innovation and Growth in China's Large State-Owned Enterprises', *World Development* 27(1): 169–200.

Nong, Jiajun (2004) 'Dianxinye gaige zaiyu dizao lixing youxu de shichang jingzheng' [The Telecommunications Industry Creating a Rational, Managed Market Competition], *Tongxin Xinxi Bao* [Communications Information Newspaper], 21 July.

North, Douglass (1990) *Institutions, Institutional Change and Economic Performance*, Cambridge University Press.

Oi, Jean (1992) 'Fiscal Reform and the Economic Foundations of Local State Corporatism in China', *World Politics* 45(1): 99–126.

Pearson, Margaret (2005) 'The Business of Governing Business in China: Institutions and Norms of the Emerging Regulatory State', *World Politics* 57(2): 296–322.

(2011) 'Variety Within and Variety Without: The Political Economy of Chinese Regulation', in Scott Kennedy, ed. *Beyond the Middle Kingdom: Comparative Perspectives on China's Capitalist Transformation*, Stanford University Press.

Pei, Minxin (2006) *China's Trapped Transition: The Limits of Developmental Autocracy*, Cambridge, MA: Harvard University Press.

Peng, Bin (2003) 'Zai youxu jingzheng zhuang da' [Growing Big Within Managed Competition], *Renmin Youdian* [People's Post and Telecommunications], 21 March, 2.

Pierson, Paul (2005) 'The Study of Policy Development', *Journal of Policy History* 17(1): 34–51.

Polanyi, Karl (2001) *The Great Transformation: The Political and Economic Origins of our Time*, 2nd edn, Boston: Beacon Press.

Przeworski, Adam (1991) *Democracy and the Market: Political and Economic Reforms in Eastern Europe and Latin America*, Cambridge University Press.

Qin, Min *et al.* (2014) 'How Telecom Graft in China Tripped up Telstra', *Caixin*, 17 April.

Qiu, Xiaohan (2002) 'Hangkongye da xipai' [The Big Reshuffle in Airlines], *Sichuan wujia* [Sichuan Pricing] 4: 8–13.

Qiu, Zhaoxiang (1988) 'Xinxihua he wo guo xiandaihua' [Informatization and China's Modernization], *Makesi Zhuyi Yanjiu* [Studies on Marxism] 3: 93–107.

Qiushi (2014) 'Shenme shi hunhe suoyouzhi jingji?' [What is a Mixed Ownership Economy?], 16 April.

Quanguo jianshe shichang xinxi [National Construction Market Information] (1997) 'Wo guo zhengzai shishi de ba da 'jin'zi gongcheng' [Eight Big 'Golden' Projects Now Being Implemented in China] 15: 71.

Rabinovitch, Simon (2012) 'Private Sector Battle March of Chinese State', *Financial Times*, 11 November.

Ramo, Joshua C. (2004) *The Beijing Consensus*, London: Foreign Policy Centre.

Reny, Marie-Ève (2011) 'Review Essay: What Happened to the Study of China in Comparative Politics?' *Journal of East Asian Studies* 11(1): 105–35.

Reuters (2015) 'China Plans Mergers to Cut Number of Big State Firms to 40: State Media'. Available at: www.reuters.com/article/2015/04/27/us-china-soe-idUSKBN0NI09A20150427.

Rutherford, Malcolm (2008) 'Old Institutionalism', in Steven Durlauf and Lawrence Blume, eds. *The New Palgrave Dictionary of Economics*. Available at: www.dictionaryofeconomics.com/dictionary.

Salidjanova, Nargiza and Iacob Koch-Weser (2013) 'Third Plenum Economic Reform Proposals: A Scorecard', *US–China Economic and Security Review Commission*, 19 November.

Schonhardt-Bailey, Cheryl (2006) *From the Corn Laws to Free Trade: Interests, Ideas and Institutions in Historical Perspective*, Cambridge, MA: MIT Press.

Schmidt, Vivien A. (2008) 'Discursive Institutionalism: The Explanatory Power of Ideas and Discourse', *Annual Review of Political Science* 11: 303–26.

(2010) 'Taking Ideas and Discourse Seriously: Explaining Change through Discursive Institutionalism as the Fourth "New Institutionalism"', *European Political Science Review* 2(1): 1–25.

Bibliography

(2011) 'Reconciling Ideas and Institutions through Discursive Institutionalism', in Daniel Béland and Robert H. Cox, eds. *Ideas and Politics in Social Science Research*, Oxford University Press.

Searle, John R. (2005) 'What is an Institution?' *Journal of Institutional Economics* 1(1): 1–22.

Shen, Tu (1992) *Zhongguo minhang zai gaige kaifangzhong qianjin* [Civil Aviation Progress in China's Reform and Opening], Beijing: China Civil Aviation Publishers.

Sheng, Guojin (1997) 'Lüelun guoyou jingji de kongzhili' [Strategic Discussion of Controlling Force of the State-Owned Economy] *Neibu wengao* [Internal Reports] 22: 1–3.

Sheng, Hong and Zhao Nong (2012) *China's State-Owned Enterprises: Nature, Performance and Reform*, Singapore: World Scientific.

Shepsle, Kenneth (2006) 'Rational Choice Institutionalism', in R. A. W. Rhodes, Sarah A. Binder and Bert A. Rockman, eds. *Oxford Handbook of Political Institutions*, Oxford University Press.

Shi, Shih-Junn (2006) 'Left to Market and Family – Again? Ideas and the Development of the Rural Pension Policy in China', *Social Policy and Administration* 40(7): 791–806.

Shih, Victor (2006) 'Partial Reform Equilibrium, Chinese Style: Political Incentives and Reform Stagnation in Chinese Financial Policies', *Comparative Political Studies* 20(10): 1–25.

(2008) *Factions and Finance in China: Elite Conflict and Inflation*, Cambridge University Press.

Smyth, Russell (2000) 'Should China be Promoting Large-Scale Enterprises and Enteprise Groups?' *World Development* 28(4): 721–37.

SPC Macroeconomic Research Group (1999) 'Shiwu qijian wo guo jiaotong yunshuye fazhan yu gaige de jiben silu' [The Basic Train of Thought for Development and Reform of the Transportation Industry in the Fifteenth Planning Period], *Hongguan jingji yanjiu* [Macroeconomic Research] 8: 30–4.

State Assets Supervision and Administration Commission (SASAC) (2007) *Wo guo guoyou jingji buju he jiegou tiaozheng ruogan zhongda wenti de yanjiu* [Research on Remaining Serious Problems in the Layout of China's State-Owned Economy and Restructuring], internal document.

State Council Development Research Center (2005) *Haihang xianxiang* [Hainan Airlines Phenomenon], Beijing: China Development Publishers.

Steinberg, David and Victor Shih (2012) 'Interest Group Influence in Authoritarian States: The Political Determinants of Chinese Exchange Rate Policy', *Comparative Political Studies* 45(11): 1405–34.

Steinfeld, Edward S. (2006) 'Market Visions: The Interplay of Ideas and Institutions in Chinese Financial Restructuring', in Lowell Dittmer and Guoli Liu, eds. *China's Deep Reform: Domestic Politics in Transition*, Lanham, MD: Rowman & Littlefield.

Steinmo, Sven (2003) 'The Evolution of Policy Ideas: Tax Policy in the 20th Century' *British Journal of Politics and International Relations* 5(2): 206–36.

Sullivan, Michael T. (1994) 'The Impact of Western Political Thought in Chinese Political Discourse on Transitions from Leninism, 1986–1992', *World Affairs* 157(2): 79–91.

Sun, Dekai *et al.* (2001) 'Zhuoyan guoji jingzheng, gao hao dianxinye gaige' [Focusing on International Competition, Do a Good Job of Telecommunications Industry Reform] *Renmin Youdian* [People's Post and Telecommunications], 6 June, 1.

Sun, Xiaoliang (1992) 'Fazhan qiye jituan de ruogan lilun he fangzhen zhengce wenti' [Some Theoretical and Policy Questions Regarding the Development of Large Enterprise Groups], *Jituan Jingji Yanjiu* [Enterprise Group Economic Research] 3: 26–30.

Sun, Zhixin (1987) 'Zhongguo de xinxing jingji zuzhi – qiye jituan' [China's New Economic Organization – Enterprise Groups] *Jingji yanjiu cankao ziliao* [Reference Materials for Economic Research] 31 (25 February): 3–11.

Sutherland, Dylan (2001) 'Policies to Build National Champions: China's "National Team" of Enterprise Groups', in Peter Nolan, ed. *China and the Global Business Revolution*, New York: Palgrave Macmillan.

—— (2003) *China's Large Enterprises and the Challenge of Late Industrialisation*, London: Routledge Curzon.

Sutherland, Dylan, Lutao Ning and Sam Beatson (2011) 'Productivity Performance in Chinese Business Groups: The Positive and Negative Impacts of Business Group Affiliation', *Journal of Chinese Economic and Business Studies* 9(2): 163–80.

Tai, Zhanxin (2004) 'Zhongguo minhang yunshuye zhengfu guanzhi gaige yanjiu' [Research on Regulatory Reform of China's Civil Aviation], Ph.D. dissertation submitted to Northwest University (China), Political Economy Department.

Tian, Guoqiang (2011) 'Zhongguo jingji fazhan zhong de shen cengci wenti' [Deep Problems in Chinese Economic Development] *Xueshu Yuekan* [Academic Monthly] 43(3): 59–64.

Tong, Dalin and Song, Yanming (1986) 'Horizontal Economic Integration is a Beachhead to Launch Urban Reform', *Chinese Economy* 20(2): 26–35.

Tongxin Xinxi Bao (2002) 'Wu jichuan: jin yi bu shenhua dianxinye gaige, zujian tedaxing tongxin qiye jituan' [Wu Jichuan: Further Deepen Telecommunications Reform, Establish Telecommunications Large Enterprise Groups], 15 May, A01.

US Congress (2008) 'The Financial Crisis and the Role of Federal Regulators'. Hearing before the Committee on Oversight and Government Reform, Washington, DC.

Walter, Carl and Fraser Howie (2010) *Red Capitalism: The Fragile Financial Foundations of China's Extraordinary Rise*, Hong Kong: John Wiley & Sons.

Wang, Chunjun (2014) 'Hunhe suoyouzhi chanquan shi zhongguo dianxin gaige de zui you xuanze' [Mixed Ownership is The Best Choice for China's Telecommunications Reform], *Nanjing youdian daxue xuebao* [Nanjing Post and Telecommunications University Journal] 16(1): 6–12.

Wang, Hongqi (2010) 'Guoqi shi "zuoda" haishi "longduan"?' [Are SOEs "Going Big" or "Monopolies"?], *Zhongguo Jingji Zhoukan* [CE Weekly] 11: 16–17.

Wang, Huijiong and Li Boxi (1989) *China Towards the Year 2000*, Beijing: New World Press.

Wang, Huijiong *et al.* (1990) 'Chanye zhengce de zongti gouxiang' [The Overall Concept of Industrial Policy] *Guanli Shijie* [Management World] 6: 25–33.
Wang, Junhao *et al.* (2008) *Zhongguo longduanxing hangye guanzhi jigou de sheli yu yunxing jizhi* [The Establishment and Operation of Regulatory Agencies in China's Monopoly Industries], Beijing: Commercial Press.
Wang, Ou (2001) 'Zhongguo dianxinye de fazhan yu tizhi bianqian' [Development and System Changes in China's Telecommunications Industry], Ph.D. dissertation submitted to Modern Economic History Department, Chinese Academy of Social Sciences.
Wang, Shaoguang (2011) 'Tansuo zhongguoshi shehuizhuyi 3.0: Chongqing jingyan' [Exploring Chinese-style Socialism 3.0: The Experience of Chongqing], working paper. Available at: www.usc.cuhk.edu.hk/PaperCollection/Details.aspx?id=7985.
Wang, Shaoguang and Hu Angang (1999) *The Political Economy of Uneven Development: The Case of China*, Armonk, NY: M. E. Sharpe.
—— (2001) *The Chinese Economy in Crisis: State Capacity and Tax Reform*, Armonk, NY: M. E. Sharpe.
Weber, Max (1946 [1915]) *From Max Weber: Essays in Sociology*, ed. H.H. Gerth and C. Wright Mills, Oxford University Press.
Wei, Xinghua and Zhang Fujun (2010) 'Dangqian "guojin mintui" zhishuo bu neng chengli' ['The Advance of the State, Retreat of the Private Sector' Cannot be Established], *Makesi zhuyi yanjiu* [Marxist Studies] 3: 5–11.
Wildau, Gabriel (2014a) 'China Announces Plan for Reform of State-Owned Enterprises', *Financial Times*, 15 July.
—— (2014b) 'China Kicks Off Second Wave of Privatization', *FT.com*, 10 August.
Wines, Michael (2010) 'China Fortifies State Business to Fuel Growth', *New York Times*, 29 August.
Woo, Wing Thye (1999) 'The Real Reasons for China's Growth', *China Journal* 41: 115–37.
Woods, Ngaire (1995) 'Economic Ideas and International Relations: Beyond Rational Neglect', *International Studies Quarterly* 39: 161–80.
World Bank and Development Research Centre of the State Council (2012) *China 2030: Building a Modern, Harmonious, and Creative High-Income Society*, Washington, DC: World Bank.
Wu, Guogang and Helen Lansdowne, eds. (2008) *Zhao Ziyang and China's Political Future*, London: Routledge.
Wu, Irene S. (2008) *From Iron Fist to Invisible Hand: The Uneven Path of Telecommunication Policy Reform in China*, Stanford University Press.
Wu, Jichuan (1997) *Zhongguo tongxin fazhan zhilu* [The Development of China's Communications], Beijing: Xinhua Publishers.
—— (1998) 'Xinxi chanye bu buzhang wu jichuan zhichu – xinxihua jianshe yao zhua san ge zhongdian' [MII Minister Wu Jichuan Points Out – Informatization Construction Must Stress Three Essential Points], *Lingdao juece xinxi* [Information for Deciders] 46: 8.
—— (1999) 'Jiji tuidong dianxin shiye de gaige he fazhan' [Enthusiastically Push for the Reform and Development of Telecommunications] *Qiushi* [Seeking Truth] 12: 18–21.

Wu, Jichuan *et al.*, eds. (2008) *Da kuayue: Zhongguo dianye sanshi chunqiu* [The Great Leap: Thirty Years of Reform in China's Telecommunications Sector], Beijing: People's Publisher.
Wu, Jinglian (2009) 'Zhongguo jingji 60 nian' [The Chinese Economy at 60], *Caijing*, 28 September.
—— (2011a) 'Economics and China's Economic Rise', in Masahiko Aoki and Wu Jinglian, eds. *The Chinese Economy: A New Transition*, Basingstoke: Palgrave Macmillan.
—— (2011b) 'Xunzu pengzhang wuyi fujia gaige xuyao ding ding ceng sheji' [Rent-Seeking in the Extreme: Reform Needs a Top Top-Level Design], *Zhongguo Gaige* [China Reform] 12, 1 December.
Wu Jinglian and Chen Jiyuan (1980) 'Genju difang tedian jianli heli de gongye jiegou' [Establish a Rational Industrial Structure According to Local Characteristics] *Zhongguo Shehui Kexue* [China Social Sciences] 3: 205–12.
Xia, Shiying (1999) 'Fangzhe ming jingji xuejia zhang jun jiaoshou' [An Interview with Economist, Professor Zhang Jun], *Juece Shikong* [Decision-Making Time and Space] 5: 4–6.
Xiao, Donglian (2006) 'Zhongguo gaige chuqi duiwai jingyan de xitong kaocha he jiejian' [The Systematic Investigation and Use for Reference of Foreign Experience in the Early Days of Reform], *Zhonggong Dangshi Yanjiu* [Communist Party History Research] 4: 23–32.
Xinhua (2006a) '"Teshu liyi jituan" shehui hexie de dadi' [Special Interest Groups are the Enemy of Social Harmony], 5 October.
—— (2006b) 'Wo guo mingque qi da hangye jiang you guoyou jingji baochi juedui kongzhili' [China Makes Clear the Seven Industries in which the State Economy's Absolute Control will be Preserved] *Xinhua Wang*, 19 December.
—— (2014a) 'China's Mixed Ownership Reform Advances Against Headwinds', 15 June.
—— (2014b) 'Anti-Corruption Campaign Forcing Change in SOEs', 3 July.
—— (2014c) 'China Focus: China Targets High Salaries at State Firms', 19 August.
Xuan, Yu'en (2003) *Zhongguo minhang yunshu shichang fazhan yu chuangxin* [Development and Innovation in China's Civil Aviation Transport Market], Beijing: China Civil Aviation Publisher.
Xü, Xiangyi (1989) 'Guowai qiye jituan de zuzhi yu guanli' [Organization and Management of Foreign Enterprise Groups], *Jingji yanjiu cankao ziliao* [Reference Materials for Economic Research] 166: 16–22.
Yao, Ying (2004) 'Dianxin gaige guanjian zaiyu youxu jingzheng' [The Key to Telecommunications Reform Is in Managed Competition], *Tongxin Xinxi Bao* [Communications Information Newspaper], 7 April, A1.
Yan, Huai and Suisheng Zhao (1993) 'Notes on China's Confidential Documents', *Journal of Contemporary China* 2(4): 75–92.
Yang, Dali (2006) *Remaking the Chinese Leviathan: Market Transition and the Politics of Governance in China*, Stanford University Press.
Yang, Jisheng (1998) *Deng Xiaoping shidai* [The Deng Xiaoping Era], Beijing: Zhongyang Bianyi.
Yeo, Yukyung (2009) 'Between Owner and Regulator: Governing the Business of China's Telecommunications Service Industry', *China Quarterly* 200: 1013–32.

Yin, Guanghua and Jia Heliang (1987) 'Dali fazhan wo guo de qiye jituan' [Vigorously Develop China's Enterprise Groups], *Jingji yanjiu cankao ziliao* [Reference Materials for Economic Research] 25 (15 April): 2–7.

Yiu, Daphne *et al.* (2007) 'Business Groups: An Integrated Model to Focus Future Research', *Journal of Management Studies* 44(8): 1551–79.

Youdian Shangqing [Post and Telecommunications Market Conditions] (1999) 'Wu jichuan da zhongwai jizhe wen' [Minister Wu Jichuan Responds to Questions from Chinese and Foreign Journalists] 8: 9–11.

Yu, Fei (2000) 'Jiaru WTO, zhongguo dianxinye maixiang xin zhengchang – fangwen xinxi chanyebu dianxin yanjiu kan kaili boshi' [WTO Entry, Chinese Telecommunications Embarks on a New Journey – An Interview with Ministry of Information Industry Telecommunications Researcher Dr Kan Kaili], *Shijie Dianxin* [World Telecommunications] 1: 6–7, 37.

Yu, Jianming (1998) 'Shenhua daxing qiye jituan shidian tuijin liang ge genbinxing zhuanbian' [To Deepen the Large Enterprise Experiment Adopt Two Fundamental Transformations], *Hongguan Jingji Guanli* [Macroeconomic Management] 254: 4–9.

Yu, Zhongyi (1983) 'Qiye zuzhi jiegou helihua yu jingji xiaoyi' [The Rationalization and Efficiency of Enterprise Organization], *Caizheng Yanjiu* [Finance Research] 3: 44–51.

Zhan, Huaxiu (2013) 'Lun "guojin mintui" de zhengjie yu fazhan fangshi de zhuanbian' [On the Crucial Reason for 'Advance of the State, Retreat of the Private Sector' and Development Style Transformation], *Jingji Yanjiu Daokan* [Economic Research Guide] 9(191): 6–8.

Zhang, Fan (2000) 'Moni jingzheng shichang de jianli yu shengzhang – Zhongguo minyong hangkong yunshuye de guanzhi gaige he shichang jingzheng' [A Simulated Competitive Economy's Establishment and Growth: China's Civil Air Transport Regulatory Reform and Market Competition], in *Zhongguo jingji yanjiu* [China Economic Research], Beijing: University Publishers.

Zhang, Kenny (2005) *Going Global: The Why, When and How of Chinese Companies' Outward Investment Intentions*, Asian Pacific Foundation of Canada. Available at: www.asiapacific.ca.

Zhang, Qi and Mingxing Liu (2010) 'Local Political Elite, Partial Reform Symptoms, and the Business and Market Environment in Rural China', *Business and Politics* 12(1), article 5.

Zhang, Weiying (2006) 'Lixing sikao zhongguo gaige' [Rational Thoughts on Chinese Reform] *Caizheng jie* [Money China] 6: 72–9.

—— (2012) *Shenme gaibian zhongguo* [What Changes China], Beijing: China CITIC Press.

—— (2013) 'Guoqu shi nian, women de linian da da daotui le' [Over the Past Decade our Thought has Greatly Moved Backwards], *IT shidai zhoukan* [IT Time Weekly] 16: 15.

Zhang, Xingxiang (2007) 'Zhengqi fenkai de jiannan tansuo: yi zhongguo minhang jipiao jiage guizhi wei shijue' [Exploring the Difficulty of Government–Enterprise Separation: The Example of China's Civil Aviation Ticket Pricing Regulation] *Gongfa yanjiu* [Public Law Research] 0: 72–3.

Zhang, Yuanyuan Sophia and Steven Barnett (2014) 'Fiscal Vulnerabilities and Risks from Local Government Finance in China', IMF Working Paper WP/14/4.
Zhang, Yuzhe and Eva Wu (2009) 'China Probe into Airlines' Fuel Hedging Continues', *Caijing*, 9 November.
Zhang, Zhijin and Liang Xian (1995) 'Ba wo guo qiye jituan jianli zai xiandai qiye zhidu de jichu shang' [Establish Chinese Enterprise Groups on the Basis of the Modern Enterprise System], *Jingji yanjiu cankao ziliao* [Reference Materials for Economic Research] 132 (26 August): 16–23.
Zhao, Hejuan (2011) 'Wrong Key Fumble for China Mobile in Pakistan', 1 August. Available at: www.cnbc.com/id/43147906.
(2012) *Tianxia you zei* [The Invisible Thief] Guangzhou: Nanfang Daily Press.
Zhao, Suisheng (2010) 'The China Model: Can it Replace the Western Model of Modernization?' *Journal of Contemporary China* 19(65): 419–36.
Zheng, Yongnian (2010) *Zhongguo moshi* [The China Model], Hangzhou: Zhejian Publishing United Group.
Zhengquan Ribao (2007) 'Baolu zijin lian kunjing haihang zujian "da xinhau" huo you yinqing' [HNA's Capital Chain Difficulties Exposed: Formation of 'Grand China' May Have a Hidden Reason], 20 November.
Zhi, Bi and Wang Xiaoqiang (1998) 'Zhongguo dianxun chanye de fazhan zhanlüe' [Development Strategy of the Chinese Telecommunication Industry], *Guangbo dianshi xinxi* [Radio and Television Information] December: 5–19.
Zhongguo Daqiye Jituan [Large Enterprises of China] (2007) Beijing: National Bureau of Statistics.
Zhongguo Xinwenwang (2008) 'Minhang zongju chute shi xiang cuoshi yingdui jinrong weiji cu hangye fazhan' [CAAC Introduces Ten Measures to Address Financial Crisis, Promote Industry Development], 9 December.
Zhou, Da (2000) 'Shidu Longduan: Hangkong yunshuye youxiao de shichang zuzhi jiegou xingshi' [Moderate Monopoly: An Effective Market Structure for the Air Transport Industry], *Minhang jingji yu jishu* [Civil Aviation Economics and Technology] 225: 11–15.
Zhou, Fangsheng (1995) 'Lun qiye jituan muzi gongsi chanquan guanxi' [On Enterprise Group's Ownership Relations Between Parent Companies and Subsidiaries], *Jingji yanjiu cankao ziliao* [Reference Materials for Economic Research] 190 (11 December): 2–50.
Zhou Qiren (1998) 'San wang fu he, shu wang jingzheng' [Convergence of Three Networks, Competition between Multiple Networks], *Dianzi Zhanwang yu Juece* [Network and Computer Security] 6: 25–39.
Zhou, Ruijin (2009) 'Qiege yu "teshu liyi jituan" de lianxi' [Cut Ties that Bind to Special Interests], *Caijing*, 20 October.
(2009) *Zhu rongji da jizhe wen* [Zhu Rongji Answers Journalists' Questions] Beijing: People's Publishers.

Government data sources

Cong Tongji Kan Minhang (CTJKMH) [Seeing Civil Aviation From Statistics] various years, Beijing: China Civil Aviation Publishers.

Zhongguo Caizheng Nianjian (ZGCJNJ) [China Finance Yearbook] various years, Beijing: China Finance and Economics Publisher.

Zhongguo Daqiye Jituan (ZGDQJT) [Large Enterprises of China], various years, Beijing: National Bureau of Statistics.

Zhongguo Daqiye Jituan Niandu Fazhan Baogao (ZGDQYJTNDFZBG) [Annual Report on the Development of China's Large Groups], various years, Beijing: Economic Management Publishers.

Zhongguo Guoyou Zichan Jiandu Guanli Nianjian (ZGGYZCGLNJ) [Yearbook of State-Owned Assets Supervision and Administration Commission], various years, Beijing: SASAC.

Zhongguo Tongji Nianjian (ZGTJNJ) [China Statistical Yearbook], various years, Beijing: National Bureau of Statistics.

Index

advance of the private sector, retreat of the state, 1, 121
advance of the state, xiii
advance of the state, retreat of the private sector, 1–2, 115
in the airline industry, 76
Air China, group structure, 59, 70
Air Force, control of civil aviation bureaucracy, 55
airline ticket pricing, deregulation of, 62
anti-corruption campaign, 19, 122
Asian Financial Crisis, 30, 37, 47, 62
Association for the Promotion of Business Groups, 45
authoritarian resilience, 110

Beijing Consensus, xii, 15
Béland, Daniel, 23
Big Four airlines, 69
Big Three state-owned airlines, 53
consolidation plan (2000), 65
Global Financial Crisis, 74
inclusion in trial group, 59
Blyth, Mark, 22–3
Bo, Xilai, 113
on state ownership, 113
Bo, Yibo, support for telecommunications development, 82
Bremmer, Ian, xiii, 15
Brødsgaard, Kjeld Erik, 19
business groups, 11–14
pilot group, 45, 48
private, 13
pyramidal, 12
trial group, 50

centralization of capital, 40
Chen, Qingtai, 49
Chen, Yuan, 44
Chen, Yun, 33, 35, 44
China 2030: Building a Modern, Harmonious and Creative Society, 117

China Construction Bank (CCB), 46
China Eastern Airlines, challenges, 71
China Mobile
anti-corruption campaign, 105
in Pakistan, 104
China Model, xii, 16, 111–15
China Southern Airlines, group structure, 71
China Telecom, 92
initial public offering (IPO), 103
China Towards the Year 2000, 34
China Unicom
initial public offering (IPO), 103
market entry, 86
China-China-foreign deals in telecommunications services, 93
Chinese Academy of Social Sciences (CASS) Economics Research Institute, 31
Chinese economic development theory, experimentalist vs. convergence school, 111
Chonqing Model, 113
Civil Aviation Administration of China (CAAC)
Maoist period, 53
Planning, Development and Finance Department, 69
response to Global Financial Crisis, 73
response to industry crisis, 63
Communist Party Congress, Eighteenth, 2
Third Plenum, 19, 106, 118
Communist Party Congress, Fifteenth, 5, 47, 99
Report, 48
Communist Party Congress, Fourteenth, 38
Communist Party Congress, Sixteenth, 50
Cui, Zhiyuan, 113
Cultural Revolution, impact on telecommunications, 80

Deng, Xiaoping
'Criticize Deng' campaign, 55
Southern Tour, 46

Index

support for telecommunications development, 81
Deng, Yingtao, 44
developmental states, 34, 39–40, 42
discrete planning unit, 42
disorderly competition, 101
Dongfeng Motor Company, 42
Downs, Erica, 20

East Star Airlines, 75
economic planning system, early reform period, 31–4
economic reform plan
   top-level design, 116
   top top-level design, 116
economic system, three-tiered, 33
economic theory, Marxian, 39

Ferchen, Matt, 16
'flying forth', 55
Fortune Global 500 list, 7, 114
fragmented markets
   airlines, 64
   early reform period, 31
framing, 29

Gang of Four, 55
General Agreement on Tariffs and Trade (GATT), re-entry negotiations, 37
Global Financial Crisis, xi, 1–2, 76, 111
   airline industry, 73
globalization, Chinese intellectuals' perceptions of, 37
'going big and going strong', 4, 28, 50, 101
'going forth', 6, 49
Golden Bridge initiatives, telecommunications, 88–90
'grab the large, let go the small', 47
gradualism, 18
Greenspan, Alan, xi
Gu, Chujun, 1
guidance planning, 33–4
guimo, 14
guojin mintui, 1–3
guotui minjin, 1

Hainan Airlines, group structure, 72
Halper, Stefan, xii, 15
Han, Deqiang, 95
Heilmann, Sebastian and Lea Shih, 34
Hellman, Joel, 17
horizontal economy, 41
Hsu, Robert, 31
Hsueh, Roselyn, 21, 79

Hu, Angang, 8, 20, 111
Hu, Jintao, 2
Huang, Yasheng, 4

ideas, xiv
ideational analysis, 110–11, 123–4
ideology, xi
industrial policy, 39
   airlines, 57–9
   policymaking system, 34
   telecommunications, 84–5
informatization, 87
initial public offering (IPO), 'red chip', 7
installation fees, increase of, 87
institutional analysis, 11, 109
   historical, 23
   rational choice, 23
interest analysis, 110
   airlines, 67
   consumers vs. nation, telecommunications industry debate, 93–5
   national, 21
   particularist, 17–21
interest group, 19

Jacques, Martin, xii
Japan, 39
J-curve theory, 17
Jiang, Jiemin, 122
Jiang, Zemin, 49
   support for state-controlled large enterprise groups, 43

Kan, Kaili, 97
Keister, Lisa, 11
Kennedy, Scott, 16–17
kereitsu, 41
Keynes, John Maynard, xi, 22, 116
Kingdon, John, 24

Lam, Willy Wo-Lap, 46
Lan, Shili, 75
Lang, Larry, 1, 115
Lardy, Nicholas, xiv
large enterprise strategy, xiv, 28, 39, 42, 53, 65, 97, 109
Leonard, Mark, 15
Li, Jiaxiang, 68–9
Li, Peng, 35, 44
Li, Rongrong, 8, 50
Li, Xiannian, 55
Li, Zheng, 3
liberals
   view of China Model, 114
   view of Chinese economy, 114–18

Index

lifeline industries, 47, 53, 99
  telecommunications, 94
Lin, Kun-Chin, 21
List, Friedrich, 64
lobbying
  corporate, 17
  local governments, to set up airlines, 61
longduan hangye, 4

Ma, Hong, 46
'macro control and micro flexibility', 34, 87
managed competition, 14, 101
management buyouts (MBOs), 1
mandatory plan, 32
market authoritarianism, 15
market vision, 15, 17
Mehta, Jal, 24
mergers between SOEs
  forced marriages, 51
  strong–strong, 51
Miao, Wei, 106
Ministry of Industry and Information Technology (MIIT), 106
Ministry of Information Industry (MII), 92
Ministry of Post and Telecommunications (MPT), 80
mixed ownership, 106, 119–21
  China Telecom, 122
  Sinopec, 122
model threat, xii
monopoly capitalism, 40
monopoly sectors, 4, 19–20, 123
'muddling through', 110

national champions, xiii, 37
National Development and Reform Commission (NDRC), 20, 69
National Oil Companies (NOCs), 20
national team, 12–13
Naughton, Barry, 16, 19, 118
neoconservatives, 30, 43
  support among political elite, 46
New Left, 16, 95, 112, 115
  distinction from China Model school, 113
New Right, 16, 20
Nolan, Peter, 11
nomenklatura, 19
non-state sector, perceived threat to SOEs, 35–6

oligopoly, 67

Partial Reform Equilibrium (PRE) model, 17, 26
Pearson, Margaret, 14

Pei, Minxin, 18
plane crashes, 61
policy solutions, 24, 38–51
price wars, airline industry, 63
problem definition, 24
  1980s, 35
  1990s, 35–8
provincial teams, 13
Przeworski, Adam, 17

Ramo, Joshua Cooper, 15
regulatory state, tiered, 14
rent-seeking, 20
Rizhao, 2

Schmidt, Vivien, 23
selective withdrawal, 18
Shen, Tu, 55
Shih, Victor, 18
short-term winners, 18
Singapore, large enterprise groups, 42
small and complete, large and complete enterprises, 30, 40
soft budget constraint, state-owned airlines, 62, 64
state capitalism, xiii, 15, 110
State Commission for Restructuring of the Economy (SCRE), 40, 116
State Council Development Research Centre (SCDRC), 34
State Economic and Trade Commission (SETC), report on low industry concentration (1996), 37
State Import and Export Committee (SIEC), 85
State-Owned Assets Supervision and Administration Commission (SASAC), 6, 16, 19, 50, 68
  limits to control of central SOEs, 51
  role in airline industry during global financial crisis, 74
  role in telecommunications industry, 104–5
state-owned economy
  adjusting the layout of, 47–8
  policy debate in 1990s, 46
state-owned enterprises, revitalization plan, 45
state-owned enterprises, central, 1, 4, 6, 16
State Planning Commission (SPC), 42, 67
  role in Golden Bridge initiatives, 88
State Price Control Bureau, 61
state–society relations, 17
Steinfeld, Ed, 15
strategic sectors, 79

Index

study trips, 45
   East Asia, 33
   Japan, 33
Sutherland, Dylan, 11

Ten Industries Revitalization Plan, 2
Tian, Guoqiang, 8
Tiananmen Movement (1989), 35
translation, 29
transnational diffusion, 29
'trapped transition', 18
triangular debt crisis, 36
'tunnelling', 12
Two Airlines Uprising, 54
two-legged system, 113

uncertainty
   before WTO entry, 49
   Knightian, 23
Unirule Institute, 3

vicious competition, 101

Walter, Carl and Fraser Howie, 19
Wang, Hongqie, 3
Wang, Huijiong, 34
Wang, Junhao, 19
Wang, Minsheng, 85
Wang, Shaoguang, 113
   socialism 3.0, 113
Wang, Zigang, 81
Weber, Max, 22
Wen, Jiabao, xii, 20

World Trade Organization (WTO)
   China's Accession Agreement, 37
   pressure of entry on airline industry, 65
Wu, Jichuan, support of large enterprise strategy, 97
Wu, Bangguo, 48
Wu, Jichuan, 81
   conflict with Zhu, Rongji, 96
Wu, Jinglian, 8, 19, 116
Wu, Jinglian and Chen Jiyuan, 31

Xia, Bin, 117
Xiao, Donglian, 33

Yao, Yilin, 35

Zhang, Chunjiang, 106
Zhang, Qi and Liu Mingxing, 18
Zhang, Weiying, 20, 115, 118
Zhao, Hejuan, 106
Zhao, Zhenhua, 120
Zhao, Ziyang, 35, 82
Zheng, Yongnian, 112
Zhou, Enlai, influence on civil aviation development, 55
Zhou, Qiren, 94
Zhou, Yongkang, 122
Zhu, Rongji, 18, 47
   on making telecommunications cheaper, 94
   support for Golden Bridge initiatives, 88
zou chu qu, 6
zuo da zuo qiang, 4